TEA ROOM IN A DEPARTMENT STORE
Designed and managed by one of Miss Bradley's pupils

COOKING FOR PROFIT

CATERING AND FOOD SERVICE MANAGEMENT

BY

ALICE BRADLEY

PRINCIPAL OF MISS FARMER'S SCHOOL OF COOKERY, BOSTON; CULINARY
EDITOR "WOMAN'S HOME COMPANION"; AUTHOR OF THE
CANDY COOK BOOK; COMPANY COOKING;
ECONOMICAL MENUS, ETC.

A CORRESPONDENCE COURSE

ON PROFESSIONAL COOKING—THE PREPARATION AND MARKETING OF HOME-
COOKED FOOD; ON CATERING FOR RECEPTIONS, PARTIES, DINNERS,
BANQUETS, SCHOOLS, CAMPS; ON THE MANAGEMENT OF
TEA ROOMS, CAFETERIAS, LUNCH ROOMS,
BOARDING HOUSES, FAMILY HOTELS
AND INSTITUTIONS.

Creative Cookbooks
Monterey, California

Cooking for Profit:
Catering and Food Service Management

by
Alice Bradley

ISBN: 1-4101-0608-X

Reprinted from the 1922 edition

Creative Cookbooks
An Imprint of Fredonia Books
Monterey, California
http://www.creativecookbooks.com

In order to make original editions of historical works
available to scholars at an economical price, this
facsimile of the original edition of 1922 is
reproduced from the best available copy and has
been digitally enhanced to improve legibility, but the
text remains unaltered to retain historical
authenticity.

CONTENTS

CONTENTS

COOKING FOR PROFIT
I

ALWAYS USE ACCURATE MEASUREMENTS

COOKING FOR PROFIT

PART I

COOKING AS A PROFESSION

COOKING is essentially woman's profession. From the dawn of history she has prepared the food for the family. Good cooking is a fine art. It is as well the most useful of the arts. Of the old time arts, it alone remains for the most part in the home. The final preparation of food to eat only has not been nearly completely commercialized and made a factory industry. The demand for home-cooked food still remains well nigh universal.

If you are about to choose a useful profession, if you are suddenly thrown on your own resources and need to earn money, then, provided you have a love for cooking and some proficiency in it, a wide field of service is open to you. People must eat to live. Everyone likes good things to eat and many are able and willing to pay liberally for well cooked food. Good cooking is the first essential to success in all lines of food service. Many a woman today enjoys a good income because she was in the first place a good cook.

PROFITABLE OPENINGS FOR AN EXPERT COOK

The following are some of the avenues open to the woman who can cook some particular things particularly well:

1. Regularly cook special dishes to fill private orders.
   - a. At your own home.
   - b. In the home of your patrons.
2. Sell cooked food on a commission to Woman's Exchange

   Grocery store
   Department store
   Soda fountain
  For a lunch room in a
   School
   Business block
   Factory

Breads, cakes, salad dressings, sandwiches, jellies, jams and marmalades are the commonest things sold in these ways.

3. Prepare and pack lunches to be sold at
   Railway stations
   On automobile routes
   At pleasure resorts
   In office buildings
   In schools
4. Cater for
   Children's parties
   Company lunches and dinners in private homes
   Card parties and receptions, preparing and serving all
    or part of the refreshments
   Prepare regular dinners, to be sent in special contain-
    ers, to private homes
5. Open a Cooked Food Shop
   Candy kitchen
   Community kitchen
   Delicatessen shop
   Tea room
   Lunch room for women
   Lunch room for business men
   Cafeteria
6. Become the manager of the kitchen in a
   Summer camp
   Institution
   Hotel

Club House

7. Conduct a guest house, summer camp, or small hotel. The place where you live will in some instances determine the line of work to be taken up. Many women cannot leave their homes but can, in their own kitchens, follow one of the above avenues and build up a successful business. If you must seek a new location you should choose it with due regard for the thing you plan to do and the kind of patronage desired. You can do different things if you are on an automobile road in the country than you can do in a crowded section of the city.

QUALIFICATIONS ESSENTIAL FOR SUCCESS

Do not undertake to earn money by cooking unless you have certain qualifications, many of which can be developed even though they are not very apparent in the beginning.

Training for the work either in the home or in an accredited school.

Experience—A person with training only and no experience cannot expect to make a great success until she has had experience.

Confidence in yourself, your business, and your ability to succeed; self-reliance.

High standards—Your work should be considered as a fine art to be developed and improved.

Honesty—Do the things as you advertise to do them.

Ideals—Willingness to work steadily and diligently until the ideal is reached. Striving toward high ideals makes work more interesting as well as more remunerative.

Love for the work, belief in it, enthusiasm for it.

Far-sightedness in starting and developing the business.

Progressiveness—not willing to stay always in one place unless to improve or enlarge it, but ambitious to go ahead in your particular line or to undertake something larger.

Executive ability—The power to do things yourself and to get others to do things for you.

Intelligence in purchasing and adapting equipment and supplies.

Ability to use time, energy and materials to the best advantage, wasting nothing, making the best use of everything; practice thrift.

Ability to handle money wisely—Spend it for things that are necessary to the business with no wasting of funds; be prompt in paying your bills and meeting obligations expect no favors, be careful to collect what is due you.

Ability to keep simple accounts and correctly add and subtract, multiply and divide .

Good judgment in deciding all of the many questions that come up; the determination to "never get left."

Adaptability to conditions, including the condition of having poor or insufficient help, of not having the supplies on hand that were expected, of not having the utensils that are required.

Tact in meeting people, shown in saying and doing the proper thing, especially avoiding what will offend or disturb.

Skill in dealing with men or emergencies; ability to talk or write to people, including business people, women of leisure, people who are not normal, people with plenty of money, people with little money.

Sympathy and *consideration* for employees, for trades people and for patrons. It is absolutely necessary to be able to put yourself in other people's places. Run your business on the Golden Rule—"Do unto others as you would have them do unto you," or "Love your neighbor as yourself." It need not be more; it should not be less.

Service your standard—service to the people with whom you are working and for whom you are working. You are a servant—one who serves—no matter what you are doing. Make every effort to please and satisfy your patrons; to do things as they wish them done.

Concentration on the thing in hand. Do not allow yourself to be turned aside to something else when you are sure of what your are doing.

Pleasing personality, necessary if you are to come in contact with your patrons.

Neatness and cleanliness—in appearance always suitably dressed and well-groomed.

Good health with a determination to maintain it. In order to do this you should have a hobby outside of your business. The person who has a hobby and rides it seldom "goes to smash" physically. Do not overwork; it does not pay in the long run.

Belief in the axiom *"Trifles make perfection, and perfection is no trifle."* Perfection of flavor and texture; attractive serving, garnishing and decorating; absolute uniformity; scrupulous cleanliness.

These are among the trifles that make or mar one's reputation and product. The best food will always sell the best.

If you haven't all these characteristics, associate with you someone who has them. All of these qualifications are not necessary in every avenue that is open to the woman who can cook, but cultivation of those that are not natural tendencies will result in increased business.

It is true that these qualifications, with a determination to succeed, will bring success in almost any line of work, but they are specially needed in the management of a business of your own.

Perfecting a Specialty

If you have the ability to cook some special thing particularly well, look around and see if there is a possibility of marketing it.

You may be able to use foodstuff grown in your own garden or orchard or farm, or in your immediate vicinity.

You may have a formula that has been handed down in your family or worked out from much experimenting that you can develop as your specialty. Is it a thing that appeals to the needs or desires of the people in your neighborhood, or your town, of your city? Perhaps your jellies, marmalade and preserves are already famous. Instead of preserves it may be mincemeat, or a particular kind of cake (one woman I know of makes a splendid living with only a delicious chocolate cake as her specialty), or a cake with a very nice frosting or filling or attractive and unusual decorations; it may be candy, or bread, or sandwiches, or doughnuts that you make so well that a market for it can be built up. Many such specialties will be suggested, but make a beginning the easiest way.

Characteristics of Food to be Sold

In order that you may sell any kind of food at a price sufficiently high to make a profit it must be

Something that people want, made especially well.

Superior to that sold in the ordinary shop.

Made of choice materials.

Made exactly from a definite formula so that results will always be the same.

Kept up to a high standard.

Labeled truthfully as to quality, weight, kind of product.

Prepared systematically and efficiently.

Always ready at the time agreed upon.

A specialty—Make only one or two things at first; "specialize" and again "specialize."

How to Market Your Specialty

First prepare a sample of the dish in which you plan to specialize. Place it in the kind of a container you plan to use—jelly glass, or fruit jar, or paper carton, or box—label it, wrap and tie it as it should be.

Show it and offer to prepare it for families in your immediate neighborhood, using your materials or theirs, or buying it in the market, or better still, from a farmer near by. You can charge for this so much a jar, or so much an hour or a day, plus the cost of all materials used—jars, rubbers, fuel, etc.

Talk your plans over with your friends and tell them what you propose to do, and let them ask their friends to give you orders.

Take your sample to a private boarding or day school and ask if there is a chance there for your specialty to be put on sale. Some people make sandwiches, cakes or candy for sale at schools where the children cannot go home to lunch.

Take your samples to a shop or factory where it can be sold at noontime.

Take samples to the largest grocers or soda fountain shops in your town or in a neighboring city. Ask them to exhibit and take orders for you, or rent you space where you can offer it for sale.

If there is a woman's exchange show them what you can do and talk over with the manager the possibility of a market there for your wares, or ask them to suggest something that you could make.

Place a sign in front of your house if you are on an automobile road. State what you have to sell. Show samples on a neat, attractive stand under a large shade tree if convenient.

Advertise in the local or city papers.

Send announcement cards to people whom you think would be most interested in the kind of thing you propose to make.

Send business-like typewritten letters to stores, restaurants, hotels, boarding houses and private families whom you haven't time or opportunity to call upon.

Coöperate with other people in your neigborhood who have products to sell similar to yours, and either hire a room and sell direct to automobile tourists or solicit patronage from some large firm in a neighboring city.

ESTABLISHING A REPUTATION

If your specialty is delicious and superior to or different from others, and of uniform quality, there will be purchasers who will tell others who will buy, and they in turn will tell others, and before long your reputation will be established and a market will have developed for your output.

One person will write to another about it, and you will have orders from other places if your goods can be shipped. If you keep up your high standard you will be asked to make other similar things and then different things. Do not try to do too many different kinds of things. It is a mistake to let your business grow so large that you cannot continue to give your personal touch and oversight to everything that goes out from your home and later on, perhaps, from your factory. Attention to every detail, even though the work must be done by others, can give a home touch to even a large business.

PERCENTAGE OF PROFIT

Before you have decided definitely on the thing in which you wish to specialize you should know its cost and its usual selling price. The difference between the cost and the price which you get for it will be your profit and should be sufficient to pay you well for your time and labor. Usually the wholesale selling price must be about double the cost of raw materials.

How to Figure Cost

Many women in figuring the cost of an article think only of the materials of which it is made. In addition to that they should consider the cost of conducting the business, (the overhead and operating expense), as well as the containers, wrappings, string, etc.

The overhead includes *rent of workroom*. If you own the house or building, the interest, repairs, taxes and insurance for a year should be estimated. If you propose to use only one room in an eight-room house, only one-eighth of the rent need be charged as overhead. If two rooms in a five-room apartment will be used, two-fifths of the rent will be your share.

It includes *interest* and *depreciation* on the equipment. Equipment includes stove, tables, sink, utensils, etc., used chiefly in your business. Make a list of them with their value. Figure interest on the amount of money you could get if your equipment were sold and the money were placed in the bank. Add to this figure one-fifth (20%) of the value you have put upon it as depreciation, or for a sinking fund with which to replace equipment. This should be counted as part of the overhead expense. Even though that equipment has been in use for years, you should consider what it is worth now and what it would cost to replace it.

The *cost of coal, gas, electricity, gasoline* or other fuel which you will use in your cooking must be included; also

Lights, if you have to work after dark.

Water, if it is taxed.

Ice, if used in keeping your supplies in good condition.

Telephone; you can do little business without one.

Advertising, if you plan to advertise in any way, including stationery, and postage if you send out announcements.

Estimate the *cost of help,* including any assistance you plan to have in cooking, packing, delivering, soliciting business, etc. If perchance a member of your own family is your assistant, figure that at a definite amount, probably at what it would cost you to get the work done by someone from outside.

Total up estimated expenses for one year, divide by 12 or by the number of months you plan to work each year. This will give you the *overhead and operating cost for one month.*

Divide by the number of working days in a month to learn the cost of doing business *each day.*

Next estimate the *amount of food* that you could prepare in an ordinary working day of eight or nine hours. How many jars or loaves can you make? What will be the *cost of the raw material,* that cost being based on wholesale prices? What will be the cost of *containers, labels, string,* etc.? What will be the cost of *commissions?*

Add these sums together, then add the overhead for one day. This will show you the total cost per day of what you propose to cook.

Now put down what you expect to receive for the finished product per jar or per loaf. Then estimate the selling price of all that you could prepare in a day. Is this more or less than the total cost of the product as estimated above? If more, subtract the day's cost from the expected receipts. Is the difference (this is the profit) enough to pay you for the time and labor you will spend in preparing and selling it?

The amount of profit you should receive should be not less than the wages or salary you would receive for doing the same amount or kind of work in another home or factory, or other place of business. Thirty to forty cents an hour is the wage, paid in 1921 to houseworkers sent out from a first-class office.

If there seems to be not enough profit in it after paying these expenses, think of some other product you might make. Do not cook all day without the probability of a reasonable profit.

Every bit of the food material and other supplies should be utilized. The cost is based not alone on what goes into the product, but on what is wasted as well. Be careful that nothing is wasted.

You may make "pin money" and gain experience without reckoning your overhead expense, but you cannot call it "Cooking for Profit."

Necessary Equipment

Before going very far in the production in your own kitchen of some special foodstuff, you want to look around your kitchen and think of it as a workshop where you can do a maximum amount of work with a minimum amount of time and strength. See if there are any ways in which the equipment in your workshop can be improved. Are the tables and sinks of the right height? Is the equipment that best adapted for the kind of work you propose to do? Think of any kind of a shop in which a man works, how he has his tools arranged so he can get at them most easily, and plan your workshop so that you will save the greatest number of steps.

There are some things that can be changed for a small amount of money and will mean the saving of time and much more money to you. If you are going to do your best work it is absolutely essential that you plan your workshop. Most efficient arrangements are described in *Household Engineering,* by Christine Frederick.*

---

* Published by American School of Home Economics.

Note the lines of travel and be sure the ingredients that you are going to use are grouped together close to the utensils that you are going to use; that these are close to the stove and that there is a shelf or table near the stove to which they can be removed from the stove and finished, wrapped or boxed, etc. Make your shop a model for convenience in order that you may get the greatest possible amount of work done.

The equipment will depend on the product which you decide to make. You will need a range; use gas if it is available,—because it is easily regulated and saves much time. If electric current is very cheap it may be practical to adopt that. At any rate use gas or electricity if you can, depending on which is the cheapest or most available. Coal or wood require more time and effort and results are not so regular. Vapor gasoline stoves are very successful if you cannot get gas. Gasoline is better than kerosene for professional cooking.

The water supply is important. There should be hot running water as well as cold to make your work easier, and the sink should be at the right height to save the strain on the back; i. e., bottom of sink, 30 to 33 inches from the floor.

The work table should be of some material that does not need to be scrubbed. Marble, or porce-namel, or heavy glass are very good.

The utensils should be of the best possible materials so that they will last, aluminum or agate, depending on the amount of work you are going to do. For some things tin is better. Copper or heavy steel are necessary for some kinds of cooking, as will be explained. Have assorted sizes that you may be able to prepare large or small amounts of food. Standardize your equipment in kind and number as quickly as possible, and have as much as you need but no more, so that a minimum amount of time and energy will be used in caring

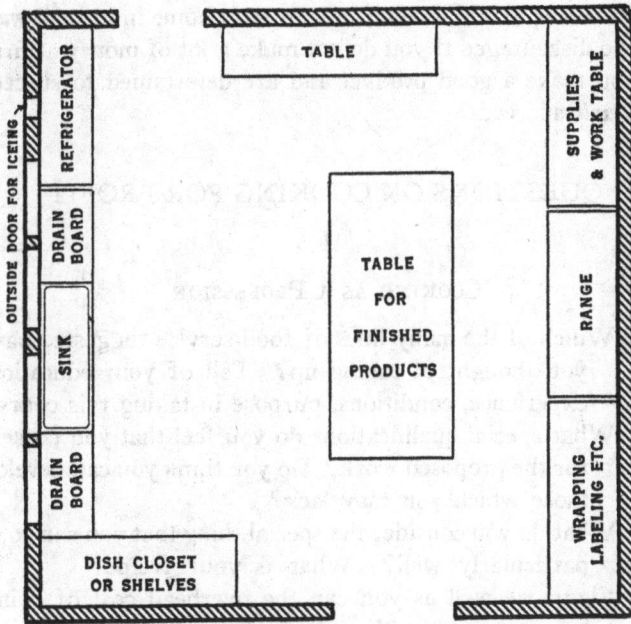

A WELL PLANNED WORKSHOP
(Adapted from Miss Bradley's Kitchen)

for them. Proper care should be taken of utensils that they may last as long a time as possible; the wrong kind of care will make short the life of the best utensil.

An electric egg beater, chopper, etc., may be purchased as soon as your business warrants it, as well as a meat and bread slicer.

Inlaid linoleums make about the best floor covering if well cemented to the floor. The walls should be easily cleanable and the color scheme attractive—light rather than dark. Plenty of light and cross ventilation are very necessary. A ventilating hood over the stove is particularly desirable.

Do not be afraid to start in your own home in a small way, nor be discouraged if you do not make a lot of money at first. If you make a good product and are determined to succeed you *will* succeed.

QUESTIONS ON COOKING FOR PROFIT

I

COOKING AS A PROFESSION

1. Which of the many lines of food service suggested have you thought of taking up? Tell of your education, experience, conditions, purpose in taking this course.
2. What special qualifications do you feel that you possess for the proposed work? Do you think you can develop those which you may lack?
3. What do you consider the special thing that you can cook particularly well? What is your recipe?
4. Figure as well as you can the overhead cost of doing business per month and per day, where you are now located, or in a home kitchen. Give all.
5. How much spare time can you give to cooking for profit?
6. What volume of business in quantity of product and amount of sales must you do to give a fair profit on the time you can spend?
7. What sales plans can you think of to market your product?
8. Draw a plan of your own kitchen (or a kitchen you would like to have). Draw in the things you might cook for profit.
9. What new equipment would you need? What would such additional equipment cost?
10. What question have you to ask on this lesson?

COOKING FOR PROFIT

II

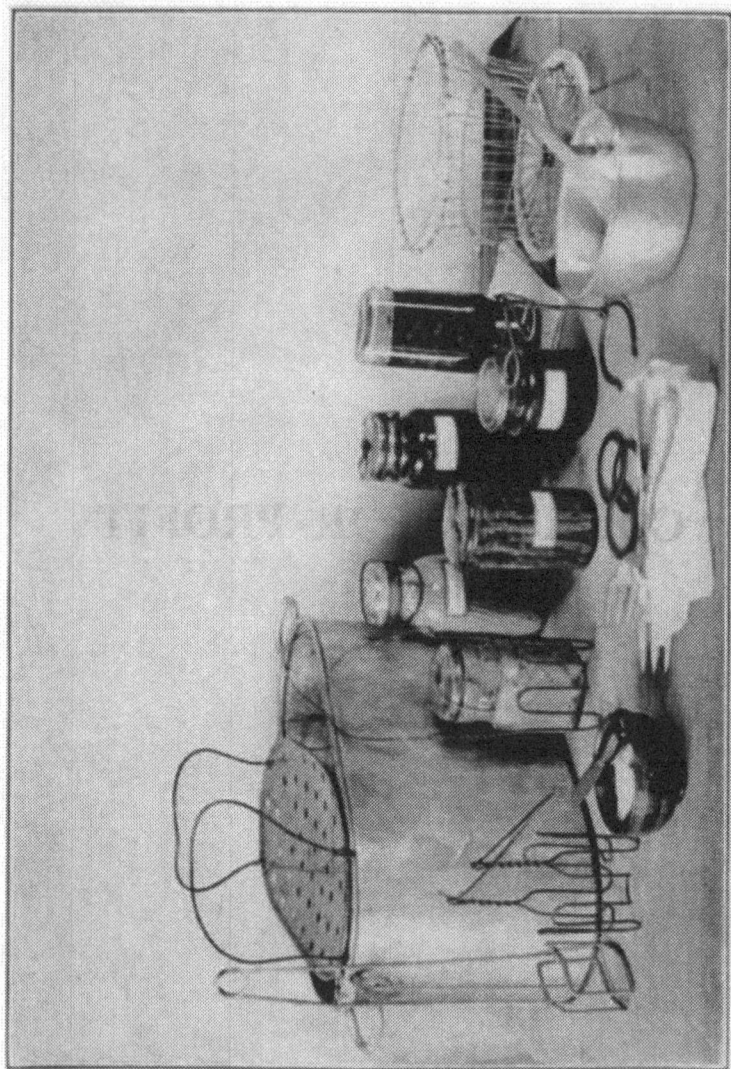

EQUIPMENT FOR HOME CANNING, COLD PACK METHOD

COOKING FOR PROFIT
PART II

SPECIALTY COOKING

CANNED FOODS; STANDARDIZING RECIPES; METHOD OF CAN-
NING; KINDS OF PRESERVES; CONSERVE, JELLIES; PICKLES
AND RELISHES; SALAD DRESSINGS; BREAD, ROLLS; COFFEE
CAKE AND BRIOCHE; BRAN MUFFINS; SANDWICHES; COLD
MEATS; HOW TO BUY.

THE cooked product upon which you decide to specialize should find a market if it is:

1. Something that you can make unusually well.
2. Something unusual that nobody else makes.
3. Something that is not put out by the large manufac-
   turers, as you probably cannot compete in price.
4. Something that people will be eager to buy.
5. Something that you raise in your garden or on your
   farm.
6. Something that can be kept without deterioration and
   can be easily used by the purchaser.

Following are lists of some foods in which others have
specialized with retail prices charged at high class stores or
food shops at the present time.

CANNED FOODS
In Glass

Fruits—$1.25 to $1.40 a quart jar, 40c, 65c, 70c a pint jar.
Vegetables—$1.00 a quart jar, 60c, 70c, 75c a pint jar.
Meats—$1.30 a large jar, 40c a small jar.
Chafing Dish Mixtures (in tins) 25c to 45c.
Grape Juice—75c a quart, 40c a pint, 15c a 4 ounce bottle.
Jellies—50c a 9 oz. jar, 35c 6 oz. jar, 30c 2 oz. jar.
Marmalades—45c a 9 oz. jar, 30c 6 oz. jar, 25c 2 oz. jar.

Preserves—85c to $1.00 a pint.
Jams—85c a small crock, 60c a half pint.
Conserves and Spiced Fruit, 50c a half pint.
Pickles and Relishes—80c to $1.00 a quart, 45c to 55c a pint.
Salad Dressings—Mayonnaise 90c to $2.00 a quart, 50c to 60c a
    pint, 35c a half pint.
Tartare Sauce—60c a pint.
Russian Dressing—75c a pint.

BREAD, ETC.

Bread—17c a 1 pound loaf.
Boston Brown Bread—8c a small loaf.
Assorted Rolls—24c to 40c a dozen.
Sandwiches—96c to $1.20 a dozen.

Miscellaneous

Boston Baked Beans—60c a quart, 35c a pint.

To Order

Beef Tea up to $2.50 a quart.
Broths for Invalids up to $2.50 a quart.
Cream Soups for Invalids up to $2.50 a quart.

The cost of selling is 25% to 40% of the retail price,
therefore if you put your product in a shop you will get
less than these prices. If possible sell direct to private trade
and get all the profit yourself.

One woman who is putting up 28,000 jars of canned fruits,
vegetables and jellies in a season charges $5.85 a dozen pints
and delivers direct to housewives. She takes orders and gets
her empty jars in the spring.

Standardizing Recipes

As soon as possible standardize your recipe, file all data
on cards, and purchase or improvise a box to hold the cards
as they accumulate.

Amounts, cost, et cetera, may be on one side; the method
of preparation may be on the other side of the card, with
other notes. Other cards may have the addresses of firms
from whom supplies are purchased, the names and addresses
and other data regarding your customers, the amounts of
food prepared at different times, et cetera.

SAMPLE CARD

Recipe			GRAPEFRUIT MARMALADE				Date..............	
Material	Amount	Weight	Unit Cost	Total Cost	Overhead Charges	Other Charges	Selling Price	Profit
Grapefruit	1	1 lb.	$1 00 doz.	$0 084				
Orange	1	6 oz.	60 doz.	.05				
Lemon	1	4 oz.	.35 doz.	.03				
Sugar	1½ qts.	3 lb.	.10 lb.	.30				
Water	3 qts.	6 lb.						
Jars	8	6 oz.	7 00 gross	388				
Paper	4 sheets		4 50 per M	.018				
Alcohol		3 grams	10 oz.	.01				
Labels	8		5 00 per M	04				
8 glasses			$0 11½ Ea.	$0 92				

Cards may be purchased in lots of 100 or more. A 4x6 inch card is a good size.

Cost of the 8 glasses of marmalade $0.92. You can add overhead charges, say 2 hours at 20c per hour, (40 cents); your labor, say 2 hours at 40c (80 cents), and sell the 8 glasses for $2.12 (27 cents a glass), or, if you double the cost of materials, as is quite often done, you will sell for $1.84 and will have 92 cents or 20 cents per hour for overhead and 26 cents per hour for your time.

If you sell at retail, charging 35 cents a glass or $2.80 for 8 glasses you will have a margin of $1.88 or 20 cents per hour for overhead, and 74 cents per hour for your time, but you will have to pay for box, paper and string, and maybe delivery charges.

REVERSE SIDE OF THE CARD

DIRECTIONS: Cut fruit in quarters and slice very, very thin, rejecting only seeds of the fruit and the core of the grapefruit. Add water and let stand in an earthen dish over night. Next morning boil until tender and again let stand over night. Boil 10 minutes, add sugar and boil, stirring occasionally that it may not burn, to 220 degrees Fahrenheit. Pour into sterile glasses, let stand, covered with cheesecloth until firm. Cover glasses and label.

Buying supplies in larger quantities at lower rates, slicing fruit with a machine instead of by hand, and otherwise lessening the time consumed, putting the product into larger or smaller jars, would decrease the cost and thus increase the profit.

Hotels and Pullman dining cars are good customers for individual jars of marmalade.

CANNING

Fruits may be canned by the cold pack or the open kettle method. Strive for appearance, flavor and just the right degree of tenderness.

The cold pack method is the best to use for vegetables. They must be canned within a few hours of the time they are picked. Be sure to use new rubbers of a make that will withstand the processing. For full directions send to U. S. Department of Agriculture, Washington, D. C., for Bulletins 839 and 853, also for Bulletins telling about "Canning Clubs," and to your State College for all bulletins they have issued on canning and preserving.

INTERSTATE SALES

Send to your State House and to the United States Bureau of Chemistry, Washington, D. C., for information regarding the requirements of canned goods that are to be sold that you may not unknowingly do anything that will prevent the sale of your goods from one state to another. Briefly, the label must tell the truth and give the net weight in the container.

Read everything you see that can help you in your work. There are several excellent books recently published, which are listed at the end of this lesson.

Kinds of Preserves

In preserves the shape of the fruit should be retained. It is not necessary to follow the old rule—a pound of sugar to a pound of fruit; many people prefer them made with ¾ pound sugar to each pound of fruit. In jams the fruit is mashed and the same proportion of sugar used as in preserves.

Spiced fruits are preserves seasoned with spices and vinegar.

Conserves are preserves to which orange juice and rind, lemon juice, raisins and nuts are added, although nuts may be omitted.

Recipe for Conserve

An acid fruit is ordinarily used for a conserve and a formula something like this:

4 to 5 pounds fruit,—rhubarb, plums, cranberries, peaches, etc.

1 to 2 pounds raisins, stoned and put through food chopper or seedless raisins left whole.

2 to 3 oranges thinly sliced as for marmalade.

1 lemon thinly sliced, if needed for flavor.

5 pounds sugar.

1 pound nut meats.

Water if the fruit is not sufficiently juicy.

Cook fruit until tender, add sugar and cook until it jellies; add nuts just before pouring into glasses.

Many kinds of preserved fruits can be prepared with rhubarb used up to 50% of the total fruit, to reduce the cost and the selling price.

The greatest demand is for standard preserves and canned goods. You might specialize in old fashioned family recipes.

Always use the same kind of jar and glass and cover.

Labeling

Have attractive printed labels after your business becomes established and, if you like, adopt a trade name. Labels are cheaper in lots of 2½ thousand than in thousand lots.

Try to attend exhibitions of canned fruit and vegetables and to exhibit your own products, as you will learn by observation and comparison to tell good canned products when you see them. When starting out to sell your products, it will give you confidence if you know that you have an article that is extra fine.

PACKING FOR MARKET

When packing glass jars for market, the corrugated cardboard boxes, in which the new jars come, will be found to be the best containers. The jars should be wrapped in paper and then placed in the sections of the box. If this box is then packed in a wooden box, there will be little danger of breakage.

CANNING IN OTHER PEOPLE'S HOMES

Many people have large gardens and will gladly pay wages of three, four or five dollars a day to someone who will go to their homes and can fruits and vegetables and make their preserves, jellies and pickles. Assistance will be provided when necessary. The money is all clear profit. A small advertisement in the paper should bring all the customers one could assist.

JELLIES

Jellies and marmalades are stiffened by the pectin which is present in certain fruits, particularly when they are not quite ripe. The pectin must be cooked out of the fruit, but it is weakened or partly destroyed by too long boiling. Jelly results from boiling the pectin containing juices with the proper proportion of sugar, provided acid is present. Commercial pectin may be added to any kind of fruit juice and with sugar very quickly makes a firm jelly.

After preparing the fruit, it is cooked gently till tender in its own juices or with a small quantity of water, 1 to 3 cups

HOMEMADE GOODIES BEING PACKED FOR SHIPMENT

HOMEMADE STUFFED FRUITS, ATTRACTIVELY PACKED

per pound, then allowed to drip through double cheese cloth or through a flannel bag. The clear juice is next measured, boiled 10 minutes or longer according to the density of the juice, and combined with the proper proportion of sugar, after which it is boiled again to the jelly point and poured into sterilized jelly glasses, cooled quickly and sealed.

The amount of pectin present can be judged by adding a spoonful of alcohol to an equal quantity of cooled fruit juice. The pectin is not soluble in this mixture and forms a more or less dense mass. The less pectin present, the less sugar should be used. Three-quarters of a cup of sugar to one cup of juice should make a clear sparkling jelly of the right consistency and flavor. Use a thermometer in making your jellies and, after adding the sugar, boil to 220 to 221 degrees Fahrenheit for a firm jelly.

By covering the fruit pulp with a little water and heating after the first draining, a second and sometimes a third extraction can be made which doubles the amount of jelly secured from a given amount of fruit, without lessening the quality of the jelly. It is best to combine the second and third extractions and boil down until the pectin test shows the correct proportion of pectin present to make a jelly uniform with the first lot.

In making jellies, jams and marmalades, it is best to cook only small quantities at a time. Enough juice for twelve half pint glasses of jelly is a sufficient amount for each kettle. Use a broad bottom kettle filled not more than one-third full and work quickly for best results. By planning the work, at least 100 glasses of jelly can be made in a day.

Fruit juice for jellies may be canned in glass jars during the fruit season, and made up into jelly with the sugar, later on, to fill your orders.

The cost of materials, if all must be purchased, should not be more than one-third of the retail selling price or two-

fifths to one-half the wholesale price. Unless you are near
the source of supply and can obtain fruits at low prices,
your costs may be too high to sell standard goods at a fair
profit.

The most popular jellies are currant, grape, apple, apple
and mint, and quince. Some combinations of fruit are
especially good as:

> Currant and raspberry,
> Quince, apple and cranberry,
> Apple and grape,
> Apple and rhubarb.

FILLING JELLY GLASSES

When filling the glasses pour the jelly first into a teapot
or pitcher and then into the hot glasses which should be
standing in a pan so that no jelly will be lost in case a
glass breaks.

When jelly is cold and firm, fasten a swab of cotton on
a skewer, dip in pure alcohol and wipe over the top of the
jelly, to destroy any germs that might cause fermentation.

Cut glazed paper to fit inside the glass, dip in alcohol,
and lay on top of the jelly. Cover each glass with a larger
piece of glazed paper with edges clipped and paste firmly
to outside of glass.

Paraffin may be used for sealing but is less attractive, and
may not prevent fermentation around the edges, and it costs
more. If the jelly is to be shipped some distance it may be
necessary to supply metal covers.

SPECIAL CONTAINERS FOR JELLIES

Jellies may be put up in unusual sized glasses or jars.
Boxes or baskets holding 6 2-oz. glasses of jelly, each a
different color and flavor, are very popular as gifts.

STANDARDIZATION

Quality and appearance are of the greatest importance. For this the raw materials must be in perfect condition. Satisfy your customer at whatever cost to yourself.

Standardize your product—

Know how many glasses or jars of a jelly or a marmalade or other product you should get from a known weight of fruit and of sugar.

Make every effort to secure the same results each time you make a batch; the difference of one glass will make much difference in your profit.

Weigh a glass that is filled to the right height and be sure that every other glass offered for sale contains exactly the same amount and exactly the same quality of product.

PICKLES AND RELISHES

There are many delicious home made pickles and relishes that are seldom found in the retail stores. If your garden produces a surplus of small cucumbers or tomatoes and you can make your own cider vinegar, your specialty may be right there.

The following pickle is easily prepared and very satisfactory.

Saco Pickle

Sell for $2.00 a dozen in 5½ ounce jars.

Wash and wipe small fresh green cucumbers, pack in glass jars and pour over them the following mixture.

Sift together

1 cup sugar.
1 cup salt.
⅞ cup mustard. Add slowly while stirring constantly
1 quart vinegar. When smooth add
3 quarts vinegar. Have the liquid fill jars to overflowing and cover closely.

SALAD DRESSINGS

A few years ago it was considered necessary to use pure olive oil in mayonnaise and French dressings, but there are several other vegetable oils, including cottonseed, peanut and corn oils, now found to be perfectly satisfactory. Do not, however, charge olive oil prices for a dressing made of a cheaper oil. Salad oil may be purchased in five gallon tins for much less than retail prices.

One Gallon of Mayonnaise

3 tablespoons salt.
3 tablespoons powdered sugar.
3 tablespoons mustard.
½ teaspoon cayenne. Mix well, add
1½ dozen egg yolks, beat until light, add
1¼ cups vinegar. Add very slowly
3½ quarts salad oil. As it thickens, add, a little at a time,
1 cup lemon juice. Add
1 cup boiling water, if desired.
This quantity makes about 9 pints. The cost today is about 33 cents a pint, and it sells for 60 cents a pint.

You may find some sale for Sauce Tartare or Russian Dressing made with a basis of mayonnaise dressing.

Sauce Tartare

To one quart mayonnaise dressing add 3 tablespoons each capers, pickles, olives, parsley, shallot or onion, all finely chopped and ⅛ cup tarragon vinegar.

Russian Dressing

To one quart mayonnaise dressing add slowly
1 cup chili sauce.
⅔ cup pimientos cut in small pieces.
⅛ cup tarragon vinegar.
2 tablespoons chives cut in tiny pieces.
4 teaspoons table sauce, Worcestershire or Escoffier.

An electric mixer, although expensive, is a great help in beating mayonnaise where large quantities are to be made.

BREADS

There is not much profit on plain bread unless made in very large quantities as is done in the large bake shops and factories. However, orders may be secured for breads that are delicious and unusual for use in sandwiches for afternoon tea and other parties.

Yeast breads of different kinds can be developed from a standard formula.

Foundation Recipe for Bread

Put
2½ teaspoons salt
2 tablespoons sugar and
2 tablespoons shortening in mixing bowl; add
2 cups scalded liquid, water, or milk and water, or all milk; when the shortening is melted and the liquid is lukewarm add
Yeast cake dissolved in
¼ cup lukewarm water. If mixed over night use ¼ yeast cake; if mixed in the morning use 1 whole yeast cake. Add
3 cups flour, beat until smooth, add
2 cups flour, stir with a knife until thoroughly mixed, and add about
1 cup flour slowly, using just enough to make dough of such consistency that it may be kneaded without sticking to the board or cloth. Knead until smooth and elastic. Let rise until double in bulk, knead again, shape in two loaves, let rise and bake in a moderate oven about 50 minutes.

Orange Bread

Dissolve
1 yeast cake in
¼ cup lukewarm water; add
1 egg, well beaten,
1 tablespoon melted butter,
1 tablespoon melted lard,
1 teaspoon salt
2 tablespoons sugar
Grated rind 2 oranges
¾ cup orange juice and
3 cups flour. Beat until smooth, adding more flour if necessary; knead until smooth and elastic; let rise until double its bulk; shape in double loaf; put in bread pan; let rise again to double its bulk; and bake 1 hour in a moderate oven.

Whole Wheat or Graham Bread

Add
3 tablespoons molasses and
1 tablespoon shortening
1 teaspoon salt to
1 cup scalded milk; cool, and when lukewarm add
1 yeast cake dissolved in

⅛ cup lukewarm water
1½ cups bread flour and
1½ cups graham or whole wheat flour; beat well, cover, and let
    rise to double its bulk. Again beat, and turn into greased
    bread pans, having pans one-half full; let rise and bake.
    Whole wheat bread should not quite double its bulk during
    last rising.

Orange Peel Bread

To graham bread add before rising.
½ cup candied orange peel cut in small pieces.
½ cup nut meats cut in small pieces.
    When risen cut down with case knife, fill small greased baking
    powder boxes ⅛ full, let rise to double its bulk and bake in
    moderate oven. This is delicious made into sandwiches with
    a filling of creamed butter and orange marmalade.

Prune Bread

Soak
½ cup prunes in
1 cup cold water over night. Cook in same water until soft and
    remove stones. To prune juice add
Boiling water to make 1 cup, bring to the boiling point and pour
    over
½ cup rolled oats. Let stand until water is absorbed, add
¼ cup sugar
½ tablespoon salt
1 tablespoon shortening
½ yeast cake dissolved in
¼ cup lukewarm water and the prunes. Then add
2¾ cups flour, mix thoroughly, let rise, add
¼ cup walnut meats cut in pieces; turn into greased bread pan or
    round greased baking powder boxes, let rise again and bake.

Cornmeal Bread

Mix
½ cup cornmeal
½ cup molasses
2 tablespoons shortening
1 teaspoon salt and
2 cups boiling water. When lukewarm break in
1 yeast cake and let stand until yeast comes to the top. Add
Flour to knead, let rise, shape, put in pans, let rise and bake.

Oatmeal Bread

Mix
1 cup rolled oats
½ cup corn meal
1½ teaspoons salt and

1 tablespoon shortening, add
2 cups boiling water and let stand 1 hour. Add
½ yeast cake dissolved in
¼ cup lukewarm water
¼ cup molasses
3 cups flour and
1 cup rye flour. Mix well, cover, and let rise until double in bulk;
beat well, turn into two greased pans, let rise, and bake in
moderate oven 50 minutes.

A bread that has been popular for many years at a large
Woman's Exchange we call

Winchester Nut Bread

Pour
¾ cup cold water over
½ cup brown sugar; as soon as lumps in sugar are dissolved add
½ cup molasses and
¾ cup milk. Sift together
1 cup bread flour
1⅛ teaspoons salt
2½ teaspoons baking powder
¾ teaspoon soda and add
2 cups Graham flour unsifted. Combine mixtures, and add
¾ cup walnut meats cut in rather large pieces. Bake in a greased
bread pan from 1½ to 2 hours in a slow oven.

Raisin Bread

Make Winchester nut bread omitting the nuts, or make
plain white bread, and add ¾ cup seedless raisins.

Bran Bread

Sift together
2 cups flour
3 teaspoons baking powder
1 tablespoon sugar and
½ teaspoon salt. Add
2 cups bran and rub in
1 tablespoon shortening with tips of fingers. Beat
1 egg yolk, add
1 cup milk, combine mixtures, add
½ cup seedless raisins, and mix well. Bake in greased bread pan
in moderate oven for 1 hour.

Rolls

If you decide to specialize in rolls, purchase as many kinds
as are for sale in the community where you plan to sell yours.

Experiment with the following formula and shapes until
you achieve if possible something that is superior to any
roll that you are able to purchase.

Make your price, as suggested in Lesson I. It will doubtless be higher than the price asked for other rolls that are
for sale, but there should be people glad to pay what they
are worth.

Biscuits and Rolls

(A good foundation recipe)

1 cup milk scalded and cooled. Add
2 to 4 tablespoons butter substitute
2 to 4 tablespoons sugar
1 teaspoon salt
¼ to 1 yeast cake dissolved in 2 tablespoons lukewarm water.
    Use ¼ yeast cake if to rise overnight, 1 yeast cake if mixed
    in the morning.
1½ cups flour. Mix well, let rise and add flour to knead (about
    1½ cups). Knead, let rise again, shape and bake in hot
    oven 15 to 20 minutes.

Experiment with different shortenings and use the cheapest shortening that will give you good results. Use as
much more as you wish up to 8 tablespoons, which will give
a very rich roll.

Variations

2 tablespoons sugar give a good flavor. More may be used up
to 1 cup which makes a sweet bun.
1 or more egg yolks, or from 1 to 3 whole eggs may be added
with excellent results.
1 egg white beaten stiff gives a deliciously crisp crust.

All these suggestions add to the expense of the rolls and
should not be used unless patrons are willing to pay the
price.

Flavor for Rolls

Attractive flavorings which add a distinctive touch.

Grated rind one lemon, or
½ teaspoon lemon extract, or
1 teaspoon vanilla, or
¼ to 1 teaspoon cinnamon, or
½ cup seedless raisins

Add the flavorings after the sponge is light.

SHAPING OF ROLLS

There are many different shapes—one, two or three balls baked in muffin pans, finger rolls, knots, four inches long with pointed ends and cuts across the top. Parker House and cinnamon rolls are the most popular.

The unbaked rolls may be brushed over with melted butter, milk and sugar or beaten egg to soften the crust or to make a glaze, just before they are put into the oven or just before they are done.

Coffee rolls are spread with thin confectioner's frosting after baking. They may be made from Brioche, a rich yeast mixture, or from the recipe given above with two eggs added.

The following rules for Brioche or Coffee Cake are taken from the Boston Cooking School Cook Book.

Coffee Cake I (Brioche)

Scald
1 cup milk; cool, and when lukewarm add
2 yeast cakes; when dissolved add
4 egg yolks
3 eggs
⅔ cup butter
½ cup sugar
½ teaspoon lemon extract or 2 pounded cardamon seeds and
4⅔ cups flour. Beat thoroughly with the hand for 10 minutes and
    let rise for 6 hours. Keep in ice box over night; in morning
    turn on floured board, roll in long rectangular piece ¼ inch
    thick; spread with
Softened butter, fold from sides toward center to make 3 layers.
    Cut off pieces ¾ inch wide; cover and let rise. Take each
    piece separately in hands and twist from ends in opposite
    directions, coil and bring ends together at top of cake. Let
    rise in pans and bake twenty minutes in a moderate oven;
    cool and brush over with
Confectioners' sugar moistened with
Boiling water to spread and flavored with
Vanilla.

Coffee Cakes II

Scald
1 cup milk, add
¼ cup sugar and
1 teaspoon salt; when lukewarm add

1 yeast cake dissolved in
¼ cup lukewarm water and
1½ cups flour. Cover and let rise, then add
¼ cup melted butter
2 eggs well beaten
Few gratings from rind of lemon and
2½ cups flour. Let rise again and finish like Coffee Cakes I.

MIXING AND WEIGHING THE DOUGH

Bread and rolls may be mixed by hand, in an ordinary bread mixer, or in an electric mixer.

Loaves of bread and individual rolls should be weighed before the dough is shaped.

Standardize the weight and size. It must not vary from day to day.

OTHER GOOD SELLERS

Hot Boston brown bread and baked beans are popular sellers in New England on Saturday evenings.

Bran muffins, especially with raisins, prunes or dates, are purchased as a laxative.

Bran Muffins

Sift together
1 cup flour
1 teaspoon soda and
1 teaspoon salt. Add
2 cups bran
1¼ cups milk and
½ cup molasses. Bake in individual tins. This recipe will make one dozen muffins.
¾ cup raisins, dates or soaked prunes, stoned and cut in pieces may be added.

SANDWICHES

There is a market for sandwiches if they are supplied regularly to people who work in large office buildings, factories or schools near your home. A neat basket filled with sandwiches, each one freshly made and wrapped in wax paper, is very quickly emptied. In addition to the sandwiches you may include half pint bottles of milk, homemade cookies, cakes, turnovers and candy if you have time to make them. You might each day supply cooked food, sandwiches, cakes, pies and doughnuts, to soda fountains where luncheonettes are served. Orders can be taken for sandwiches for afternoon teas and receptions.

Use for sandwiches what is known as a sandwich loaf, a loaf of bread square at each end and about 13 inches long.

Purchase a bread slicer to secure ease and uniformity in the slicing of bread.

Learn the number of sandwiches you should get from:

    1 loaf of bread
    1 pound of butter or oleomargarine
    1 pound of cheese
    1 ham, best part sliced, poorer pieces chopped
    1 roast of beef—the face of the rump will do very nicely
    1 fowl
    1 head lettuce
    1 dozen eggs

Use plenty of butter on your bread, especially on the corners. Use plenty of filling in your sandwiches.

Moisten chopped mixtures with mayonnaise dressing.

Use a leaf of lettuce and plenty of salad dressing with your chicken and egg sandwiches.

Occasionally add a new sandwich to the list of old reliable ones.

Know the cost, including butter, wax paper and seasonings, of each sandwich you make and fix your selling price accordingly. One slice bread, doubled and filled, may sell for ten cents.

Computing the Cost of Cooked Meat

Learn the difference in weight between a piece of meat raw and the same piece cooked, the amount of salable cooked edible meat that can be obtained from a given weight and cut of raw meat, and estimate the value per pound of the cooked meat, exclusive of the overhead and labor costs. You will be amazed at the shrinkage. Tabulate your results on a card, and be careful not to lose money if you are asked to sell cooked meat!

Did you know, for example, that cooked chicken meat is worth $2.00 a pound when chicken sells for 50c a pound?

HOW TO BUY

The amount you pay for your raw material will make a big difference in the profit you are able to make. As soon as you find your business is actually started, food stuffs and wrappings should be purchased at wholesale prices. The amount you buy should be governed by

> The size of your storage space.
> The amount that you expect to sell.
> The length of time you expect it to take to use up that material.

With perishable material, order only as much as you can use in a day.

Sugar should be bought in the original packages (100 pound bags or in barrels).

Supplies that come by the case should be bought by the case.

Butter and shortening can be bought in tubs, and in time of plenty and cheap prices can be placed in storage and then taken out as required.

Eggs should be bought by the case, and it may be possible to buy enough for the entire year when they are cheapest and most plentiful and keep them in waterglass, or in storage. Frozen eggs are satisfactory if contents of container can be used as soon as opened.

The containers that you propose to use for your product should be purchased in large quantities, probably after your business is established, in sufficient quantity to last six months or a year. The amount purchased at first should depend on the amount necessary to start your business. If you are starting in a small way you will not buy as much as you will later on when you have become known.

Buy as many supplies as you can direct from the factory, in case lots, so that you will have everything that you need when you need it.

THE STOCK ACCOUNT

There should be a check-up system for supplies. The stock book should usually be balanced daily. Use a double page for each food stuff, etc., which you purchase. On the left side of the book record all the stuffs that are received, whether paid for or not. The page may be ruled into six columns headed as follows:

PASTRY FLOUR RECEIVED
Month, Day, Purchased From, Amount, Unit Cost, Total Cost.

On the right side of the book record food stuffs, etc., that are used and go out, with the cost and with the value of your product, so that you can check up every day and know whether the amount for which you are selling your product is more than sufficient to pay for the supplies that you are using each day.

If preferred, cards may be used for the stock record, one column for goods received, two columns for goods used.

A bill should come with the goods that you order which can be O. K.'d when they are received. You should make a strong point of the way bills come in and are checked up so you will pay for nothing that you do not actually receive. Mistakes are sometimes made by the most reliable concerns.

In the front of the book you may figure what you expect your overhead and operating expenses are going to be, leaving room to figure out accurately what they are. Then right at hand will be the amount per day that must be taken in to cover your daily overhead and operating expenses. When you total up your expenses for the day and your income for the day, you can quickly reckon whether you are making or losing money on each day's product.

Keep your business on a cash basis and pay bills by bank check.

It is a very good plan to deposit *all* receipts in the bank and make *all* expenditures by check. This method, with the use of a Self-Accounting Check Book,* will give you a permanent, classified record of all expenses and receipts.

INVENTORY

The amount of material on hand should be found and entered in the stock book each month before the orders for the next month are given. These figures will be known if you balance daily.

The cost of supplies actually used can then be figured and the total expense, receipts and profit for the month can be accurately determined.

REPAIRS AND EQUIPMENT

Repairs and new equipment should not be entered with the daily food stuffs, but should appear by themselves. They may follow the inventory of the equipment with which you start.

At the end of the year you can estimate whether the

---

* The Office or Household Accounting Check Record, which may be used with the checks of any bank, may be obtained from American School of Home Economics, Chicago. $1.00 postpaid.

amount of depreciation as figured was sufficient to cover the cost of repairs and replacement. Your profit should be sufficiently large for you to have a new stove, work table, etc., if you should need them, and to keep your equipment up-to-date.

REFERENCE BOOKS

NOTE. The following books (and many others listed later) will be loaned to *Members of the School,* one at a time. Send postage with request—8 to 20 cents, according to distance and size of book. They will be sent to anyone on receipt of price and postage.

Successful Canning and Preserving, Ola Powell, $2.50.
Canning, Preserving and Jelly Making, Janet M. Hill, $1.60.
Every Step in Canning, Grace Viall Gray, $1.25.
Everywoman's Canning Book, Mary B. Hughes, $0.90.

Bulletins

For the free Farmers' Bulletins, send to the Department of Agriculture, Washington, D. C. The Bulletins on which a price is given may be obtained by sending currency (not stamps) to Superintendent of Documents, Washington, D. C. For College Bulletins, send direct to the colleges named.

Home Canning of Fruits and Vegetables, Farmers' Bulletin. Free.
Homemade Fruit Butters. Farmers' Bulletin No. 900. Free.
Canned Fruit, Preserves and Jellies. Maria Parloa. Farmers' Bulletin No. 203. 5 cents.
Canning Vegetables in the Home. J. F. Breazeale. Farmers' Bulletin No. 359. 5 cents.
Canning Peaches on the Farm. Gould and Fletcher. Farmers' Bulletin No. 426. 5 cents.
Manufacture and Use of Unfermented Grape Juice, H. Husmann, Farmers' Bulletin No. 644. 5 cents.
Canning Tomatoes at Home and In Club Work, O. H. Benson, Farmers' Bulletin No. 521. 5 cents.
The Preservation of Food in the Home, Stanley and McDonald, University of Missouri, Columbia, Missouri.
Jellies, Preserves and Marmalades. Agnes Ellen Harris, Florida State College for Women, Tallahassee, Florida.
Canned Foods: Fruits and Vegetables. Florence R. Corbett, Teachers College, Columbia University, New York City.
Principles of Jelly Making. N. E. Goldthwaite, Cornell University, Ithaca, New York.
Preserving Fish for Domestic Use. Bureau of Fisheries, Dept. of Commerce, Washington, D. C.

QUESTIONS ON COOKING FOR PROFIT

II

SPECIALTY COOKING

1. Why does jelly "jell"?
2. What are the essential factors for successful jelly making?
3. What are the advantages of canning by the cold pack method? How much canning have you done by this method?
4. Have you special recipes for something canned that you feel might be marketed? If so, what is the recipe? How might this product be marketed?
5. Make an investigation of the quality and price of bread and rolls for sale in your neighborhood and report. Do you think there would be a sale for a better product at a higher price?
6. Would it be possible to build up a trade in sandwiches where you are now situated? If so, what varieties would you make?
7. Make a list of twelve kinds and shapes of rolls and biscuits.
8. Make out a card showing weight of a piece of meat.
   (a) as purchased and cost per pound.
   (b) after cooking and cost per pound.
   (c) edible or salable portion, and cost per pound.
9. Make a sketch of the two sides of a page of a stock book.
10. What bulletins have you sent for on canning, etc? Have you any questions to ask on this lesson?

COOKING FOR PROFIT
III

DIFFERENT TYPES OF COOKIES ATTRACTIVELY DISPLAYED

COOKING FOR PROFIT

PART III

COOKING FOR THE FOOD SHOP

THE FOOD SHOP; DOUGHNUTS, CRULLERS, ECLAIRS, COOKIES
(PLAIN AND FANCY); PLAIN PASTRY,—PIES AND TURN-
OVERS; PUFF PASTE,—PATTY SHELLS, VOL AU VENT, FRENCH
PASTRY; QUANTITIES THAT PAY; CHANGING SMALL RECIPES
TO LARGE ONES; THE DELICATESSEN SHOP.

IN most cities and in many towns there is a food shop
to which consignors may take their products, the shop
selling the food on a commission, or buying it outright.
If there is no food shop in your neighborhood it might be
profitable for you to open one. Perhaps one room in your
home can easily be arranged with tables or counters and
shelves, and as the income increases, glass show cases and
other equipment can be added.

LOCATING A FOOD SHOP

A food shop should be on a main thoroughfare or good
automobile road, where there is constant passing. If you
rent a place for your food shop try to have it on the side
of the street or a corner where people pass in greatest
numbers.

Have an attractive show window with something different
each day, or the arrangement changed, so that there will
be no danger of people thinking that the same food has
been in the window for days at a time. Patrons will come
in because the window appeals to them.

A kitchen shut off by glass partitions only from the food shop is very effective. For such a kitchen the best and most attractive equipment would be required.

To have patrons come again and again the food should be beyond reproach and above criticism.

THE INTERIOR OF THE SHOP

The shop itself should be attractive with the attractiveness that comes from

> The use of broom, dust cloth, soap and water.
> Simple fresh curtains at the windows.
> Neat and polite sales girls.
> Tables and counters thoroughly scrubbed.
> Glass and china clean and shining.
> Silverware thoroughly polished.
> An attractive arrangement of boxes, paper and twine.
> Quick, efficient and agreeable service.

At first you may be able to prepare all the food sold and fill the orders that are taken. If the business grows, as it should, you will find other women who are glad to send in cooked foods, or to fill orders left at your shop. You can charge them a certain per cent of the selling price of the foods they send in, or you can pay them a stipulated price and sell the cake or other food at a profit to yourself, probably an increase of 20% to 40%, depending on your overhead costs.

CONSIGNORS

The selection of the consignors should be most carefully made. The people themselves should be very neat and clean in person. Regular inspection should be made of the consignor's kitchen or work shop that you may know if her product is made under sanitary conditions.

Consignments

Have a definite time when products must be brought in.

Be critical in passing upon consignments,—do not accept anything that is not up to your standard, and have that a high one.

Return consigned articles that are not absolutely right.

Wrappings

Have the paper, boxes, twine and labels standardized for your shop, and supply them to the consignors. Order these supplies where you can get the best prices, and reorder from the same firm or firms if their goods are satisfactory.

The Proprietor's Problem

The proprietor of a cooked food shop must consider costs from a different angle than the consignor. You will have to pay for what you get, but you must make some arrangement for disposing of what remains unsold. You may be able to use it in a tea room or sell it to your employees or to outsiders for the cost of the raw material, or serve it to your help.

You must learn as soon as possible to judge accurately of the amount that you can sell each day.

Good Sellers for a Food Shop

In addition to the canned foods, breads, etc., mentioned in Lesson II, good sellers include doughnuts, cream puffs, pies and turnovers of all kinds, puff paste patties, and of course, all varieties of cakes, cookies and candies. It is wise to have but one consignor for each kind of food.

The Special Dish

In your food shop have special things that it is difficult to get anywhere else. Occasionally have something different, and as your business grows, find new consignors.

DOUGHNUTS AND CRULLERS

One woman earned enough from the sale of doughnuts to support herself and children and send them through college. In some parts of the country the doughnut is called a cruller and in others the cruller is called a doughnut.

This is the recipe for our newest doughnut and the one we like best of all.

Best Ever Doughnuts

Beat slightly
1 egg and
1 egg yolk, adding slowly
½ cup sugar, then add
2 tablespoons heavy cream
⅜ cup milk and
½ teaspoon lemon extract. Sift together four times
2½ cups bread flour
½ teaspoon salt
3 teaspoons baking powder and
¼ teaspoon nutmeg. Combine mixtures. Toss on floured cloth, knead slightly, shape, fry in deep hot fat and drain on paper. For a richer doughnut add
2 teaspoons melted butter.

If this doughnut is too expensive, use a cheaper recipe; one extra egg yolk is a valuable addition to any recipe. The whites can be used in frosting, meringues or cake.

A plain raised doughnut with jelly or jam inside is a good seller.

Doughnuts sell for 40c to $1.00 a dozen.

The cost of doughnuts should be figured per dozen, not forgetting to include in the cost the fat absorbed in the frying.

The homemade doughnut is one for which people are willing to pay an extra price. Where large quantities of doughnuts are made daily, a special equipment for cutting the doughnut, putting it in and taking it out of the fat is used. When this equipment is located in a store window, large numbers of patrons are attracted to buy coffee and doughnuts to eat on the spot, or to purchase doughnuts to take home.

CREAM CAKES AND ECLAIRS

Choux paste is the name given to the mixture from which cream cakes and eclairs are made. It is unlike any other mixture used in cookery. There are many sizes and shapes in which choux paste may be formed by means of a pastry bag and plain tube. It can be made into regular cream puffs and eclairs, into tiny cream puffs one inch in diameter with colored frosting that are nice for afternoon teas, into eclairs three inches long filled and then dipped in frosting of various colors. The tops when frosted can be decorated with nuts or with tiny candies. The filling may be a cooked cream filling, whipped cream or fruit, forced through a pastry bag and plain tube into the cake. They should not look or taste like the variety that can be bought in the ordinary bake shop. The prices charged range from 5 cents to 10 cents each.

COOKIES

You can have a standard formula for cookies, since many cookies can be made from approximately the same rule. The less milk used the better and richer the cookie. Tie them in bundles of 1 dozen each, with coarse thread, each shape by itself. Two cookies with frosting between and on top are attractive. Many mothers will buy oatmeal and ginger cookies for their children. Thick, rich hermits are good sellers.

Cookies

Work until creamy

1 cup butter substitute, and add
2 cups sugar gradually.
4 eggs well beaten
3 cups flour, sifted with
4 teaspoons baking powder
1 teaspoon salt and
1 teaspoon nutmeg if desired. Add
4 tablespoons milk and
3 cups flour and flavoring.

Put in ice box or in a cool place until thoroughly chilled, when mixture should be quite stiff. Take out a small portion at a time, on a floured cloth, roll until thin as paper, shape as desired. Place on greased tin and bake 8 minutes in a moderate oven.

Fancy Cookies

1. Sprinkle mixture generously with cocoanut when partially rolled out, finish rolling.

2. Sprinkle mixture with cinnamon and sugar before cutting out.

3. To ¼ the mixture add 1 cup chopped nut meats, roll thin, shape, sprinkle with chopped nuts and bake.

4. Put a few currants in the center of each cookie before baking.

5. Put 1 teaspoon caraway seed in ¼ the mixture before chilling.

6. To ¼ mixture add 1⅓ squares melted chocolate before chilling.

7. Use maple sugar instead of plain sugar and sprinkle cookies with maple sugar and chopped pecan nut meats.

8. Flavor cookies with grated orange rind.

9. To ¼ mixture add 1 cup chopped candied ginger.

10. Shape cookie mixture with heart, diamond, club and spade cutters. When baked spread hearts and diamonds with frosting colored red, and clubs and spades with melted sweet chocolate.

11. Decorate frosted cookies with leaves and stem of green citron, and flowers made of candied caraway seeds.

12. Cut cookie mixture in circles. On one-half the pieces put 1 teaspoon of raisin or conserve filling, cover with another cookie and press together.

PASTRY

Pastries of all kinds are very good for consigning. The pastry for pies should be a good plain paste, not a puff paste, except for the upper crust of mince pies. For shortening use all lard, or lard and butter, or substitute for either. The formula must be standardized and then followed. BE SURE TO MEASURE ACCURATELY. Standardize by weight the amount of crust that is used for the lining of the pie plate and for the upper crust, so that the crust will always be of uniform thickness. When baking pies have a hot oven at first to cook under crust and prevent escape of juice.

Quick Plain Paste

Put
1 cup lard in a chilled bowl, work until creamy, using a wooden
    spoon. Add
½ cup ice water
3 cups pastry flour and
1 teaspoon salt and mix by cutting with a knife.
    Bind a strip of wet cheesecloth around juicy pies to keep juice
    from coming out.

Selling Price of Pies

The price of 65c for an apple pie and 70c for most of the others is the ordinary charge. Mince pie is more expensive and may have a puff paste upper crust. Individual pies or tartlets can be easily sold in some localities.

Apple, mince, raspberry, pineapple, lemon and banbury tarts sell for from 72c to $1.08 a dozen, or from 6c to 9c each. They should be made of a more flaky pastry than pies, and may be made of puff paste if desired. They should be standardized as to size and the amount of filling used in each.

Puff Paste

Puff paste patty shells, and vol au vents, which are large patties, can be made to order. Puff paste requires experience in making, dexterity in handling, rapid manipulation, ice for chilling and an oven that can be easily regulated. First class puff paste must be made of real butter.

Puff Paste Recipe

2 cups butter, wash, and pat and shape in circular shape. Reserve two tablespoons and put remainder between two pans of ice. Work the reserved butter into

3 cups bread flour, mix to a dough with

1¼ cups ice water, knead 5 minutes, cover and let stand for 5 minutes. Pat and roll ¼ inch thick with square corners. Place butter in center of one side of the pastry, fold other side over butter pressing edges firmly together. Fold one end over butter, other end under butter, pressing edges together. Turn ¼ way round, pat with rolling pin, lift, roll, fold in 3 layers and turn one-fourth way round. Repeat four times, chilling when necessary between pans of ice and folding the last time in 4 layers. Chill, roll out, shape, chill again and bake in hot oven, reducing heat after pastry has risen.

FRENCH PASTRIES

Among the novelties that can be made from puff paste are the following:—

MARSHMALLOW TARTS. Line small patty pan with pastry, then with wax paper, fill with raw rice or beans, bake, remove rice, put in layer of jam, fill with stiff marshmallow cream, and cover with confectioners' frosting flavored with lemon and colored yellow.

MARLOWE TARTS. Prepare cases as for Marshmallow Tarts and cut covers to fit. Bake, fill with fruit, put on cover, frost, and decorate with green cocoanut in narrow border around the top.

AN ATTRACTIVE DISPLAY OF FRENCH PASTRIES

APRICOT TARTS. Line a 2-inch round shallow tin with pastry, fill with marmalade, cover with lady finger mixture, sprinkle with chopped almonds and bake.

APPLE BOATS. Cover small boat-shaped tins with pastry, prick and bake. Remove pastry. Fill with apple sauce, decorate with sections of apple, half of them cooked in plain and half cooked in syrup colored red.

FILENE TARTS. Bake 2 pieces pastry 3 inches long and 1½ inches wide, put together with jam, and decorate top with meringue. Bake until delicately brown.

PASTRY STICKS. Cut pastry in strips 3 inches long and 1 inch wide. Bake, split, fill with jelly, cover with confectioners' frosting and sprinkle ends with chopped nuts.

PETITE GATEAU. Cut pastry 2 inches in diameter. Put border of choux paste around edge, bake, fill centre with jam, and garnish with whipped cream and glacé fruit.

MARMALADE BASKETS. Cut oval pieces of puff paste, score the top one-third inch from edge and bake. Cut strips of paste for handles and bake separately over a stiff piece of paper, the diameter of the paper roll being the same as the width of the oval. Remove centers from baskets and fill with orange marmalade mixed with ¼ the amount of blanched and shredded almonds. Insert handles, decorate with whipped cream sweetened and flavored with very strong coffee and shredded almonds slightly browned.

CREAM HORNS. Roll pastry ⅛ inch thick, cut in strips ¾ inch wide. Roll over forms of stiff paper, bake in hot oven until well puffed and slightly brown. Brush with egg white slightly beaten and diluted with 1 teaspoon cold water. Sprinkle with sugar, return to oven, finish cooking and remove from forms. When cold fill with whipped cream, sweetened and flavored.

PALM LEAVES. Roll remnants of puff paste ⅛ inch thick; sprinkle ½ surface with powdered sugar, fold, press edges together, pat and roll out, using sugar for dredging board; repeat 3 times. After the last rolling fold 4 times. The pastry should be in a long strip 1½ inches wide. From the end cut pieces 1 inch wide; place on baking sheet, cut side down, 1 inch apart, and separate layers of pastry at one end to suggest a leaf. Bake 8 minutes in hot oven; these will spread while baking.

TURNOVERS. Roll pastry ¼ inch thick, and put in pieces 6 inches long and 3 inches wide with round ends. Lay on tin sheet, make a 1-inch cut one inch from each end, put jam or cooked fruit in the centre, bring one end of pastry through hole in other end, press edges together and bake.

QUANTITIES THAT PAY

Of different foods, different amounts will have to be made by a consignor to cover cost of overhead, cost of material used and value of time consumed.

Take, for example, Mock Cherry Pies.

Recipe			MOCK CHERRY PIES					Date	
Materials	Amount	Weight	Unit Cost	Total Cost	Overhead Charges	Other Charges	Selling Price	Profit
Flour	9 cups	2¼ lb.	$15 00 bbl.	$0 172				
Lard	2¾ cups	1¼ lb.	.19 lb.	253				
Water	1½ cups							
Salt	1 T	½ oz.	02 lb.	.001				
Cranberries	4½ qt.	4½ lb.	14 00 per 100 lb.	63				
Sugar	8 cups	4 lb.	.10 lb.	40				
Cornstarch	½ cup	2¼ oz.	.10 lb.	014				
Molasses	1 pint	1½ lb.	1 19 Gal.	15				
Raisins	4 cups	2 lb.	25 lb.	.50				
Salt	2½ T	1¼ oz.		.002				
Water	3 cups							
Pies	8 pies		26 Ea	$2 122				

The recipe costs about $2.12 and makes 8 pies.

This makes 26c as the cost of 1 pie to which must be added 6c as the cost of box, paper, plate and string, 32c as the total cost of each pie to the maker.

Selling price of each pie, if the cost is doubled, 64c.

Allowance per pie for overhead and labor, 32c.

Overhead costs, are, say $1.60 per day, if you hire no help.

Dividing $1.60 by 32c, the cost of 1 pie, shows that 5 pies would cover the cost of overhead for 1 day.

In order to make $3.20 clear (8 hours at 40c an hour), to pay for your labor, would take 10 pies more; that means a total of 15 pies a day.

How long does it take to make 1 pie?

Could you dispose of 15 pies a day?

Then it might be worth while to work up a business in pies, making different kinds according to the season of the year.

If you are operating a food shop yourself, the rent, light, heat, depreciation, labor, advertising, etc., must be considered as your overhead, as explained in Lesson 1.

In your own home, with the simplest equipment, the daily expenses may be no more than $2.00 a day.

Perhaps you plan to specialize in doughnuts. They will cost about 21 cents a dozen; box and string 6 cents more, which makes 27 cents the cost. Selling price $0.60 sold direct to customer. Cost, 27 cents; 33 cents margin.

If you make 33c on each dozen it will take 6 dozen to pay your overhead expenses of $2.00 per day.

If your labor for 8 hours is worth $3.20, it will take 10 dozen to pay for your labor.

This makes a total of 16 dozen for the day.

Or, if you are selling doughnuts for a consignor, you may get 12c for each dozen you sell. Then with overhead and labor at $5.20, dividing by 12 gives $43\frac{1}{3}$ dozen which must be sold daily. If that is not feasible, add other consigned articles to your list, until you are selling enough to pay you for your time and trouble.

CHANGING SMALL RECIPES TO LARGE ONES

In making some kinds of foods for a food shop, just as good results can be secured by making a large quantity as by making a small quantity.

Experiment with your equipment and your strength, making a little more each time, until you discover how much you can make at once without becoming overtired, or changing the quality of your product.

Increase the proportions of each thing, writing down the amounts on paper and verifying your multiplications to be sure they are correct before beginning to cook.

Increasing a Recipe

CREAM CAKES

For 1 doz. large or 3 to 4 doz. small.	For 4 doz. large or 12 to 16 doz. small.
½ cup butter substitute.	2 cups or one pound.
1 cup boiling water.	1 quart.
4 eggs.	16 or 1⅓ dozen.
1 cup bread flour.	1 quart or 1 pound.

CREAM FILLING

For 1 doz. cakes.	For 4 doz. large cakes.
1 cup milk.	1 quart.
⅛ cup flour.	⅔ cup or ⅛ pound.
½ cup scant sugar.	1¾ cups.
1 egg yolk.	4 egg yolks.
¹⁄₁₆ teaspoon salt.	¼ teaspoon.
½ teaspoon vanilla.	2 teaspoons.

Scald milk, add flour, sugar and salt; stir until thickened, cover and cook 15 minutes. Add egg yolk slightly beaten, stir and cook 2 minutes. Cool and add vanilla.

CHOCOLATE CREAM FILLING

For 1 doz.	For 4 doz.
Cream filling 1 cup.	4 cups.
Sugar extra 1 tablespoon.	¼ cup.
Chocolate bitter ¾ ounce.	3 ounces.

Add melted chocolate and sugar to cream filling before adding the egg.

COFFEE CREAM FILLING

For 1 doz.	For 4 doz.
Milk for cream filling 1 cup.	4 cups.
Ground coffee 1 tablespoon.	¼ cup.

Scald milk with coffee, strain and proceed as in cream filling.

CREAM FILLING WITH WHIPPED CREAM

For 1 doz. cakes. | For 4 doz. large cakes.
Cream filling 1 cup. | 4 cups.
Heavy cream ⅓ cup. | 1⅓ cups.

Beat heavy cream until stiff, and add to cold cooked cream filling just before using.

TABLE OF WEIGHTS AND MEASURE

Learn by heart this table of measures adding to it the particular things you use so you can quickly write a large recipe in large terms.

3	teaspoons	equal	1 tablespoon
16	tablespoons	"	1 cup
2	cups	"	1 pint
4	cups	"	1 quart
4	quarts	"	1 gallon
8	quarts	"	1 peck
4	pecks	"	1 bushel
1	cup butter or substitute	weighs	8 ounces
1	cup flour	"	4 ounces
2	cups granulated sugar	"	1 pound
2⅔	cups powdered sugar	"	1 pound
3½	cups confectioners' sugar	"	1 pound
2⅔	cups brown sugar	"	1 pound
2½	cups baking powder	"	1 pound
16	ounces of anything dry	"	1 pound
1	peck apples	"	12 pounds
1	peck cranberries	"	8 pounds
1	peck potatoes	"	15 pounds
1	barrel flour	"	196 pounds
1	barrel potatoes	"	165 pounds

DELICATESSEN SHOP

A delicatessen shop may be desirable in your neighborhood, where people can buy enough food for an entire meal cooked and ready to take home. In such a shop the following foods should sell well, in addition to those suggested in this and other lessons. Have a few different dishes each day, not all the same day.

SOUPS

Meat soups: Consommé, Bouillon, Chicken broth with rice, Lamb broth with barley.
Cream soups: Potato and other vegetable soups.
Chowders: Fish, clam, corn, etc.

SUBSTANTIAL SALADS

Potato.	Moulded salmon.
Chicken.	Cole Slaw.
Crabmeat.	Mixed Vegetables.

MEATS

Roast Stuffed Chicken.	Roast Pork.
Roast Lamb.	Boiled Ham.
Roast Beef.	Corned Beef.
Roast Veal.	Meat Loaves.

MISCELLANEOUS

Corned Tongue.	Fish Balls.
Chicken Stew.	Croquettes.
Lamb Stew.	Macaroni and Cheese.
Beef Stew.	Scalloped Dishes.
Veal Stew.	Potato Chips.
Chicken Pie.	Ice Cream.
Creamed Chicken.	Chocolate sauce for Ice Cream.
Stuffed Peppers.	Butterscotch sauce for Ice Cream.
Goulash.	Charlotte Russe.
Scalloped Oysters.	Rice Pudding.
Baked Beans.	Hot Coffee.

The foods that will sell best depend on :—

> Locality in which the shop is located.
>
> Whether the people in the neighborhood are high salaried or poorly paid.
>
> Their food habits.
>
> Their likes and dislikes.
>
> Their nationality and the season of the year.

Prices must be regulated by :—

> The cost of material used.
>
> Cost of overhead.
>
> The class of people for whom you cater.

SPECIAL BREAKFAST COMBINATIONS

You might have special breakfast combinations such as:

Fruit.

Cooked or individual packages of cereal and one-fourth pint jar thin cream.

Rolls with small portions of butter.

2 eggs or
Sliced bacon or
Fish cakes
Coffee in cheesecloth bags holding 1 ounce (enough for 2 cups).
Sugar, ¼ lb. in paper carton.
Jam or marmalade, individual jars.

DINNER COMBINATIONS

1 hot dish.
Salad.
Salad dressing.
Fresh hot rolls.
Dessert in individual dishes.
Coffee.

Have a distinctive note in your delicatessen to distinguish it from common, ordinary, only half-clean eating places.

REFERENCE BOOKS

Boston Cooking School Cook Book, Fannie Merritt Farmer, $2.50.
New Book of Cookery, Fannie Merritt Farmer, $2.00.
Paul Richards' Pastry Book, $2.50.
Lessons in Cooking Through Preparation of Meals, Robinson and Hammel, $2.00.
Practical Cooking and Serving, Janet M. Hill, $3.00.
Pies and Pastry Desserts, Alice Bradley, In Woman's Home Companion, Nov. 1919.
Puff Paste, Alice Bradley, In Woman's Home Companion, March, 1921.

(The above books may be borrowed, one at a time, by *Members of the School*. Send 12 to 20 cents in stamps, according to distance for each book. Return or purchase within one week of receipt.)

QUESTIONS ON COOKING FOR PROFIT

III

COOKING FOR THE FOOD SHOP

1. How much fat is used in frying two dozen doughnuts?

2. How many cookies can you make from the recipe given in this lesson?

3. What is the cost of cookies per dozen if plain? With three of the variations? Send in all figures arranged on cards as shown on page 48.

4. Change your favorite recipe for one lemon pie to enough for eight pies and figure the cost. How much profit is there on eight pies after deducting overhead costs figured as in Lesson I? Send in all details and figures.

5. Do you make good puff paste? Have you a cook book with directions for making patties?

6. Is there an opening for a cooked food shop or delicatessen in your neighborhood? Your reason for thinking so.

7. Suggest list of foods that might be sold in the Food Shop. In the Delicatessen Shop in your community.

COOKING FOR PROFIT

IV

HANDSOMELY DECORATED WEDDING CAKE

COOKING FOR PROFIT

PART IV

CAKES AND CAKE MAKING

LOAF AND LAYER CAKES; SPONGE AND SUNSHINE CAKE;
ANGEL FOOD; POUND CAKES; FRUIT CAKES (PLAIN AND RICH);
SMALL RECEPTION CAKES; AFTERNOON TEA CAKES; FILLINGS;
FROSTINGS; CAKE DECORATION; RECIPES; HOW TO FIGURE COST
AND SELLING PRICE.

THERE is undoubtedly a market for cake in almost any community of moderate size. Many women have not the time or do not know how to bake cake themselves, and are only too glad to purchase a superior article regularly or when they entertain.

You might in the beginning make cakes to order for your friends and their friends. At first there may be only 3 or 4 orders a week. Before long orders may come for cakes for receptions, lodge suppers, afternoon teas and parties; orders which are large enough to require more than a day for their preparation. Perhaps this may lead to the establishment of an attractive cake shop on the best street of a large city, or to a real catering business where all the other dishes required for a party are provided in addition to the cakes.

No one should expect to make cakes that are good enough to sell at a profit unless she has had some previous experience and success in making cakes.

A cake to be called successful should have these characteristics:

1. Light when handled, except dark fruit cake.
2. Light brown crust on all sides, showing that cake is neither under-baked nor over-baked.
3. Even surface, no cracks or humps.
4. Fine grain.
5. Smooth velvety texture.
6. If frosted, frosting that is attractive in appearance and that does not crack or stick when cut.

Selling Cake

Each specialty shop and home cake maker has her own names and variations in the style of cakes for sale, and in the flavor and character of the filling, frosting and decorations.

Perfect your own specialty; the kind of cake that your patrons like because it is especially good and different, and give it an attractive name in addition to its class name, as pound, sponge, white, et cetera.

In the beginning you will probably make your cakes in the ordinary family quantity. As your orders increase you can increase your quantities until you are mixing perhaps enough for 5 loaves at a time.

With an electric mixer you may be able to make 20 loaves at once, or 40 layers.

Standardize the size of your pans. Always use the same pans for the same kind of cake, unless you have orders for a special size.

Individual cakes, muffin pan size, smaller cakes for afternoon teas, loaf and layer cakes, all are popular.

Cakes may be sold through a food shop, a store, to a lunch room or directly to your customers.

A card in the local paper should secure orders in a community where much entertaining is done.

A dainty folder listing the kinds of cakes you will make to order could be mailed to such people as you think would be interested.

A neighborhood of high class apartment houses is a good field in which to start a business in cake making or other cooked food project.

Quality should be your first consideration, and patrons will be found among people of discriminating taste, who have money to gratify their taste.

After your business is started take note of customers' tastes, and cater to them. Some cakes will sell well, and others will not sell even in different sections of the same city. Keep watch of the sales.

Never sell a stale cake or one that is not up to your standard.

How Many Cakes Ahead

Cakes will keep better without frosting than with it. If you have a large cake shop, keep about 3 dozen individual cakes and 2 loaf cakes a day ahead of your orders. Macaroons will probably all be sold every day.

Use for Stale Cakes

Cakes may be sold at cost at the end of the second day, or stale cake, crumbs and ends of cake that result from cutting cake in fancy shapes, may be rubbed through a coarse sieve, or when dry, run through the food chopper. Such crumbs may be substituted for half the flour in hermits, spice cakes and Boston brown bread.

Profit on Cakes

The most common way of charging for cakes, if they are to be sold, is to estimate the cost of materials and double it.

If elaborately decorated, an extra charge should be made proportionate to the time consumed in decorating. If original designs are worked out the price should be proportionately graded.

The cake shop may add an extra charge of 30% to cover cost of selling. This 30% you may add to double the cost of your materials to make your price, when you sell direct to the consumer.

Cake when cut and sold in a lunch or tea room must be priced higher than by the loaf.

Cake Prices

The following list of cakes, popular in a high-class food shop, may help you to choose your specialty in this line.

The small cakes are sold at from 60 cents to $1.44 per dozen. The loaf cakes, which vary in size from 8 by 4 inches to 9 inches square or 9 inches in diameter, sell for from 50 cents to $1.75 each, according to the size and the variety.

Rich dark fruit cake brings from $1.00 to $1.90 a pound.

Small decorated cakes sell for from $1.50 a dozen up, and large decorated cakes up to $10.00 or more each.

POPULAR CAKES

Name	Style	Filling and Frosting
WHITE CAKES		
Angel cake	Round loaf, hole in center	Japanese frosting
Angel cakes	Individual	Japanese frosting
Bride's cake	White loaf	White ornamental frosting
Caramel cake	Loaf	Nut caramel frosting
Caramel layer	3 layers	Nut caramel frosting between and on top
Caramel cakes	Individual	Nut caramel frosting
Chocolate layer	3 layers	Boiled chocolate frosting between and on top
White fruit	Loaf with almonds, citron and cherries	
White loaf	White cake with nuts	

YELLOW CAKES

Favorite loaf	Loaf	White frosting
Favorites	Individual	White frosting
Jelly	3 square layers	Jelly or jam between
Baby Baltimore	Individual	Pink boiled frosting
Lady Baltimore	3 layers	Boiled frosting with chopped nuts between layers, pink boiled frosting on top and sides
Maple layer	3 layers	Boiled frosting flavored with maple or made of maple sugar, between and on top
Owen Wister	3 layers	Boiled frosting with nuts and raisins between and a little on top; plain boiled frosting, flavored with almond and rosewater, on top and sides
Washington pie	3 round layers	Jelly or jam between
White mountain	3 layers	Boiled frosting between, powdered sugar on top
Chocolate cream	Loaf	Boiled frosting covered with melted chocolate
Currant cakes	Individual	Currants in cake
Golden puff sponge	Loaf sponge cake, hole in center	
Hazelnut cream pie	3 layers	Cooked filling with nuts between; boiled frosting on top sprinkled with chopped toasted hazel nuts
Lord Baltimore	3 layers	Boiled frosting with macaroons, nuts and cherries between; boiled frosting on top decorated with cherries and angelica
Orange sunshine	3 layers	Orange filling between layers; boiled frosting flavored with orange on top
Petit Four	Small sponge or pound cakes, assorted shapes	Covered with fondant, decorated with frosting, etc.
Pound	Very rich loaf	
Roxbury cakes	Individual spice cakes	White frosting with small circle of chocolate frosting in center
Sponges	Individual sponge	
Unfrosted walnut	Loaf	Walnuts in cake

CHOCOLATE CAKES

Columbia teas	Individual chocolate	White frosting with bit of chocolate frosting in center
Chocolate caramel	Chocolate loaf	Caramel frosting
Chocolate marshmallow	Chocolate loaf	White marshmallow frosting
Creole chocolate	3 layers, chocolate nut cake	Boiled frosting between and on top. Boiled chocolate frosting on top of white
Creole layer pie	1 yellow layer between 2 chocolate layers	Fudge frosting and marshmallows between and on top
Fudge squares	Thin chocolate nut cake cut in squares	
Fudges	Individual chocolate	Fudge frosting
Fudge cake	Chocolate cake with nuts	Fudge frosting

FRUIT CAKES

Dark fruit cake	Loaf	
Wedding cake	Very rich dark fruit cake	White ornamental frosting

Measurements and Ingredients

Be very careful and accurate in all your measurements. In all our recipes measurements are level.

A good margarine may be used in place of butter. For white cakes it need not be colored. It may be colored for yellow and dark cakes. Fewer or smaller cakes result from a mixture made with margarine in place of butter, and you may find butter more economical to use in spite of the difference in cost.

Fine granulated sugar should be used unless the recipe specifies some other kind.

Frozen egg whites and yolks may be used if the contents of a container can all be used in one day. They come in 10, 20 and 30 pound tubs. Where recipes are increased several times, the difference in the amount of egg used, if they are very large or very small, will be considerable. Break the required number of average sized fresh eggs, measure them and write the amount in your recipe. Then measure eggs thereafter instead of counting them.

Powdered milk dissolved in water may be used in place of fresh milk. It is convenient as it can always be on hand.

Use the best pastry flour, sifted once before measuring.

Use a high class baking powder and the kind with which you secure the best results. Some people prefer soda and cream of tartar in cake. You may use ½ as much cream of tartar as the amount of baking powder called for and ½ as much soda as cream of tartar if you wish. It is wise to use salt in all cake recipes.

Use good flavorings. The price you charge for your cake should cover any difference in cost between good and poor extracts.

Mixing Cake

Follow directions carefully.

With an electric cake mixer, the ingredients can be put in one at a time, and it is not necessary to beat the eggs separately. Baking powder and beaten egg whites should be beaten or folded in by hand after other ingredients are combined by the machine.

Add flavoring with the milk, then if whites of eggs or flour have to be folded in, no further mixing is necessary to thoroughly incorporate the extract.

It is a safe precaution always to line your cake pans with paper, then grease paper and sides of pan, using a rubber set pastry brush and cooking oil.

Use a spatula for cleaning your mixing bowls. Do not waste cake or frosting material.

When cake mixture is put in pan, spread it a little higher on the sides than in the middle, so that it will rise evenly.

Small Cakes

Small cakes may be baked in muffin pans of different sizes, or may be cut from a thin sheet of fine grained rich cake, like the pound cake given below.

Avoid waste in cutting cakes, and use the crumbs in making an inexpensive crumb cake or hermits.

Paper cases can be purchased to use in muffin pans for small cakes. They should be sold in the paper, which can be pulled off when cakes are served.

Baking Cake

If you use an oven with a reliable thermometer, learn at what temperature your cakes bake best and always maintain it.

If you have a gas or electric range and no thermometer, you can purchase a chemical thermometer for about $5.00. Insert it in a large cork, which will hold the thermometer upright. Have a hole made in the center of the top of the oven of the correct size to fit the cork. The thermometer can be easily read on the outside and your temperature maintained evenly and exactly.

Experiment with you cakes and your thermometer until you learn the temperature at which you secure the best results, then you need never fear failure in your baking. You will find the temperature varies with different kinds of cake. For most cakes the thermometer should register between 300 and 400 degrees.

Without a thermometer excellent results can be secured by lighting both burners of a gas oven for ten mintues, putting in the cake and turning off all the heat for five minutes with small cakes and ten minutes with large cakes. Then turn on one or both burners part way and regulate as necessary.

With coal or wood ovens have a good fire when the cake goes in, and increase heat slightly after cake has risen.

The time required for baking may be divided into quarters: during the first quarter the mixture should begin to rise; during the second quarter it should continue rising and begin to brown; during the third quarter it should continue browning; during the fourth quarter it should finish baking and shrink from pan.

When cake is correctly baked, it should shrink from sides of pan, should be of an even brown color, there should be no sound of bubbling when held close to the ear, and a toothpick inserted in the centre should come out clean.

When finished turn out the cake on a wire cake cooler that there may be a free circulation of air on all sides of the cake while it is cooling.

Shapes for Little Cakes (Petit Fours)

When a sheet of cake is cool it may be cut in the following shapes, using a sharp knife or a cookie cutter:
Square—1½ to 2 inches square.
Rectangular—2 inches by 1 inch.
Oval—2 inches long.
Circle—1 to 3 inches in diameter.
Triangle—2 inches by 1½ inches by 1½ inches.
Diamond—1½ inches on each side.
Cutlet—2 inches long.

Fillings and Frostings

Cakes may be split, and a jelly, nut or frosting filling put in between. They may be covered with **frosting on top only,** or the sides may be covered as well.

Cake Decoration

Cakes are decorated for special occasions and holidays.

Decorations may be of frosting, plain or colored, forced through pastry bags of cloth or paper.

For wedding and bride cakes, white frosting is best. For birthday cakes and cakes for holidays and other special occasions, colored decorations on a white background may be used effectively.

A cloth bag with metal tubes, the ends cut in many different ways, may be purchased of a dealer in kitchen furnishings. These are best when white frosting is used.

Paper tubes may be quickly made from a sheet of **firm** letter paper 11 by 8½ inches. Cut from corner to corner into two triangular pieces and form each into a cornucopia by holding by the two sharp ends. Turn in the edges to hold the funnel. The point of the funnel is then clipped to leave a small round opening of desired size for dots, lines and writing.

For leaves, press the point of the paper funnel flat, clip off one-fourth inch from the end, clip off the corners, making a V point, and make a slit one-eighth inch long in the point of the V. For large leaves and petals clip more from the end.

For some flower petals, flatten and clip off the point of the funnel as before and cut two notches in the end, making the shape of the letter M or W.

Paper tubes are especially satisfactory when several different colors are being used.

Color pastes or liquid colors that are certified by the Federal Government should be used, and all colors should be light and delicate.

"Half fill a paper funnel with frosting, bring edges of open end together, and fold over twice, that frosting may not come out at the top. Hold the funnel in the right hand with the little finger toward the point of the tube and the thumb and forefinger closed tightly above the frosting. Force the frosting gently through the hole in the end of the tube by squeezing with the right hand and guiding with the left hand. Allow the tube point to rest lightly on the surface to be decorated. Conventional designs may be attempted at first, and soon it will be possible to make flowers and leaves. Do not use a tube after it has become soft and out of shape at the point."
—From Candy Cook Book, by Alice Bradley.

Flowers, leaves and stems may be effectively used for cakes, especially the following. If possible copy from the fresh flowers or from good colored pictures.

Wild roses
Rose buds
Chrysanthemums
Forget-me-nots
Brown-eyed Susans

Jonquils
Bachelor buttons
Violets, yellow and purple
White wild roses with silver dragées in the centre
Lilies of the valley
Sweet peas
Holly
Poinsettias
Butterflies

Colored frosting is generally used for the above flowers, but almond paste, tiny colored candies, angelica, citron, candied fruits and nuts are also effective.

Designs can be beautifully painted with a fine brush and color paste on smooth white frosting.

FROSTINGS

For ornamental frosting decorations you can use
    Boiled frosting
    Uncooked ornamental frosting
    Butter or mocha frosting
    Japanese frosting

OTHER DECORATIONS

These may be used in regular or fancy designs on large or small cakes:
    Nuts
        Almonds, blanched and cut
        Walnuts, whole or cut in pieces
        Pecans, whole or cut in pieces
        Pistachio nuts, blanched and sliced or chopped
    Cocoanut, plain or colored.
    Candied cherries, pineapple or plums cut in small
        pieces
    Angelica
    Citron

Candies
> Candied caraway seeds
> Small red cinnamon drops
> Marshmallows, whole or cut in strips
> Almond paste colored and shaped

DELIVERING CAKES

Deliver your cakes in firm folding boxes, made to order if necessary, of a size to just hold the cake without crushing.

For decorated cakes the box should be large enough to allow for cut or crushed tissue paper between the box and the cake.

For sending fruit cakes by mail, provide tin boxes just the size of the pan in which the cake is baked.

RECIPES FOR ESPECIALLY GOOD CAKES

Boston Favorite Cake

Cream until very soft and light
⅔ cup butter, add gradually
2 cups sugar and
4 egg yolks beaten until thick; then add alternately
1 cup milk and
3½ cups flour sifted with
5 teaspoons baking powder and
½ teaspoon salt; fold in
4 egg whites beaten stiff.

This makes 2 loaves or 4 layers or 2 to 3 dozen small cakes.

Yellow Layer Pie

Cream
½ cup butter, add gradually
1 cup sugar
8 egg yolks well beaten
2 teaspoons vanilla; then add alternately
½ cup milk and
1¾ cups flour sifted with
4 teaspoons baking powder and
¼ teaspoon salt. Bake in three greased layer tins or in loaves.

This is an excellent cake and a practical one when many whites of eggs are needed for white cakes and frostings.

Light Fruit Cake

Cream

1 cup butter, add finely grated yellow rind
1 lemon and
1 cup sugar gradually. Beat
4 egg yolks until thick and lemon colored, add to first mixture and beat thoroughly. Add
1½ cups flour sifted with
1 teaspoon baking powder
¼ teaspoon salt and
¼ teaspoon cinnamon. Add
¼ cup almonds blanched and shredded and .
¼ cup mixed candied fruit; beat well, and fold in
4 egg whites beaten until stiff. Bake in a pan, lined with paper, buttered, and sprinkled with
2 tablespoons each of flour and sugar, sifted together.

Dried fruits or different nuts can be substituted for candied fruits and almonds and flavoring extract for cinnamon.

White Cake

Cream

⅔ cup butter, add gradually
1⅛ cups flour sifted with
½ teaspoon soda; then add
1½ teaspoons lemon juice. Beat
6 egg whites until stiff, add gradually
1¼ cups powdered sugar while beating constantly; combine mixtures, then fold in
⅔ cup flour.

Bride's Cake

Make the White Cake and bake in a loaf, or, if desired, in three molds of graduated size. Put together with frosting between and decorate with ornamental frosting. For a large cake three times the recipe will be needed. A Bride's Cake should contain a ring, a thimble, a coin and a button. These are very small and may be pushed into the cake just before frosting.

Pound Cake

Cream

1 cup butter less 1 tablespoon; add gradually
1½ cups flour. Beat
5 egg yolks until thick and lemon colored and add gradually
1½ cups sugar; combine mixtures, add
5 egg whites beaten until stiff
1 teaspoon vanilla and sift over
1 teaspoon baking powder. Beat thoroughly. Bake in angel cake pan or bread pan 1 hour in moderate oven, or bake in a dripping pan and when cold cut in fancy shapes, frost and decorate.

Sponge Cake

Beat

5 egg yolks until very light, then beat in gradually
1 cup sugar and
1 teaspoon vanilla. Beat
5 egg whites until stiff and dry and fold into the yolks.
Mix
1 cup flour
1 teaspoon baking powder and
½ teaspoon salt and sift and fold gently into the egg mixture.
Bake in an iron frying pan in a moderate oven and split and
fill it when cold, or bake in two layer cake pans, in a sheet, a
loaf, or in muffin pans.

Sunshine Cake

To

Whites 10 eggs add
¼ teaspoon salt and beat until light. Sift in
⅞ teaspoon cream of tartar and beat until stiff. Beat
Yolks 7 eggs until thick and lemon colored and add
2 heaping tablespoons beaten whites. To remaining whites add
gradually.
1½ cups sugar measured after five siftings. Add
1 teaspoon almond extract and combine mixtures. Cut and fold in
1 cup pastry flour, measured after five siftings. Bake in angel-
cake pan, first dipped in cold water, in a slow oven one hour.
Have a pan of hot water in oven during the baking. Frost as
desired.

Angel Cake

Beat

1½ cups egg whites until stiff, using large egg beater.
Remove egg beater and add gradually
1½ cups sugar mixed with
1 teaspoon cream of tartar, folding in with wooden cake spoon.
Cut and fold in
1 cup bread flour, mixed with
¼ teaspoon salt, and add
1 teaspoon vanilla. Turn into an unbuttered angel cake pan, cover
and bake in a moderate oven twenty minutes. Remove cover
and bake from twenty to twenty-five minutes. Invert pan on
wire cake cooler and let stand, when cake should by its own
weight drop from pan.

Fudge Cake

Melt

4 to 8 ounces chocolate over hot water, add
2 egg yolks and very slowly
1 cup milk, sweet or sour, stirring constantly. Cook and stir over
hot water until mixture thickens. then set aside to cool. Cream

½ cup butter substitute; and add
2 cups brown sugar slowly; add
2 teaspoons vanilla and
1 cup milk or boiled coffee alternately with
3 cups bread flour mixed and sifted with
1½ teaspoons soda and
1 teaspoon salt. Add chocolate mixture, beat thoroughly and bake.

Marshmallow Layer Cake

For marshmallow layer cake bake Fudge Cake in three square cake pans lined with greased paper. Remove cakes from tins as soon as they come from the oven. Place marshmallows immediately between and on top of the cakes. The heat of the cakes will cause them to melt slightly and adhere to the cake. Cover with fudge frosting.

Marshmallow Roll

Melt
1 square chocolate in double boiler, add
4 eggs and
½ cup sugar and beat with Dover egg beater over hot water until lukewarm. The mixture should be light and foamy. Remove from fire, beat until cold, add
½ cup flour sifted with
½ teaspoon salt
½ teaspoon cream of tartar and
⅓ teaspoon soda; fold over and over and turn into a dripping pan lined with greased paper. Bake in a moderate oven ten to fifteen minutes. Turn out on a sheet of paper sprinkled with powdered sugar, spread with marshmallow filling, roll up like jelly roll, roll paper tightly around cake and leave until cool. Spread with plain chocolate frosting. When ready to serve cut in diagonal slices. *Be sure to have the filling ready before cake comes from the oven.*

Fruit Cake or Wedding Cake

Cut in pieces
1 pound raisins
¾ cup citron
⅓ cup candied cherries
⅓ cup candied pineapple and soak over night in
⅓ cup grapejuice. Cut in pieces
¾ cup almonds and soak over night in
2 tablespoons rosewater. Dissolve
¼ tablespoon allspice
¼ tablespoon cinnamon
¼ tablespoon nutmeg and
¼ teaspoon clove in
2 tablespoons orange flower water and let stand over night.

Cream
½ cup butter, add
½ cup sugar and
2 egg yolks beaten until thick and lemon colored; add
Spices and orange flower water
¼ cup grape jelly
1 teaspoon melted chocolate
2 egg whites beaten stiff and a portion of
1 cup flour browned in the oven and sifted. Beat, add fruit rolled
   in remainder of the flour, almonds, and
1 cup pecan meats. Mix well, pour into a well greased pan,
   place in a larger pan of boiling water, cover with greased
   paper and bake in a slow oven about 2 hours. Spread cake
   with
Almond paste moistened with white of egg and when this is firm,
   frost and decorate as desired.

Macaroons

Break
½ pound almond paste into small pieces and mix with the hand,
   adding gradually
1 scant cup of sugar and
4 egg whites, which should be a scant half cup. When perfectly
   blended stir in
⅓ cup powdered sugar. Shape with pastry bag and plain tube on
   tin sheets covered with thin paper, and bake in a slow oven.
   Remove from oven, invert paper and macaroons, and wet
   paper with a cloth wrung out of cold water, when macaroons
   may be easily removed.
This recipe should make 2 dozen macaroons.

Fudge Squares

Melt
2 squares chocolate, over hot water, add
½ cup butter, stir until butter melts and set aside.
Beat
3 eggs, adding gradually
1 cup sugar. Sift together
¾ cup bread flour with
½ teaspoon baking powder and
½ teaspoon salt. Add to eggs with
1 cup chopped walnuts and
1 teaspoon vanilla, then add chocolate mixture. Spread in shallow
   10x15 pans, bake about ten minutes and cut in squares while
   warm.

Walnut Bars

Beat until light
2 eggs, add gradually
1 cup sifted brown sugar and beat again. Then add
1 cup chopped nut meats
1 cup chopped stoned dates
5 tablespoons flour sifted with

½ teaspoon baking powder and
Few grains salt.   Bake in a greased pan 7 by 10 inches.   When
   cool sprinkle with
Powdered sugar and cut in bars one inch wide and two inches long.

Hermits with Cake Crumbs

   Work until creamy
⅓ cup shortening; add slowly
1 cup brown sugar
1 cup molasses and
4 beaten eggs.   Beat mixture thoroughly, then add
1 teaspoon soda dissolved in
1 tablespoon cold water.   Sift together
3 cups flour
4 teaspoons cinnamon
1 teaspoon allspice
1 teaspoon mace
½ teaspoon clove
1½ teaspoons salt and add alternately with
½ cup milk.   Then add
3 cups fine dry cake crumbs
½ cup citron and orange peel cut in fine strips and
½ cup currants or raisins.   Mix well.   Spread in 4 greased dripping
   pans one-fourth inch thick, bake and cut in rectangles.

FROSTINGS

The favorite frosting on loaf and layer cakes is a boiled
frosting, light and fluffy, beaten by hand or an electric mixer.
This may be piled irregularly on top of the cakes.

Sometimes it is smoothed and covered with a thin layer of
melted bitter chocolate, or with boiled chocolate frosting, or
it is decorated in the different ways already mentioned.

Different cakes which are covered with the same frosting
may be distinguished by a different kind of scroll on the
frosting, made with the handle of a knife as soon as frosting
is put on the cake.

Japanese Frosting

   Work until very creamy
½ cup butter, add slowly while beating
1 cup confectioners' sugar.   Beat
4 egg whites until stiff, beat in gradually
2 cups confectioners' sugar; combine mixtures, add
½ teaspoon vanilla and more sugar if needed.   Use for a rough
   frosting or for decorating cakes as desired.

Chocolate Japanese Frosting

6 squares chocolate; melt over hot water and add slowly to Japanese frosting.

Boiled Frosting

1 to 2 cups sugar, put in saucepan with
½ cup water and boil. Beat
2 egg whites until very stiff, add gradually and one at a time 5 tablespoons of the boiling syrup, beating constantly. When syrup registers 240 degrees on the thermometer or it spins a very long thread, remove from fire, add gradually to the egg whites, beating constantly; add
1 teaspoon flavor and use as desired. If not stiff enough to hold its shape, place over hot water and fold over and over until mixture begins to get sugary on the inside of the bowl, then remove from fire and fold over and over until cold.
Cover with a damp cloth and use at any time during the day. If any is left over it may be used the next day for chocolate frosting.

Marshmallow Frosting

Add to
Boiled frosting while still warm
24 marshmallows cut in small pieces and fold over and over until stiff enough to hold its shape.

Maple Frosting

Use maple flavor in boiled frosting or make frosting with maple sugar in place of granulated sugar.

Chocolate Frosting

Add to boiled frosting enough chocolate melted over hot water to give the desired color and flavor.

Boiled Frosting with Electric Beater

Put in saucepan
3 cups water add
8 cups sugar, stir until dissolved and bring to boiling point.
Put in beater
1½ cups egg whites and begin beating. Add to syrup
1 teaspoon cream of tartar and boil to 228 degrees F. Pour over egg whites, which should be very stiff. Beat until very light.

Nut or Fruit Frosting

To boiled frosting add chopped nuts of any kind, desiccated cocoanut or figs, dates or raisins, or pounded macaroons, alone or in combination.

Pink Frosting

To boiled frosting add rose color paste and flavor with raspberry extract.

Caramel Frosting

Use all brown sugar or part brown sugar and part white sugar in making boiled frosting.

Coffee Frosting

1 cup sugar
½ cup brown sugar
½ cup coffee infusion
2 egg whites
½ teaspoon vanilla
Few grains salt

Make like boiled frosting.

Fudge Frosting

Melt

2 squares chocolate over hot water. Add

1 cup sugar

1 tablespoon flour and

Few grains salt mixed together. When smooth add

⅓ cup milk slowly. Cook until it spins a thread one inch long. Add

2 tablespoons butter and

¼ teaspoon vanilla, cool, beat until of the right consistency to spread without running and pour over cake. If frosting becomes too thick set the pan of frosting over hot water and stir until frosting softens and then pour over the cake.

REFERENCE BOOKS

Lessons in Cooking, through Preparation of Meals, Robinson and Hammel, $2.00.

Boston Cooking School Cook Book, Fannie Merritt Farmer, $2.50.

A New Book of Cookery, Fannie Merritt Farmer, $2.50.

Paul Richards' Pastry Book, Paul Richards, $2.50.

Boston Cook Book, Mrs. Mary J. Lincoln, $2.25.

Practical Cooking and Serving, Janet McKenzie Hill, $3.00.

Choosing Oven Temperatures, Minna C. Denton, in The Journal of Home Economics, December, 1920.

The Candy Cook Book, Alice Bradley, $1.75.

Cake Lesson, Alice Bradley, in Woman's Home Companion, January, 1920.

Frostings, Alice Bradley, in Woman's Home Companion, March, 1920.

(The books in the above list may be borrowed, one at a time, by *Members of the School*.)

QUESTIONS ON COOKING FOR PROFIT

IV

CAKES AND CAKE MAKING

1. What experience have you had in making fine cakes?
2. (a) Do your cakes ever crack open in the middle? Why?
   (b) Do they ever overflow the tin when baking? Why?
   (c) How may you be reasonably certain of an even surface on your cake?
3. (a) What kind of an oven have you, and how do you regulate the baking of cake?
   (b) When is it safe to turn a cake in the oven?
   (c) What test do you use to determine when cake is sufficiently baked?
4. (a) Are you successful in making boiled frosting?
   (b) What do you do if frosting is too stiff or too soft?
5. Have you or can you decorate cakes effectively? Send in several designs for criticism.
6. (a) Can you successfully make a paper tube for use with ornamental frosting?
   (b) Which do you find works to best advantage, a cloth pastry bag and tubes or paper tubes?
7. (a) Estimate the cost of making and frosting one of the cakes in this lesson, including overhead, time, wrapping, et cetera.
   (b) What is the size of the cake?
   (c) What should be the selling price of the cake? Send all data, using the form given on page 48.
8. (a) What are the most popular cakes for sale or that are served in your neighborhood?
   (b) Are there plenty of opportunities for purchasing fine cakes, or do you think there may be an opening for you?
9. Suggest one or more cakes suitable to serve for an afternoon tea, with recipe for same.
10. Are there any questions about the making of cake or frosting that you would like to ask us?

COOKING FOR PROFIT

v

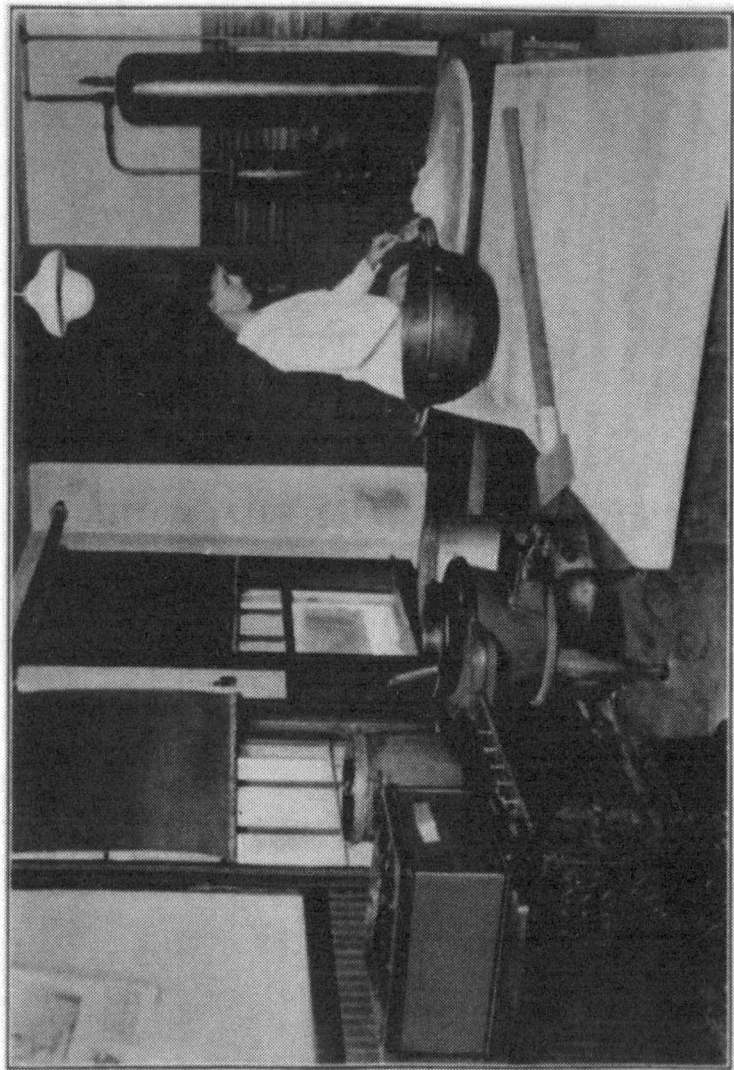

MAKING FONDANT IN KITCHEN OF A "HOME MADE" CANDY SHOP

COOKING FOR PROFIT

PART V

CANDY MAKING

OPPORTUNITY FOR HOME CANDY MAKING; EQUIPMENT; PUR-
CHASING SUPPLIES; PROFIT; USING THE SCRAPS; PACKING FOR
DELIVERY; BEST SELLERS; FUDGES; FONDANT AND ITS USES;
CARAMELS; PEANUT BRITTLE; TURKISH PASTE; BUTTERSCOTCH;
CHOCOLATES; FAVORS; NUTS.

T HE consumption of candy in the United States has
increased greatly in the past few years. The most
conservative estimate places it at 13 pounds per
person for the year at an average cost of 75c a pound. More
candy is purchased in the winter than in the summer. In the
hope of getting part of the profits on such a business, many
women have started to make candy in their own homes, and
have quickly built up a business as large as they could handle.

One woman, after eight years, is supplying candy to 120
retail stores, and at Easter sold 30,000 Easter eggs. Another
woman, one Christmas, refused orders for 4,000 pounds of
candy. A woman whose husband takes care of the sales,
chiefly to workers in offices and in banks, has been able to
purchase a seven-passenger car to use in deliveries.

EQUIPMENT

The equipment required in the beginning is not expensive.
The following articles will be found sufficient at first:

A good reliable thermometer, at least 12 inches long and
one that registers up to 420 degrees Fahrenheit. This
costs about $2.50. A smaller one may be used, but is
harder to read.

75

A set of scales

Measuring cups and quart measure

Spatula, 2½ inches wide and 6 inches long

For large batches, spade 7 inches wide with handle 2½ feet long

Case knife

A long sharp knife

Wooden spoon

Tablespoons

Teaspoons

Saucepans of agate, aluminum or copper with straight sides and smooth bottom

Double boiler

Caramel pans, 10x13 inches square

Mint dropper

Bonbon dippers may be purchased or fashioned at home from a piece of No. 14 wire. They should be 6 inches long and the open bowl of dipper ¾ of an inch across

Iron bars are convenient to have and may be bought at a blacksmith's shop at so much a pound. They should be ¾ of an inch square and as long as your table is wide. The opening between may be made of any size, and candy may thus be cooled on the table without the use of a pan

A large marble slab or table, a porceliron table or a zinc table are desirable to have, but a large enamel tray, or a large platter will be sufficient to start with, and as the business grows you can get what you need. Do not stock up with unnecessary equipment.

As your business grows you will probably need

Molds of plaster to make impression in starch, for shaping centres of chocolates

Starch trays, 2 feet square

Batch warmer, for pulled candies.

THE THERMOMETER

When using the thermometer be sure each time to place it in a saucepan of water and bring to the boiling point to see if it registers 212 degrees F. when the water boils.

If your thermometers register 210 degrees F. at boiling point, your candy has to be cooked 2 degrees less than the degree given in your recipe. If the boiling point registers higher than 212 degrees cook your candy to a higher temperature. If tested each time there is no danger of spoiling your batch of candy.

Be sure that the size of the pan is adapted to the amount of candy that is to be cooked, and that the bulb of the thermometer is covered by the mixture in the saucepan, otherwise you will not get a correct registration.

When cooking in an aluminum saucepan, remove it from the fire when the thermometer registers 2 degrees below the temperature to which the candy is to be cooked, as aluminum holds the heat and candy will finish cooking after being taken from the stove. Remove thermometer when candy is finished and place in boiling water. When not using keep hung up to prevent breakage.

WHERE AND WHAT TO BUY

Get in touch with a reliable dealer in confectioners' supplies. There are several in every large city. They can furnish special articles of equipment, flavoring oils, colors, coating chocolate, nuts, almond paste, glucose and other supplies, and the special kinds of paper, as rice paper, chocolate dipping paper, and wax paper. One woman usually has a standing order for 600 pounds of coating chocolate weekly!

Buy sugar by the hundred-pound bag or by the barrel, which holds between 300 and 400 pounds.

Buy corn syrup in No. 10 cans, by the case, or use glucose, which comes in small barrels or tubs. Use ½-pound glucose, to replace 1 cup corn syrup called for in our recipes. It is usually removed from the container with the hand which is first dipped in cold water. Before taking out the glucose, place on your scales the saucepan that you are to use and note the weight. Then add the glucose, weighing kettle, glucose and all. The difference in weight indicates the amount of glucose added, and should be the same as the amount called for in the recipe, or as suggested above, ½ pound for each cup called for. This is added to give to candies the proper texture, and keep them from becoming "grainy." White corn syrup is best.

Purchase oils for flavoring. They come in 1-pound containers. Only a few drops are required for 1 pound of fondant or other candy.

Buy vanilla by the quart or gallon. Use a first quality vanilla, not vanillin, in high-class candies.

Nuts may be purchased out of the shell. Sometimes, however, the shelled nuts are of inferior grade, and it may be wiser to purchase nuts in the shell, and shell them yourself.

PROFIT IN CANDY MAKING

Estimate the approximate cost of making the mixture which you plan to sell, the length of time required to make and pack the candies, the cost of paper, individual paper cups for holding bonbons and chocolates if you use them, and the cost of the candy boxes. When you estimate the cost of your time, materials and boxes, you will find there is a good profit in candy making. Sixty to ninety pounds of fudge a day can be made by one woman and a strong assistant.

Many women are able to get from 85c to $1.50 for almost every pound of candy they make.

The following figures will serve as an example of the profit on seventy pounds:

FUDGE

To Make 1 lb.	To Make 70 lbs.	Unit Cost	Total Cost
Margarine, 1 tablespoon.....	60T=1⅞ lb.	$0.28 lb.	$0.53
Sugar, 2 cups (1 lb.).....	120c=60 lb.	.08 lb.	4.80
Milk, ¾ cup...............	45c=11¼ qt.	.17 qt.	1.92
Chocolate, 2 squares (⅛ lb.)	120 oz.=7½ lb.	.44 lb.	3.30
Vanilla, 1 teaspoon.........	60t=20T=1¼c	3.00 qt.	.95
Boxes, 1	60	.05 ea.	3.00
Overhead—			
Making, 1 day.................		2.00	
Packing, 1 day.................		2.00	4.00
Cost		$0.22 lb.	$18.50
Selling price		.85 lb.	59.50
Difference		.63	41.00

When 70 pounds of fudge a day are made and sold for 85c a pound at an apparent profit of $41.00, it looks like a lot of money. If two people spend all one day making it, and another day packing, and someone else is spending two days taking orders and delivering the candy, the $41.00 divided by 6 days' work means $6.83 per day per person, and a good wage.

If all your candy is sold to dealers to be resold, the $10.00 which we have here figured for taking orders and delivering the fudge may be their profit: that is, they can pay you 67½ cents, or maybe 65 cents a pound and make a profit of 25% to 30% selling it at 85 cents, leaving you a profit of about 50%.

Other candies can be figured in the same way, and one should know just how one stands financially every day, or at least every week.

Some home candy makers work three days a week making candy, and spend the remainder of the week packing it in boxes. Others keep assistants busy most of the time cutting up and packing for market.

With sufficient room and equipment, and a force consisting of the woman in charge, who makes some of the candies, two other candy makers, two chocolate dippers, two packers, and a man who comes when needed to pack and nail up the wooden cases, from 700 pounds to 1,000 pounds a week of high-class homemade candies can be turned out.

Chocolates can be made up ahead; other candies are best when freshly made.

USING THE SCRAPS

Broken pieces of candy, crumbly fudges, trimmed off edges of candy, and scraps of all kinds should be saved in a sort of "stock kettle." When a sufficient amount accumulates, weigh it. For each pound add ¾ cup milk or water and two ounces of chocolate, or less, according to the amount of chocolate in the scrap. Cook and finish like fudge. Sell at a reasonable price under a particular name as Belgian Fudge.

Waste nothing—material, paper, string, boxes or time— and you will surely be able to clear a good profit on homemade candy.

PACKING AND DELIVERY

Boxes can be purchased from 2½ cents up. If you have an office trade, the cheap box is acceptable because as soon as emptied it goes into the waste basket. You will need better boxes for the home trade. These will cost from 5 cents to 10 cents each for the half-pound size, and from 8 cents to 12 cents for the pound size. Experiment with sizes until you have those just large enough to hold one-half or one pound of your own kinds of candy, then have the boxes made to order with your special name and trade-mark on the cover.

One woman who has built up a very large business has always used simple, inexpensive boxes, preferring to put her money into first-class material instead of into fancy paper, ribbon and cardboard.

Unique arrangements for packing, such as decorated tin boxes, boxes representing bales of cotton, and other unusual styles, have proved profitable to some makers.

Paraffin paper should be used to line each candy box, and may be used to wrap the boxes. A paper seal may fasten the wrapper.

For Christmas trade a red ribbon may be tied around the box under the paper.

Boxes must be wrapped again in plain white paper for delivery.

For mailing, the box should be wrapped again in corrugated paper and then in strong wrapping paper, and firmly tied with string. Make every effort to protect the candy from being broken when received.

Where many boxes go to one address they are packed in wooden cases and shipped by express.

PARAFFIN PAPER

Paraffin paper comes in several different weights and sizes. It can be cut to order to fit candy boxes, and to wrap caramels, lollypops, etc. It is sold by the ream or by the package, usually by the concern from which you get your candy boxes.

Buy the quality and size that you can use without waste.

MARKETING YOUR CANDY

Market your things neatly and attractively and be sure your profit is right from the start, so that you will not have to raise the price.

You will find you will have no trouble to market your goods if quality is your watchword.

If your business grows so fast that you have to have assistants to help you fill your orders, get people who will do the work just as you have done it; that is, do not allow your candy to deteriorate in the slightest degree because you are not doing it all yourself.

The motto of the efficient business person, whether man or woman, is "Do not do anything that you can get somebody else to do." There is more money in the management of a number of people than in doing everything yourself, but you must be very careful that your quality does not suffer in any way as your trade increases.

Best Sellers

There are many kinds of candy that should not be attempted by the inexperienced candy maker, but the following are made successfully in the home:

> Assorted chocolates
> Assorted fudges
> Cream mints
> Cream caramels
> Bonbons
> Peanut brittle
> Corn balls
> Butterscotch in different forms
> Stuffed dried fruits
> Salted nuts
> Glacé nuts and fruits

One woman who is making a great success of the candy business tells in these words what kinds of candies people like best.

"Men's taste is quite different from that of women. Men do not care so much for the rich, creamy candies which women prefer. They like something with more 'body' to it; something they can really chew on. They are fond of chocolate, but they want the center to be nuts, or nougat, or caramels, or molasses. And they like something that has salt in it."

ENLARGING THE RECIPE

Great care must be taken not to enlarge a recipe too much, as often the quality of a large batch of candy is not as good as of a smaller one, and it is more difficult to handle.

When wholesalers wish to put out a new candy, and samples are to be sent out, a small batch is made, and by hand rather than by machinery.

Always boil to the same degree on the thermometer, whether the batch be large or small.

FUDGE AND FONDANT

Fudges of different kinds are easily made, and when soft, fine grained and creamy, are good sellers. A good standard recipe is Chocolate Fudge, given below. For the trade, the recipe may be increased up to about 10 pounds in a batch. More than this is too much to be worked by hand.

Sour cream instead of milk makes a particularly good fudge.

Part water and part condensed milk may be used for fudge.

Fudges should be worked like fondants. They should be cooled before being worked in order to secure a rich, creamy consistency. If fudge becomes too hard to work easily a damp cloth may be laid over it for a few minutes to soften it.

Fudge may be put into a stone crock the same as fondant, after being worked until creamy, and can be softened over hot water. then molded and cut as orders come in.

Shape fudge between candy bars which have been placed upon a wooden table lined with heavy wax paper. Fudge cooled upon marble or in tin cools more quickly on the top and bottom than in the center, and when it is cut it is apt to crumble.

To cut fudge use a strip of wood with straight even edges cut just the width you wish to have your fudge squares, say 1½ inches wide. Lay the wood with the edge parallel with the edge of the fudge and cut fudge beside the ruler with a sharp knife.

When fudge is made in large quantities glucose is often added, but this is not desirable, as it may give your fudge a chewy rather than a creamy consistency.

Do not try to make divinity fudges and nougatines without an electric beater, as too much time is required for beating, and dampness affects the white of egg so that it takes a long time for the mixture to dry out.

Chocolate Fudge

Melt
1 tablespoon butter and
2 squares chocolate over hot water, add
2 cups sugar and
¾ cup milk and stir gently until sugar is dissolved; then bring to boiling point on the fire and boil without stirring to 234 degrees Fahrenheit, or until it will form a soft ball when tried in cold water. Remove candy from fire, pour on damp marble slab, let stand undisturbed until cool, add
1 teaspoon vanilla or
¼ teaspoon cinnamon and work with a spatula until candy begins to get sugary. Turn immediately into a buttered pan, or between bars, and mark in squares with a knife. The pan or space should be about 7 inches square, so that the fudge will be ¾ of an inch thick when cut.

Popular Fudge Combinations

Opera fudges, especially with cherries and nuts
Chocolate fudge, plain and with nuts
Marshmallow fudge
Maple fudge, with and without nuts

Opera Fudge

Put in saucepan
2 cups sugar, add
1 cup heavy cream, stir back and forth until it boils, add
⅛ teaspoon cream of tartar and boil to 238 degrees Fahrenheit,
   stirring frequently and moving thermometer about to prevent
   burning. Finish like Chocolate Fudge. When it becomes
   creamy cover with a damp cloth for half an hour, then add
½ teaspoon vanilla or other flavoring and color if desired, working
   it in well with the hands. Press into shape and when firm
   cut into squares. This may be used for centers for chocolates
   and for centers and coating of bonbons.

This is a rich soft fudge made with heavy cream instead
of milk. It may be colored and flavored in various ways.
This is the candy on which one young woman built up a
candy business that has been successful for many years.

Opera fudge may be cut like other fudge or used as
fondant is used.

Opera Fudge Variations

Color pink, flavor with raspberry, add if desired ½ cup blanched
   almonds cut in pieces, or shredded cocoanut
Color green, flavor with almond and vanilla, and add if desired ¼
   cup pistachio nuts cut in pieces
Color pale violet and flavor with violet
Color pale yellow and flavor with lemon
Color orange and flavor with orange
Add 3 tablespoons candied cherries cut in pieces, 3 tablespoons
   citron cut in pieces and flavor with maraschino
Add 12 marshmallows cut in pieces, flavor with 4 teaspoons orange
   flower water
Add chopped almonds, flavor with almond
Add chopped candied pineapple, flavor with pineapple
Add chopped candied plums, flavor with lemon
Add chopped candied ginger
Add melted chocolate with or without chopped nuts

White Fondant

Put
5 cups sugar and
1½ cups water in smooth saucepan, place on range, and stir constantly until boiling point is reached. With a damp cloth or
   pastry brush dipped in cold water, wash down the sides of
   the saucepan until every grain of sugar is removed. Add
¼ teaspoon cream of tartar, cover saucepan, and allow candy to
   steam for three minutes. Remove cover, put in thermometer.

and boil rapidly until candy forms a soft ball when tried in cold water, or until thermometer registers 238 degrees F. While syrup is cooking wipe marble slab or agate tray with a damp cloth. When syrup is ready, pour gently on the slab. Do not allow the last of it to drip out over what has been poured on the slab, and never scrape out the kettle on the first mixture. Do not disturb the syrup in any way until it is cold. Then with a broad spatula scrape and turn the syrup toward the center, and continue turning it over and over, working from the edges of the mass. Each time that the syrup is turned over, scrape clean and turn the spatula up and over the mass, occasionally scraping mixture from the spatula with a case knife. It will soon become white and creamy.

Knead with the hands until perfectly smooth, cover with a cloth wrung out of cold water, and leave for half an hour.

Cut in pieces and put into a stone jar and cover with a wet cloth and a cover. It is better to let it remain two or three days before using, and it may be kept for months in a dry cool place.

This fondant may be used for centers of bonbons and chocolates for outside coatings of bonbons or for mints.

Experiment first with the recipe for White Fondant given above. Four times this recipe or 10 pounds of sugar may be used for a batch after some experience. One-half teaspoon glycerine is sometimes added to fondant to give a fine gloss for coating bonbons.

One-third cup corn syrup put in before cooking, or 1 egg white beaten stiff and added when syrup is cold, are often used in fondant for centers.

CREAM MINTS

These are easily made from fondant, and are very satisfactory.

Put plain fondant in upper part of double boiler, and melt over hot water, stirring constantly after fondant begins to soften. Thin with a few drops of cold water or simple syrup if necessary. Flavor with a few drops of any oil, such as mint, lime, clove or cinnamon.

When you find which kind of mint your customers like best, you will, of course, supply them with that particular variety. Shape on paraffin paper or in rubber molds, using a heated confectioner's funnel, or drop from tip of spoon. They may be crystallized.

Crystal Syrup

Put in saucepan
10 cups sugar and
1½ quarts water. Stir until dissolved, bring to boiling point and keep sides of pan washed down with pastry brush to remove crystals. At 216° F., pour some of the hot syrup into graduated tube and if the Beaumé scale floats at desired degree, the syrup is ready. For a fine crystal the syrup should register 32° on this Beaumé scale and 34° for a coarse crystal. Pour syrup from graduate tube back in syrup and bring to the boil again because the least disturbance spoils the syrup. Let syrup stand until perfectly cold. Roll jelly candies such as
Gum drops or Turkish paste in granulated sugar. Place candies on trays in crystal pans, and pour over them syrup to cover. Let stand several hours or over night, then lift candies out on tray and let dry. Syrup may be reheated and used over again if more water is added and syrup tested as before.

Bonbons

These are easily made, but soon grow hard and show white spots so that they must be made fresh more often than some of the other candies.

Fondant is the base, and with nuts and candied fruits, and opera, coffee or maple fondant, a large assortment of bonbons can be made. They are more frequently used in making up attractive boxes than to be sold by themselves.

Centers for bonbons may be shaped by hand or in starch molds. The former are best as they stay soft, and creamy a longer time. With the hands fondant may be shaped in cones, balls, short strips, oval, crescent, and mint.

Bonbon Dipping

For bonbon dipping a candy dipper or a two-tined fork, and two small saucepans, one fitting inside the other, is all the equipment that is necessary. A double boiler may be used, but experience shows that the gloss of the fondant for the coating of bonbons can be better kept if only a small portion of fondant is melted at a time.

If fondant seems too thick to dip in, thin very carefully with cold water or "simple syrup" and be very careful that it does not get too warm. A good test is to drop a little on the back of the hand, and if it is warm, not hot, it is usually right for dipping.

Simple Syrup: Put in saucepan, 1 cup sugar, ⅓ cup water, ⅛ teaspoon cream of tartar, and boil to 220° F.

CARAMELS

These are good sellers. They are best made of heavy cream, although light cream gives a rich caramel. They may be made of part milk and part cream or all milk.

Milk caramels are rich enough if they are to be dipped in chocolate.

In making caramels be sure you have a pan with a smooth bottom, with a large surface exposed to the flame, and the pan only one-third full of mixture that it may not boil over.

Stir gently but firmly and back and forth rather than around.

Caramels should be made in small quantities to keep up the quality, as they are not as satisfactory when made in large quantities.

All corn syrup may be used instead of sugar, but, of course, will not make as good a caramel.

Caramels

Put
1 cup sugar
½ cup corn syrup and
½ cup cream into saucepan, stir until sugar is dissolved, bring to
   boiling point, and boil until mixture will form a soft ball when
   tried in cold water. Stir gently and constantly to prevent
   burning, making the spoon reach all parts of the saucepan.

Do not beat, as beating may cause the candy to become gran-
ular. As soon as candy forms a soft ball add

½ cup of cream. Boil again until it forms a soft ball in cold
water, add

½ cup cream, and boil until candy will form a decidedly firm ball
when tried in cold water. The caramels when cold will be
of the same consistency as this firm ball. Pour caramels into
a buttered pan or between bars 4 by 9 inches. When cool
cut in squares, and wrap in wax paper. If caramel should get
sugary, return it to kettle, add more cream and boil again.
If all the cream is added at once, caramels may be made in a
shorter time, but they will not be as rich and creamy.

Assorted Caramels

To Caramel Mixture add just before pouring into buttered pan
any of the following combinations:

1 cup cocoanut
1 cup nut meats cut in pieces
Raspberry extract and rose color paste
8 figs cut in pieces
¾ cup raisins cut in pieces
16 marshmallows cut in pieces.
3 squares melted chocolate
3 squares melted chocolate and 1 cup blanched almonds
3 squares melted chocolate and 1 cup salted pignolia nuts
1 teaspoon vanilla

NUT BRITTLES

Peanut brittle is a good seller in cool weather, but will
grow sticky in warm or damp weather.

This is best made in a cast aluminum or Scotch iron kettle,
as there is less danger of its burning.

In this recipe butter is better than margarine.

These proportions make 1½ pounds of candy.

If large peanuts are used 1½ cups are sufficient.

The brittle may be poured out upon a greased slab and
broken in pieces, or poured between bars and cut in three-
inch squares, which is the better way to market it if you sell
it by the box.

Other kinds of nuts may be used, though more expensive.

Peanut Brittle

Put
1½ cups sugar
⅔ cup corn syrup and
⅔ cup cold water in iron kettle, stir until mixture boils, cover, and
    boil 3 minutes. Remove cover, and boil to 275 degrees F.
    Add
2 tablespoons butter and
2 cups shelled raw Spanish peanuts and stir constantly about 10
    minutes or less, or until peanuts are cooked. Add
½ teaspoon vanilla and
½ tablespoon soda dissolved in
½ tablespoon cold water and
¼ teaspoon salt. Stir until thoroughly mixed, and turn on slightly
    buttered marble slab or agate tray. Spread as thinly as pos-
    sible, and lift constantly while cooling, using a spatula, and
    pull to distribute nuts evenly. Flatten with palm of hand and
    break or cut in pieces.

TURKISH PASTE

Turkish paste is a good seller, easily made at little cost,
and in great variety.

Agar agar, or Japanese gelatine, gives a paste that breaks
apart, while a sheet gelatine pulls apart. Agar agar is for
sale at drug stores or by wholesale confectioners.

Recipe for Turkish Paste

½ ounce agar agar. Put in saucepan with
1½ cups boiling water and set one side. Put
2 cups sugar and
½ cup corn syrup in another saucepan. Pour
½ cup warm water over agar agar, stir until it reaches the boiling
    point, remove from fire, stir until dissolved, and strain over
    sugar. Stir and cook mixture to 220 degrees Fahrenheit. Add
3 drops oil of lime, or peppermint, cinnamon, clove, lemon or
    orange, and color appropriately. Pour on slab ¾ of an inch
    thick between bars.
When firm cut in squares and roll in confectioners' sugar.

BUTTERSCOTCH

Butterscotch mixture can be used in different ways and is
always popular.

Butterscotch Wafers

In saucepan put

1⅔ cups sugar

½ cup corn syrup and

½ cup water, stir until dissolved, bring to boiling point and boil to
270 degrees Fahrenheit, or until it is brittle when tried in cold
water. Add

1½ tablespoons butter and

1 tablespoon molasses and cook to 280 degrees Fahrenheit, or until
it cracks in cold water, stirring to prevent burning. Remove
from fire, add

¼ teaspoon salt and

1 teaspoon vanilla. Pour from saucepan onto oiled marble slab
into wafers the size of a coin.

Scotch Squares

Make

Butterscotch Wafer mixture and pour onto oiled marble slab between candy bars placed in a square to make mixture one-
fourth inch thick. Mark while cooling, with sharp knife, starting at the outside as edges cool more quickly than center.

Scotch Mallows

Make

Butterscotch Wafer mixture. Prepare

Marshmallow by brushing and leaving exposed to air for several hours, to form a slight crust. Drop marshmallows, one
at a time, bottom side up, into mixture, press down that they
may become completely coated, lift with greased candy dipper
and put on buttered slab, bottom side down.

Lolly Pops

Make

Butterscotch Wafer mixture, pour onto oiled marble slab, cool
slighly, rool up like jelly roll, toss back and forth until cool
enough to handle, cut off with scissors in pieces 1½ inches
long, insert stick in one end. With palm of hand press into
shape. Wrap in wax paper.

Sticks for lolly pops can be purchased in lots of 5,000 from dealers
in confectioners' supplies.

Cream Butterscotch Balls

In saucepan put

1 cup white sugar

½ cup brown sugar

⅓ cup white corn syrup

⅓ cup butter

½ cup heavy cream, stir until well mixed, bring to boiling point,
stir constantly back and forth, and boil like caramels to a firm
ball. Remove from fire, add

1 teaspoon vanilla, lemon or almond extract, pour into a buttered pan and when cool shape into small balls, and roll in powdered sugar.

½ cup walnut or pecan nut meats cut in small pieces may be added when candy is removed from the fire, or balls may be rolled in chopped nut meats.

One woman supplies 3 or 4 large stores with this one candy alone.

Nougatines

Nougatines are popular, but hard to beat without machinery if large quantities must be made.

Esmeralda cream is a variety of nougatine that is successfully made by an amateur. A sufficient quantity to use for dipping in chocolate can be made by the home candy maker.

Recipes may be found in *The Candy Cook Book*.

Chocolate Dipping

Chocolate candies are undoubtedly the most popular candies that are sold, but they are difficult to make by the amateur. It is said to take a year to become an expert chocolate dipper, so it may be well in the beginning, if you decide to market chocolate candies, to hire a professional dipper for that part of the work, although you may make the centers yourself. While you are learning to dip successfully you could be making hundreds of pounds of other candies.

Chocolates should cool quickly, but if placed in the ice chest they are apt to gather moisture. In factories they usually have ammonia refrigeration, and as this is a dry cold and not a damp cold, more satisfactory results can be secured than in the home.

The room in which the dipping is to be done should be free from steam and of an even temperature of 65 degrees to 75 degrees Fahrenheit. On a hot or a rainy day chocolate dipping should not be attempted at home.

Break not less than four pounds coating chocolate in pieces, and put into a double boiler or saucepan over hot water. The two pans should fit closely, that the steam may not escape. Set both pans over the fire until water comes to boiling point in the lower pan. Remove from fire, and stir until chocolate is melted, then remove dish from hot water and beat chocolate gently until it feels a little cooler than the hand, or registers between 80 degrees and 85 degrees on the thermometer. This will take from five to twenty minutes, depending upon the temperature of the room and the amount of chocolate used. At no time should temperature of chocolate go above 125 degrees or below 80 degrees F.

Drop a center into melted chocolate, with candy dipper move it around until well covered, then lift out, upside down, draw across edge of pan to remove excess chocolate, and place on chocolate dipping paper right side up.

Popular Centres for Chocolates

Cream mints
Caramels
Opera fudge
Nuts
Butterscotch
Esmeralda cream
Apricot paste
Fondant

The way in which the chocolate is coiled on top of each piece of candy indicates to the initiated the kind of center used.

Only "coating chocolate" should be used for dipping. There are many kinds on the market from which you can select the quality which your customers prefer.

Chocolate Dipping Paper

This may be purchased in 10-pound cases from dealers in confectioners' supplies. It can be used over again many times to receive dipped chocolates. Table oilcloth is also good.

Favor Suggestions

If you can originate artistic and attractive favors made from candies or dried fruits, or if you can make candy flowers to top off a box of candy, or if you can decorate mints, you can take special orders for them from candy shops, women's exchanges, or from people who are entertaining. Some suggestions are given in *The Candy Cook Book*.

During one winter season lollypops with painted faces and elaborate dresses of crêpe paper, or with colored heads cut from magazines and butterfly bows of tulle or crêpe paper, made popular favors.

Salted Nuts

Heat

½ cup cooking oil in very small pan; when hot, put in enough nuts to cover bottom of pan, and stir until delicately browned. Remove with spoon or small skimmer, taking up as little oil as possible. Drain on brown paper and sprinkle with

Salt. Repeat until all are fried. Blanched almonds, raw peanuts with skin removed, whole pecans and other nuts may be salted in this way.

Spiced Nuts

Prepare salted nuts, and when sprinkling with salt sprinkle also with powdered clove, powdered cinnamon or a mixture of spices. Use instead of salted nuts.

Sugared Peanuts

Remove brown skins from

1 cup shelled roasted peanuts, put nuts in a saucepan and keep in a warm place. Put

1 cup sugar and

½ cup water in another saucepan, stir until sugar is dissolved, and boil without stirring to 238 degrees Fahrenheit, or until candy forms a soft ball when tried in cold water. Hold pan of peanuts several inches above the fire and shake vigorously while slowly pouring syrup over the nuts. Occasionally stir the nuts, then add remaining syrup drop by drop until all is used.

Nuts should be evenly covered with a coating of sugar. If coating is not thick enough, more sugar and water may be boiled and added as before. (One cup almonds, blanched or not as desired, may be used instead of peanuts.)

If you have had little or no experience in candy making but wish to specialize in this line it will be well for you to study *The Candy Cook Book* carefully, then experiment with the recipes therein in about this order, which is the order in which we give lessons in candy making at Miss Farmer's School of Cookery.

Sour Cream Fudge	Scotch Kisses
Opera Fudge	Butterscotch Wafers
Divinity Fudge	Toffee
Penuche	Soft Butterscotch
Fondant	Bonbon Dipping
Uncooked Fudge	Cream Mints
Vanilla Caramels	Chocolate Dipping
Esmeralda Cream	Candy Flowers
Marshmallows	Barley Sugar
Turkish Paste	Spun Sugar
Chocolate Caramels	Crystal Cups
Peanut Brittle	Cocoanut Cakes
Glacé Nuts and Fruits	

There are many things in the candy business that you must learn from experience. It is impossible to cover every point in a lesson or in a book.

Try to learn something every day from your work, your patrons, the people you meet or from the things you read.

Do not try to market great varieties of candy at first. Thoroughly master one kind at a time.

REFERENCE BOOKS

The Candy Cook Book, Alice Bradley, $1.75.
The Art of Home Candy Making, "The Home Candy Makers," with thermometer, etc., $3.75.
Candies and Bonbons and How to Make Them, Marion Harris Neil, $1.50.
Candy Making Revolutionized, Mary Elizabeth Hall, $2.00.
My Candy Secrets, Mary Elizabeth Evans, $5.00.
Rigby's Reliable Candy Teacher, W. O. Rigby, $2.00.
Candy for Dessert, Paul Richards, $1.50.
Confectioners' Journal, Philadelphia, Pa., $3.00.

QUESTIONS ON COOKING FOR PROFIT
V
CANDY MAKING

1. What experience have you had in candy making?
2. Send us the names and addresses of dealers in confectioners' supplies and in candy boxes in your locality.
3. Have you a candy thermometer or are you familiar with the use of one?
4. Have you a broad spatula, 2½ inches by 6 inches, and a bonbon dipper? If not, are you able to get them in your town? You will find them invaluable in many other cooking operations beside candy making.
5. What kind of a table or tray have you for making fondant and fudge? What will it cost to purchase what you may need?
6. Find out what are the most popular candies for sale in your locality, and by whom made. What prices are charged for homemade candies?
7. If you propose to make and sell candy, experiment with chocolate fudge, opera fudge, fondant, mints, bonbons, peanut brittle and caramels. Report as to your results, asking questions about anything that is not clear. If you wish, send us a sample of each kind of candy so that we may be able to help you if you have any difficulties, and that we may judge of the quality of the product that you propose to market.
8. Are there any favors which you have designed or which you make especially well? If so, please describe them, give their cost and probable selling price.
9. How long does it take you to make one rule of butterscotch? How many marshmallows can you dip in it? Estimate the total cost, including materials, overhead, etc. What is the selling price? What is the profit? Send in data as arranged on page 79.

COOKING FOR PROFIT

VI

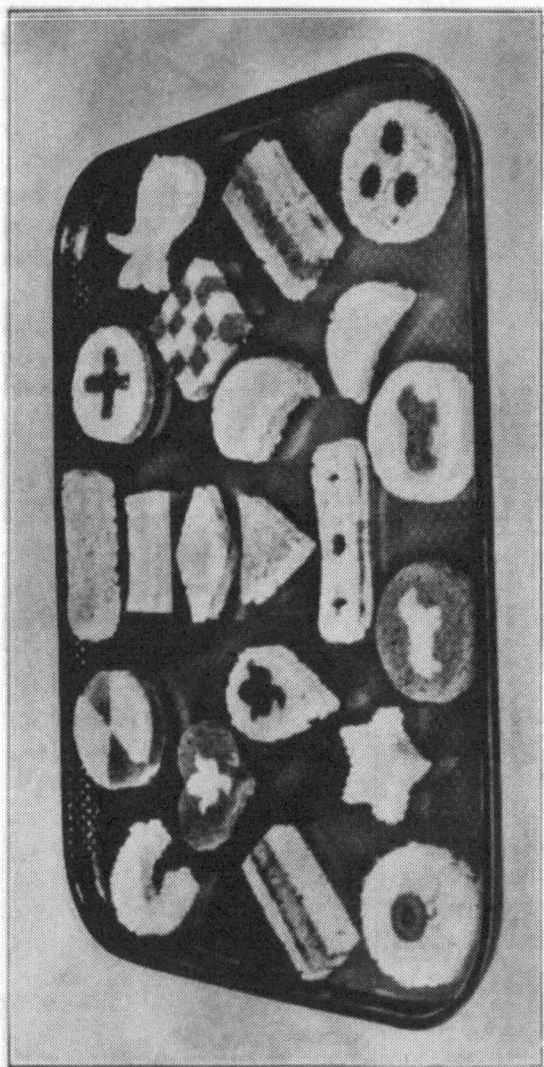

ATTRACTIVE SANDWICHES FOR AFTERNOON TEAS

COOKING FOR PROFIT

PART VI

CATERING FOR SOCIAL OCCASIONS

AMOUNTS TO SERVE; MENUS AND ESTIMATES; AFTERNOON TEAS, BEVERAGES—TEA, COFFEE, CHOCOLATE, PUNCHES; SANDWICHES; COOKIES AND CAKES; HIGH TEAS AND CARD PARTIES; THE BUFFET SPREAD, SERVICE; LAYING THE TABLE; WEDDING RECEPTIONS AND BREAKFASTS; PATTIES AND HOT DISHES; SALADS, ASPICS; DESSERTS, FROZEN DESSERTS; MENUS FOR SOCIAL OCCASIONS; FIGURING COSTS; CATERING FOR A LARGE PARTY.

IF YOU have become successful in making cakes or rolls or sandwiches or patties, or all of these things, people may already have begun to ask you to do other things, and have found that you can make many other dishes equally well. Somebody will soon want to know if you won't plan for and make all the sandwiches and cakes for the afternoon tea she is giving. If she is pleased, she or her friends will ask you to serve a more elaborate spread. Before you know it you may be doing a catering business! It is far better to let your business develop naturally in this way than to open a catering establishment unless you have had considerable experience in cooking for large numbers of people or in the executive part of such a business. Before starting in to do a regular catering business on a large scale it would be well to secure a position in a well established catering firm to learn the many phases of this line of work.

97

Catering *only* would give an uncertain income at the best. It is usually carried on in connection with a cooked food shop, a lunch room, hotel or community kitchen in order to make it a paying proposition all the year round.

Like most businesses, catering is service. It also means much testing, tasting, time, thought and hard work, and *no wasting*.

Usually all dishes are prepared by the caterer and delivered to the place where they are to be served. As a rule no cooking is done on the premises, although facilities for reheating or keeping food hot may be found or provided. Special insulated coffee urns can be purchased of dealers in hotel supplies for $20 to $30, and containers for other hot foods will be made up to order on the principle of the thermos bottle. Frozen dishes are packed in molds and in tubs of ice and salt.

Experience will be your best guide as to the number of sandwiches, cookies and cakes, the amount of salad, ice cream and coffee to provide, but careful, intelligent planning in the beginning is also necessary.

Make up a definite amount of the desired food and note the amount necessary for one portion, and the number of portions in the amount you have prepared. Calculate from this data the recipe for one and then for the whole number to be served. During and after the serving of refreshments watch carefully and correct your estimates if necessary so you will have more accurate data another time.

Basic Portions

The following figures were taken from *The Soda Fountain,* a monthly magazine, and may serve as a guide in your computations.

LEMONADE, FRUIT PUNCH, or other similar liquid beverage served in lemonade or punch cups—10 quarts for each 60 people. Mineral glass portions—10 quarts for each 56 people.

ICE CREAM. 6 standard portions to the quart. If bricks of ice cream are ordered, ready cut, they will make very satisfactory portions if each quart is divided into 8 servings. If a disher or ice cream scoop is used, know exactly how many scoops to a quart and a gallon you can get by using dishers of different sizes, and it will make a difference if these scoops are leveled off or just rounded out with all they will hold. Sometimes the profits go into careless measurements.

FRAPPÉ AND SHERBET, hard frozen—3 gallons for 50 people. Half frozen and beginning to melt—2 gallons for 50 people.

LOAF SUGAR. 1 pound to 24 people.

BERRIES, large sized ones—10 quarts for 50 people. Medium sized ones—8 quarts for 50 people. Smaller sized, sound, ripe berries— 7 quarts for 50 people. Granulated or powdered sugar for berries— 2 pounds for 50 people.

FANCY WAFERS. 3 boxes to 50 people.

BONBONS. 3 pounds to 50 people.

OLIVES of medium size will run about 75 to the pint. Allowing 3 olives to a person, a pint will serve 25.

BOUILLON, hot—12 quarts will serve 50 people, allowing about 7 ounces to a person. Jellied, 8½ quarts will serve 50 people.

WHIPPED CREAM. 1 quart will make 50 rounding tablespoonfuls. One quart refers to the unwhipped cream, and the measurement by tablespoonfuls to the result after it is whipped.

HOT CHOCOLATE. 25 to 30 cups to the gallon, depending on the cup measurement. This amount will take half a pound of chocolate.

CAKES, round loaf or layer, may be made to serve eight people if cut in triangles from the center; or 16 people if cut in quarters and then sliced from the center outward toward the edge. In this case, the pieces are not exactly uniform in size, but the smaller pieces are thicker and the larger ones thinner, so each customer gets the same amount of cake in reality.

CROQUETTES. 6 pounds of meat will make croquettes for 50 people.

OYSTERS. Oysters on the half shell are apportioned at 4 to a customer. Solid oyster meats chopped call for 4 quarts for 50 people. Oyster stew—allow 6 quarts to 50 people. If you wish a more generous allowance of oysters to a serving, allow 7 quarts.

CHICKEN, TURKEY OR ROAST MEAT. Remember that raw meats weigh from two to two and a half times their net weight when cooked. This is because so much of the moisture is evaporated when roasting. With meats which are boiled, or fried, or quickly cooked in any way, the raw meat will weigh about one and a half the cooked portions. Boiled meats will shrink almost as much as roast meats, much of the nutriment going to the gravy or broth. Twenty-five pounds of raw, dressed meat are allowed for the serving of 50 people, if the meat is hot. Cold meat goes farther because it can be sliced thinner, and 25 pounds can be made to serve from 60 to 70 people.

SALMON SALAD. This calls for 6 pounds of salmon for 50 portions.

CHICKEN SALAD. A 4-pound fowl combined with celery and the other trimmings, should make 2 quarts of salad. 2 quarts of salad should serve 12 people or 1 quart to 6 people. 8½ quarts will serve 50 people, and 8½ quarts of salad will call for 17 pounds of fowl. If larger portions are desired, and it is almost solid chicken meat, allow 20 pounds for 50 people.

SANDWICHES. An ordinary sandwich loaf will make 24 sandwiches, or will cut into 48 thin slices of bread; or if you desire a little thicker slices of bread and sandwiches with more substance, cut each loaf into 36 slices or 18 sandwiches. Each sandwich will be the full size of a slice of bread. Allow 2 sandwiches to a person. Or if the sandwiches are cut in two or in triangles, allow 4 to a person.

One pound of creamed butter should spread 3 loaves of bread. One quart of sandwich filling is the average allowance for one loaf of bread.

MENUS AND ESTIMATES

You should plan in advance several menus with standard dishes, suitable for afternoon teas, buffet spreads, wedding receptions, or other functions for which you may be asked to cater, and estimate the amounts required and the entire cost of serving fifty or a hundred or more people with these different menus. Then you will be prepared when you are called upon for an estimate of the expense for such service. With a change of menu there will probably be a change in the price, but something to work from for your patrons will be helpful both to you and to them.

When making up your estimate for any function do not forget to charge for transporting the food from your kitchen to the place where the entertainment is to be given, and do not neglect to charge for your own time including the time of consultation. The distance, the number of people to be served and the menu are important items that determine the price you must charge.

Your business may develop to such an extent that you

will be asked to provide waitresses to set the table and to serve the refreshments, and you may also be requested to provide the tables, chairs, china, silver and linen, and even the decorations.

EQUIPMENT FOR CATERING

You can probably get in touch with a caterer from whom you can hire such equipment as is necessary, on commission. In the same way you can make arrangements with one of the best florists in your vicinity, and make a commission on the flowers and other decorations that you have to provide.

If there are many people in your vicinity who entertain, it may be wise for you to purchase such equipment as is most frequently needed, as china, silver, linen, et cetera, that is not found in sufficient quantities in private homes. You can rent the equipment to your patrons, store it between engagements, and care for it instead of hiring from some one, and it will soon pay for itself, and be a distinct asset to your business.

Very careful figuring will be necessary to arrive at the proper charge to make for the equipment you lend.

The original cost, loss by breakage, loss by theft, general wear and tear, cost of transporting, cost of washing, polishing, repairing, replacing, et cetera, must all be taken into consideration. Sometimes it is necessary to charge almost as much as the original cost of the china or glass each time it is rented.

Fifteen per cent of the total charge for serving a tea may be for the dishes used, while at an elaborate banquet as much as 75 per cent of the charge may be for the equipment alone.

Prices charged for equipment vary with conditions. At one successful establishment the charges are as follows:

One cent each for flat silver.

Fifty cents a dozen for cups, saucers, plates, et cetera.

One dollar and fifty cents a dozen for camp chairs.

A very large establishment may have to furnish awnings, carpeting, dancing crash, tables, etc., and also furnish footmen, musicians, dish washers and lumpers.

There are special business houses in New York, Chicago, Cincinnati, and other large cities which will give you an estimate on the cost of such equipment as you find you need from time to time. Many of these firms advertise regularly in the Hotel and Caterers' Magazines.

Until your business has given you sufficient profit to warrant the purchase of an auto truck, you can hire a truck paying by the day or by the mile, for the transportation of food, equipment, etc. One large concern finds that waiters arrive in less dusty condition at their destination if they go by train or trolley instead of on the truck.

Help Required

One waiter or waitress will probably be needed for each six to ten guests if an elaborate spread is provided.

With simple refreshments and people coming and going during several hours, fewer waiters will be needed.

A dish washer will be necessary to scrape and rinse dishes before they are put back in their containers and returned to headquarters.

Waiters and waitresses should be well trained and know exactly what they are to do while they are in your patron's home.

What to Serve

In this lesson we are giving lists of many dishes that may be used for different menus and for different occasions.

AFTERNOON TEA

It is not necessary to set a table for an informal afternoon tea, but a table should be ready to receive the refreshments in the room in which the guests are to be entertained. The table may be covered with a dainty tea cloth or centerpiece, spotless, unwrinkled, and as elaborate as one desires. A centerpiece of flowers may be in place on the table.

Dishes Suitable for Afternoon Tea

Beverages

Tea with such Accompaniments as
> Lump sugar rubbed over the surface of a washed and dried lemon or orange
> White or red rock candy
> Lemon drops
> Cream
> Sliced lemon
> Cubes of candied pineapple
> Candied or maraschino cherries
> Whole cloves
> Orange marmalade
> Candied ginger
> Candied rose petals or mint leaves

Coffee
> With honey and whipped cream

Add to these lists dishes that you yourself or your patrons like especially, and consult these lists constantly while planning new menus. As you note the cost of each dish and the amount required for a definite number of people, the figures may be placed in columns following the dishes. You will find it of the greatest help to have such lists to work from in planning meals for all sorts of occasions.

A few notes are given to help in serving these refreshments.

> Boiled
> Filtered
> With cream and sugar
> With vanilla extract, sugar and whipped cream

Cocoa or Chocolate

>With cream
>With marshmallows
>With coffee flavor (Mexican chocolate)
>Iced chocolate

Soups

>Mock bisque soup
>Cream of chicken soup
>Beef Bouillon
>Chicken or clam bouillon with whipped cream

Punches

>Blackberry punch
>Cranberry bunch
>Cider and white grape juice punch
>Gingerale lemonade
>Gingerale punch
>Grape juice and orange punch
>Grape juice lemonade with mint
>Ginger punch
>Loganberry punch
>Lemonade
>Orangeade
>Orangeade with gingerale
>Pineapple julep
>Pineapple lemonade
>Tea lemonade
>Pineapple grape juice punch
>Tea punch
>Raspberry shrub punch

Frappés

>Café frappé with whipped cream
>Cider frappé
>Cranberry frappé
>Grape frappé
>Grape juice and mint frappé
>Orange frappé
>Raspberry frappé
>Strawberry frappé

How to Make Tea

Oolong, English breakfast, and Orange Pekoe tea are used for afternoon tea. It may be in the teapot when the tea tray is brought in. The water may be almost at the boiling point in a kettle heated by alcohol or electricity, and should be used as soon as it actually boils. It should stand on the leaves from 1 to 3 minutes only, depending on the kind of tea used. The tea should never be allowed to boil. Fresh leaves should never be added to those that have once been used for tea. Two level teaspoonfuls of tea and 1 pint of boiling water will make 3 tea cups of tea. Sugar and both lemon and cream are provided, and each guest makes her own selection. Other accompaniments are suggested above.

Where only 1 or 2 cups of tea are to be made at a time, a tea ball or perforated double teaspoon half full of tea may be used. Place in the cup, pour on boiling water, lift the ball up and down until the tea is the right strength as indicated by the color, and remove tea ball immediately to another cup or a small dish. Two to 4 cups of tea may be made without refilling the ball.

Iced Tea

In hot weather iced tea may have a greater appeal than the hot beverage. The tea should be freshly made and poured while hot over pieces of ice in tall glasses. Sugar and lemon are used with it.

Coffee

Coffee and cocoa are usually served from urns at which friends of the hostess preside.

Filtered coffee may be made in the urn if it is provided with a strainer or if a linen bag is suspended in the urn.

At a famous restaurant the rule is as follows:

One Gallon Filtered Coffee

Mix thoroughly
8 ounces medium fine ground coffee
½ of 1 egg white
½ cup cold water and
⅛ teaspoon salt; pour over
1 gallon of fresh water which is actually boiling.
Draw off the liquid and pour over and over until of the right strength, then remove bag.

If a percolator is used in which the water bubbles up and falls down through the coffee, it will probably take about 10 minutes to become of the right strength.

Special insulated coffee urns should be provided in which coffee will keep hot for a number of hours if made in one place and served in another, or if it is served at intervals for several hours.

Boiled Coffee for Fifty

Put in coffee bag
1 pound ground coffee, place in container, add
6 to 8 quarts cold water and let stand several hours or over night.
Bring to boiling point and boil 3 minutes. Remove bag and
serve coffee as required.
For After Dinner Coffee use 4 to 5 quarts of cold water.

Cocoa and Chocolate

Cocoa or chocolate may be served from the kitchen or from a
chocolate pot at the table.
Be sure the cocoa or chocolate boils with the water and sugar for
at least 5 minutes before the milk is added, and that it is then kept
hot over hot water or in a special container.

Mexican Chocolate

Scald
1 quart milk with
1 inch piece of stick cinnamon and
3 tablespoons ground coffee. Strain through cheesecloth, add
2 squares sweet chocolate melted over hot water and mixed with
½ cup boiling water. Cook three minutes over hot water, add
½ teaspoon vanilla and serve with
Whipped cream.

Soups

Delicate cream soups are sometimes served at afternoon affairs,
especially at bridge parties. A spoonful of whipped cream slightly
salted or combined with sifted pimiento may be served on the
soup.

Punch

Punch or frappé, which is a half frozen sherbet, is served with a
ladle from a punch bowl, which should be on a small table that is
covered with a luncheon cloth. Punch glasses should be on the
table around the bowl.
A block of ice should be in the punch bowl, also a garnish of
thin slices of fruit or sometimes a bunch of mint leaves. Balls of
lemon or strawberry ice may be used instead of ice in the punch
bowl.
Whipped cream may be put on each glass of some varieties of
punch as it is served.
Gingerale or charged water should not be added to punch until
just before it is served.

SANDWICHES

Five o'clock tea sandwiches should be small and dainty. The bread should be thinly sliced, and the crusts removed. The serving plate may be garnished with cress or small lettuce leaves. White, graham, Boston brown or nut bread may be used. Be careful to spread the butter and filling to the edges and corners of the bread.

Sandwiches may be cut in circles, squares, rectangles, triangles, diamonds or strips. They should be wrapped in a dry cloth, then in a damp cloth as soon as made, and put in a closely covered metal receptacle or crock or wrapped in wax paper.

Bread spread with creamed butter is always in good taste or the following fillings may be used.

Fillings for Sandwiches

Chopped olives or pimolas
Lettuce and mayonnaise dressing
Chopped nuts and creamed butter
Pimiento cheese
Marmalade or strawberry jam
Maraschino cherries and whipped cream
Chopped preserved ginger, cream cheese and chopped nuts
Cream cheese, lettuce and guava jelly
Jam and cheese
Sardine and celery
Lobster and mayonnaise dressing
American cheese and catsup
Creamed butter and anchovy paste
Radishes and mayonnaise dressing
Horseradish butter
Cream cheese and chopped olives
Cream cheese, chopped celery and pimolas
Cream cheese, chopped chicken and mayonnaise
Melted sweet chocolate between buttered bread
Strawberries sliced and mayonnaise
Chopped ham and raspberry jam
Ham and sweet pickles chopped and mayonnaise
Raisins and almonds chopped and marmalade
Raisins chopped and mayonnaise dressing
Cucumber slices and mayonnaise

Ribbon Sandwiches

Layer sandwiches or ribbon sandwiches are made with three or more slices of bread ¼ inch thick, put together with filling. They should be folded in damp cheesecloth, pressed under a weight until serving time, then cut in ¼ inch slices, and arranged on a doily-covered plate. The bread may be all white, or alternate slices of white and dark bread may be used. Nut bread, graham bread, and Boston brown bread are all attractive. The middle slice of bread should be spread on both sides with butter or other filling, and the outside slices should be buttered on one side only. The effect is like a slice of layer cake.

Piquante Ribbon Sandwiches

6 tablespoons butter, work until creamy, add
4 tablespoons grated horseradish
1 teaspoon lemon juice
6 pimolas finely chopped
Few grains salt

Spread a slice of white bread with this mixture, cover with a slice of graham bread, spread with the mixture and cover with a slice of white bread. Prepare other slices of bread in the same way. Wrap in damp cheesecloth, press under a board with a weight on top, and when ready to serve cut in thin slices.

Mosaic Sandwiches

Cut three slices each of white and graham bread one-half inch in thickness. Spread a slice of white bread with creamed butter and place a slice of graham on it; spread this with creamed butter and place on it a slice of white bread; repeat this process, beginning with a slice of graham. Put both piles in a cool place under a light weight. When butter has become firm, trim each pile evenly and cut each pile in three one-half inch slices. Spread these with butter and put together in such a way that a white block will alternate with a graham one. Place again in a cool place under a light weight, and when butter has become perfectly hard cut in thin slices for serving. Arrange on a plate covered with a doily.

Crackers

Small, toasted, unsweetened crackers may be served with soup or tea, or with a filling in place of sandwiches.

Cookies and Little Cakes

These should be small and dainty for an afternoon tea. Cut cake with a soft frosting is difficult to handle, and had best be kept for some other occasion.

Small cakes may be plain or frosted, and sometimes may be decorated.

Recipes and suggestions for cookies and cakes are found in Chapters III and IV, or in standard cook books.

Make up your own list of these cakes and add to it other small cakes that you have found popular. Use this list in planning your menus.

A cross between a wafer and a cracker are the dainty Swedish Tea Cakes.

Swedish Tea Cakes

Beat slightly
1 egg, add
½ teaspoon salt and
Flour enough to make a very stiff dough.
Knead, roll mixture very thin, cut out with small round fluted cutter, fry in hot oil and sprinkle with cinnamon and powdered sugar.

HIGH TEAS AND CARD PARTIES

At an elaborate tea you should not attempt to serve too many dishes, but whatever is served should be as attractive and appetizing as possible.

The menu may consist of sandwiches or rolls, a hot dish, a salad, a jellied or frozen dessert, cakes, bonbons, salted nuts and tea or coffee. If the salad is a frozen one, the dessert should not be frozen; a charlotte russe, or a jellied or fruit dessert, will be satisfactory.

At a card party the card tables are often covered with dainty cloths, and the same kind of menu as suggested above is served at each table.

The salads and desserts should all be served individually.

Refreshments at card parties and club meetings may be easily served from the kitchen on individual trays containing the three or four dishes of the menu.

THE BUFFET SPREAD

At a formal reception, a wedding, a dance or other large party, a buffet spread may be served. At noon it may be called a wedding breakfast, at one or two o'clock a luncheon, in the afternoon a high tea, in the evening a spread or a reception.

At any of these functions the guests may partake of the refreshments standing.

BUFFET SERVICE

When buffet service is used the food is placed upon an attractively laid table, usually all at the same time, although it may be brought to the table and served in courses. Plates, silver and napkins are arranged upon the table to make the service as quick and simple as possible.

The arrangement and service of a buffet luncheon and a buffet spread or supper are practically the same, except that the luncheon often presents heavier and more varied courses, and in the evening lighted candles are used.

The arrangement of the dishes depends largely upon the menu and the number of guests to be served. Rather than have the table appear crowded, it is better to have a maid replenish the dishes and supplies from the serving table or pantry.

The menu may consist of one or two hot dishes, one or two cold dishes, hot rolls and sandwiches, one or two frozen desserts, or one dessert frozen and the other an attractively garnished mold of jelly or cream; cakes, olives, bonbons, nuts, coffee or chocolate and punch. All food should be such as can be easily eaten with a fork or spoon.

The laying of the table should be as follows: After laying the luncheon cloth or the silence and dinner cloth, place the floral decoration in the center, and the candlesticks, two or four, about the centerpiece (these may be omitted for a midday spread). Four dishes of bonbons, or two of bonbons and two of salted nuts or olives should be placed just outside the candlesticks for an evening spread. Next, place two chafing dishes or platters at ends of the table in direct line. These should be filled just before the guests arrive. Each may contain a different mixture, or each may contain the same kind of mixture. The platters for the salad or salads are placed next, at opposite sides of the table. Around these platters and chafing dishes group the forks attractively and the plates in one or two piles. Place the serving silver in the most convenient position, fork at the left and spoon at the right of the salad platters and chafing dishes.

Rolls and sandwiches are arranged on doily-covered plates and placed not too far in from the edge of the table; rolls are served with the hot course, and sandwiches with the salad.

Place small napkins piled diagonally, side and corner alternating, not too high, on two or four opposite corners of the table.

After the hot and salad courses have been served and removed, the ices, with serving silver, are brought in. Cakes arranged on doily-covered plates may be previously placed on the serving table, and passed or placed with ice cream on the dining table. Coffee alone, or coffee and chocolate, may be provided. Either one or both may be served from an urn placed at one end of the table, or the filled cups, either large or small, may be brought in on a tray from the pantry. Punch is usually served from a punch bowl placed with the necessary glasses on a small table in another room.

Friends of the hostess usually serve; sometimes the host and hostess assist, although a waitress may do the passing, removing all soiled dishes, bringing fresh ones and replenishing supplies. A buffet spread for a large reception, where people are coming and going during certain hours, varies from the spread served at a definite hour to a definite number in that all refreshments (hot, cold and frozen) and also the beverages are put upon the table at once.

WEDDING RECEPTIONS AND BREAKFASTS

The refreshments served at a wedding may be simple or elaborate. A Bride's Cake or a Wedding Cake or both may be used with a simple menu or omitted if more convenient. With an elaborate menu they may both be included. If only ice cream and cake are served the ice cream may be brought from the pantry on individual plates by waiters, members of the family or friends, or it may be served in the dining room.

A folded napkin may be under each plate and a teaspoon, or an ice cream spoon may be on each plate as it is passed. The cakes arranged on doily-covered plates may then be passed.

If served in the dining room the arrangement is the same as suggested under a Buffet Spread.

The decorated Bride's Cake may be used as the centre piece.

DISHES THAT MAY BE SERVED AT A BUFFET SPREAD

Patties and Hot Dishes

Any delicate meat or fish, heated in a rich white or cream sauce, may be served in patty cases, timbale cases, ramekin dishes, from a chafing dish or as a croquette.

Mushrooms, truffles, pimientos, green pepper or cheese may be added for flavor and garnish.

Timbales are made of finely chopped chicken, sweetbreads, ham, veal, salmon, or delicate white fish combined with eggs, cream and crumbs, baked in timbale molds, turned out and served hot with a rich sauce. They may take the place of patties.

Suggestions for Hot Dishes

In the chafing dish or in patty cases

Creamed chicken
Russian oysters
Creamed sweetbreads
Creamed oysters
Chicken à la King
Crab meat à la King
Creamed sardines and eggs
Shrimps and peas in white sauce
Chicken and mushrooms
Lobster or other shellfish à la Newburg
Cheese Rarebit
Oyster Rarebit
Tomato Rarebit

Croquettes

Chicken	Chestnut
Lobster	Chicken and mushroom
Sweetbread	Egg
Oyster	Oyster and Macaroni
Salmon	Salmon
Cheese	Veal

Scalloped Dishes

Oysters
Scallops
Fish

Timbales

Chicken
Halibut
Ham
Lobster
Sweetbread and Mushroom

Rolls and Sandwiches

The rolls served at a buffet spread should be small, light, a delicate brown in color, and buttered before they are served, or made so rich with butter that none is necessary. Cream fingers, Parker House rolls or luncheon rolls are usually served.

Sandwiches may be the same as suggested for teas.

Salads

Salads may be made of vegetables, fruit, fish, meat, nuts or cheese, alone or in combination, mixed with salad dressing and served on lettuce or other green.

Mayonnaise dressing, alone or combined with whipped cream, or a cooked dressing may be used.

Every leaf of lettuce should be carefully washed and dried. The ingredients of which the salad is made should be cut in regular pieces of uniform size. The salad filling should be most carefully placed on the green used. Avoid any appearance of carelessness in the arrangement.

Salads are very attractive if the ingredients are combined with 1 tablespoon gelatine soaked and dissolved in 3 tablespoons liquid for each cup of mayonnaise used. They may be molded in individual forms or in large decorated molds.

Frozen salads are popular. For a frozen salad as much cream should be whipped as you will use of mayonnaise dressing. Combine and mix with the fruit, vegetables, lobster, chicken, or whatever is used. Put into small brick molds or baking powder boxes, cover, pack in 1 part ice to 2 parts salt and leave about 2 hours or until frozen. Salad may then be sliced and served on lettuce leaves.

For a very elaborate affair whole small salmon, boned chicken or turkeys may be molded in aspic jelly. The molds are usually elaborately decorated and when turned out are garnished with cress or other green and mayonnaise dressing and make an attractive addition to a buffet table.

Aspics

Highly seasoned soup stock made from beef, veal, chicken or fish, is used for aspic jelly.

Gelatine is dissolved in the stock; it is then cleared, cooled and used in a mold with boned chicken or turkey, salmon, eggs, lobster, chicken salad or other delicate ingredients.

The mold may be a large one and garnished with hard cooked eggs, capers, olives, pickles, truffles, parsley, bits of cooked vegetables, et cetera. It should be well chilled before being turned out on a platter.

A FEW SALADS THAT MAY BE SERVED

Lobster salad
Pear salad—half pears on lettuce, center filled with nuts and mayonnaise
Tomatoes stuffed with chicken or vegetable salad
Alligator pear salad with pineapple and fresh lime dressing
Frozen fruit salad
Mixed vegetables molded in jelly
Sweetbread and celery or cucumber salad
Chicken and celery or cucumber salad
Lobster and celery or cucumber salad
Molded salmon with cucumber sauce
Salmon in aspic
Duck and orange molded in jelly
Molded chicken and celery
Mock lobster salad (cooked halibut, celery and pimientos)
Fresh crab meat salad

Chicken salad molded in frozen tomato
Fresh crab meat salad
Shrimp salad

Frozen Fruit Salad

Mix well
1½ tablespoons flour
¾ tablespoon mustard and
½ tablespoon salt; add
¼ cup condensed milk
½ cup vinegar
½ cup water and
1 egg yolk slightly beaten. Cook over hot water fifteen minutes, stirring constantly until thickened. Remove, strain, add
2 tablespoons butter, and
¼ teaspoon celery seed. Cool, then fold in the stiffly beaten white of
1 egg
½ cup cream beaten stiff and
1½ cups fruit, using oranges, bananas, white grapes and maraschino cherries. Put in small baking powder boxes, cover with buttered paper, then with tin cover, and pack in 2 parts crushed ice to 1 part rock salt for 2 hours. Remove from molds, cut in slices and serve on lettuce leaves.

Dessert

The dessert served at a buffet spread is usually frozen, but jellies, charlotte russe, and Bavarian creams may be used. They should be attractively molded and decorated. They are frequently placed on the table on large platters and should be pleasing to look at as well as to taste.

Jellies

The jellies used are stiffened with gelatine. Powdered gelatine is especially satisfactory as it is quickly softened and dissolved. For flavor lemon juice, orange juice or almost any fresh or canned fruit juice may be used except fresh pineapple juice which has the property of digesting gelatine, thus preventing the hardening of the jelly.

Spanish Cream

Spanish cream is boiled custard stiffened with gelatine and made light and fluffy by the addition of beaten egg whites. The custard may be made of all milk and flavored as desired, or of part milk and part coffee.

Bavarian Cream

Bavarian creams are like Spanish creams with whipped cream folded in just as they are beginning to stiffen. Cooked fruit juices, as pineapple and apricot, may be used instead of milk.

Charlotte Russe

Charlotte russe is made of cream or fruit juice sweetened and flavored, stiffened with gelatine and combined with whipped cream. The mold is usually lined with lady fingers or thin slices of sponge cake.

Fancy Molded Desserts

Jellied desserts may be molded in layers. The mold should be placed in ice water and a thin layer of jelly put in the bottom. This may be decorated with fruit, nuts, etc. Then jelly should be carefully put over the decorations to hold them in place. When firm, more jelly may be added, or beaten jelly, a whipped cream mixture or fruit may be used alternately with the jelly until the mold is full.

Artificial colors, as scarlet, rose, green, orange, etc., may be added to the mixture before it is stiffened.

Fruits or nuts in small pieces may be folded into the mixture, may be arranged in the bottom of the mold, or may be used as a decoration on it or around it, when the mold is turned out.

FROZEN DESSERTS

Recipes for many kinds of frozen desserts may be found in any good cook book.

If two or three kinds of ice cream or ice cream and

sherbet are to be packed in one mold they must each be frozen separately and then packed in alternate layers. This is called Neapolitan ice cream.

Sherbet. A sherbet is a mixture of fruit juice, water and sugar frozen like ice cream.

Frappés. A coarsely frozen water ice or sherbet. Equal parts ice and salt are used and mixture is stirred occasionally until frozen.

Ice Cream. Ice creams are mixtures of cream, sugar and flavoring, turned into the can of a freezer, surrounded with a mixture of 3 parts ice and 1 part rock salt, and frozen while being constantly stirred. Fruit ice creams are made by combining thin cream with sifted fruits and sweetening to taste.

An ice cream stiffened with rennet or junket requires less cream than most other kinds of frozen desserts.

Sometimes flour and eggs are both used to thicken the custard for ice cream.

Ice cream made with many egg yolks is called French ice cream.

Many commercial ice creams contain gelatine or other preparations to prevent their melting too rapidly.

When it is impossible to get cream for frozen desserts evaporated milk may be successfully substituted.

When served with whipped cream and lady fingers a mold of ice cream becomes a charlotte glacé.

Bisque Ice Cream. Ice cream to which chopped nuts or pounded macaroons are added is called bisque ice cream.

Mousses are mixtures of whipped cream, sugar and flavoring. The mixture is put into a mold, covered with greased paper and with the tin cover, and packed in 2 parts ice to 1 part salt and left for 2 hours or longer.

Parfaits are made by pouring hot syrup over beaten yolks or whites of eggs and combining it with whipped cream and flavoring. They may be frozen withou an ice cream freezer. Turn into a mold or empty baking powder boxes, cover with greased paper and with tight tin cover. Surround with 2 parts crushed ice and 1 part rock salt, and leave 2 hours or longer. The salt water that accumulates should be occasionally poured off to prevent the possibility of its getting into the mold.

Bombe. A bombe is made by lining a bombe, melon or other mold with frozen sherbet or ice cream, and filling the center with frozen ice cream or unfrozen mousse or parfait of a contrasting color. Many attractive combinations are possible. Pack for two hours or more before serving.

Variations. Any plain ice cream may be served with whipped cream or with a sauce. Many sauces are served warm and stiffen when poured over the cream. Nuts may be sprinkled on top of the sauce. Fresh or candied fruit may be used in a sauce, especially with vanilla ice cream.

Sundaes. Ice cream molded with a scoop, covered with a sauce and sprinkled with nuts.

How to Freeze Ice Creams, Etc.

Ice cream freezers to be turned by hand come in sizes from 1 quart to 25 quarts. Where ice cream must be made daily and in large quantities, it is desirable to have a freezer that runs by electricity, and special methods for storing the frozen cream. Coils through which flows ammonia gas are frequently used instead of ice and salt in ice cream factories.

The Ice Cream Scoop

Ice cream scoops come in different sizes so that six, eight or twelve portions may be taken from one quart of cream.

Some scoops are half spheres, and some are cone shaped. They insure uniformity in the size of the portions served. A large mixing spoon may also be used.

When serving, use two scoops or spoons and change them frequently, keeping one in hot water, while the other is being used to serve the cream, so that the ice cream will slide easily from the hot scoop or spoon into the serving dish.

MOLDED ICE CREAMS

Ice cream molds come in individual shapes. The best ones are made of lead and cost from one to three dollars each. Larger molds come in sizes holding from one pint to two quarts or more in many different shapes, such as brick, melon, heart shaped, et cetera.

Individual ices are of course served one to a person. Large molds should be cut in slices for serving. Molds are filled to overflowing with the frozen mixture, covered and packed in 4 parts ice and 1 part rock salt until time for serving.

The rim where the mold and the cover join may be bound with a strip of cheesecloth dipped in melted fat to prevent the entrance of salt water into the mold.

TURNING OUT A MOLD OF JELLIED OR FROZEN MIXTURE

A mold should be oiled and the oil wiped out with soft paper before a mixture is put in. Wet with cold water the platter on which the mold is to be served and do not dry it. If it does not fall directly in the center, it can then be easily moved into place. If the mixture does not readily come out of the mold, dip it for an instant in warm water or lay over it a cloth wrung out of hot water. A thin knife run around the edge will help to loosen it.

Garnishing a Mold of Jellied or Frozen Dessert

The turned out mold may be decorated with:

Whipped cream forced through a pastry bag in which a rose tube
  has been inserted
Candied or maraschino cherries
Candied pineapple, plums and apricots cut in pieces
Whole or chopped nuts, especially green pistachio nuts, toasted
  almonds and pecans
Fresh or canned fruits especially strawberries and apricots
Lady fingers
Macaroons
Kisses
Marshmallows
Spun sugar
Candy flowers

Frozen Desserts Attractive for High Teas or Buffet Service

Vanilla ice cream plain or with chocolate or butterscotch sauce
Chocolate ice cream with marshmallow sauce and nuts
Strawberry ice cream
Coffee ice cream
Banana ice cream
Vanilla ice cream with strawberries
Strawberry ice with center of vanilla or strawberry mousse
Macaroon ice cream
Lemon ice with center of maraschino mousse
Coffee caramel parfait
Vanilla mousse with broken meringues frozen in it
Pistachio ice cream with nuts or with peaches
Neapolitan ice cream (three kinds of ice cream molded in brick
  mold)
Café parfait
Frozen pudding
Strawberry mousse
Caramel bisque
Orange ice cream with crushed strawberries
Strawberry ice cream between slices of angel cake, covered with
  chopped sweetened strawberries

The most popular sauces to serve on ice creams are:

        Butterscotch Sauce
        Marshmallow Sauce
        Chocolate Sauce
        Nut and Fruit Sauce
        Fresh fruit crushed and sweetened

These sauces sell separately for about eighty cents a pint.

Butterscotch Sauce

In saucepan put
1¼ cups (½ pound) brown sugar
⅔ cup (½ pound) corn syrup and
4 tablespoons butter. Boil to 230 degrees F., and add
¾ cup thin cream. Serve on ice cream and sprinkle with
Chopped nuts. This sauce may be kept for some time. Stir well
just before using.

Nut and Fruit Sauce

Wash, stone and cut in pieces
½ pound dates; cut in pieces
1 cup maraschino cherries; mix and add
½ cup maraschino syrup
1 10-ounce can of preserved figs cut in pieces and
Syrup in which they are preserved. Chill thoroughly and just
before serving add
⅔ cup almonds blanched, halved and browned in the oven.

If you have not the facilities for making or molding large
quantities of ice cream, you can get in touch with a large
city manufacturer who has the reputation of making the
best ice cream of anyone about, and order from him as
required. He will doubtless give you a commission, probably of 12½ per cent, on all that you sell for him.

Cakes

Little cakes and cut cake may be served at the Buffet Spread.
To the list of cakes that you have made up for afternoon teas,
you may add:

Pound cake   Angel cake
Devil's food cake   Bride's cake
Sponge cake   White fruit cake

Accompaniments

Olives   Mints
Stuffed olives   Bonbons
Salted nuts   Tiny hard candies
Candied ginger   Chocolates

MENUS FOR SOCIAL OCCASIONS

Following are menus for different types of functions. Some are a trifle unusual and especially delicious. Others are standard and submitted by first-class caterers. Where possible the cost of serving, as estimated by a caterer, is included as a guide to you, when you do work of this kind.

Afternoon Tea

Menu I

MARMALADE AND STRAWBERRY JAM SANDWICHES
CHOPPED NUTS AND CREAMED BUTTER SANDWICHES
LITTLE CHOCOLATE CAKES
TEA WITH ORANGE SUGAR
SALTED ALMONDS

Menu II

CHOPPED OLIVE SANDWICHES
TINY CREAM PUFFS WITH CHOPPED PRESERVED GINGER AND
CREAM-CHEESE AS FILLING
SWEET CHOCOLATE SANDWICHES
HAZEL NUT CAKES   BONBONS   SALTED NUTS
TEA WITH SLICED LEMON AND WHOLE CLOVES

Menu III

PIMIENTO CHEESE SANDWICHES
LETTUCE AND MAYONNAISE DRESSING SANDWICHES
FROSTED WAFERS   NOUGAT   SWEDISH TEA CAKES
BOILED COFFEE WITH CREAM

Menu IV

MOSAIC OR RIBBON SANDWICHES
CHICKEN AND CREAM CHEESE SANDWICHES
FROSTED AFTERNOON TEA CAKES   FUDGE SQUARES   SALTED NUTS
ORANGE FRAPPÉ
BONBONS
COFFEE   TEA

A Formal Tea

ASSORTED SANDWICHES
FANCY ASSORTED CAKE
FRESH STRAWBERRY FRAPPÉ
OLIVES
SALTED ALMONDS   BONBONS
PRESERVED GINGER
COFFEE   TEA
100 persons—$1.00 a Plate

The More Elaborate Tea

MENU I

LOBSTER SALAD   TINY BUTTERED ROLLS
JAM AND CHEESE SANDWICHES   RIBBON SANDWICHES
STRAWBERRY BOMBE   LITTLE NUT CAKES
SPONGE SQUARES   SALTED ALMONDS
TEA WITH CLOVES   COFFEE WITH CREAM
BONBONS

MENU II

MOLDED CHICKEN SALAD   CHOPPED OLIVE OR PIMOLA SANDWICHES
BROWN BREAD SANDWICHES   HORSERADISH BUTTER SANDWICHES
MACAROON ICE CREAM   LITTLE SPONGE CAKES
FROSTED TEA CAKES   GLACÉ FRUITS
TEA WITH LEMON SUGAR   CHOCOLATE WITH CREAM
CANDIES

MENU III

CHICKEN AND CLAM BOUILLON
TOASTED CRACKERS
PINEAPPLE MOUSSE SALAD
CREAM CAKES WITH CHEESE FILLING
FRUIT PUNCH

Prices with Buffet Service

One successful caterer sends out the following menus. The cost includes the use of necessary china, silver and linen; also the services of two men and one maid to assist in the kitchen.

Menu I

SALMON CUTLETS AND PEAS
ROLLS
SELECTED ICE CREAM
FANCY CAKE
COFFEE

50 persons or more—$1.60 each

Menu II

CHICKEN PATTY A LA KING
ASSORTED SANDWICHES
SELECTED ICE CREAM
FANCY CAKE
COFFEE

50 persons or more—$1.80 each

Menu III

SWEETBREAD CUTLETS
FRUIT SALAD
ROLLS
SELECTED ICE CREAM
FANCY CAKE
COFFEE

50 persons or more—$1.85 each

Menu IV

TIMBALE OF CHICKEN—MOUSSELAINE SAUCE
WHOLE SALMON MAYONNAISE
ROLLS
SELECTED ICE CREAM
FANCY CAKES
COFFEE

50 persons or more—$1.90 each

Menu V

LOBSTER A LA NEWBERG IN RAMEKIN
CHICKEN SALAD
ROLLS
SELECTED ICE CREAM
FANCY CAKES
COFFEE

50 persons or more $2.50 each

Evening Receptions

Menu I

NEAPOLITAN ICE CREAM
CAFÉ PARFAIT
FROZEN PUDDING
STRAWBERRY MOUSSE
RASPBERRY BISQUE
FANCY FRUIT AND FLOWER ICES
FANCY ASSORTED CAKE
COFFEE   FRUIT LEMONADE

100 persons—$1.00 a Plate

Menu II

LOBSTER SALAD   CHICKEN SALAD
ROLLS
NEAPOLITAN ICE CREAM
CAFÉ PARFAIT
FROZEN PUDDING
STRAWBERRY MOUSSE
RASPBERRY BISQUE
FANCY FRUIT AND FLOWER ICES
FANCY ASSORTED CAKE
COFFEE   FRUIT LEMONADE

100 persons—$1.50 a Plate

Wedding Receptions and Breakfasts

A Simple Menu

PINEAPPLE PUNCH
SPONGE CAKES

It is permissible to serve only a punch or frappé and sweet crackers or cakes, whether the wedding takes place during the day or in the evening. If the weather is cool, coffee or cocoa may be more acceptable, with sandwiches and wafers or cakes.

Simple Menu for Cool Weather

COFFEE WITH WHIPPED CREAM
CHERRY AND NUT SANDWICHES
WEDDING CAKE BONBONS

More Elaborate Menus
Menu I

RASPBERRY BOMBE
BABY BALTIMORE CAKES
CHOCOLATE PEPPERMINT PARFAIT
BRIDE'S CAKE
GRAPE JUICE PUNCH   COFFEE

Menu II

LOBSTER SALAD
WATERCRESS SANDWICHES
NEAPOLITAN ICE CREAM
LITTLE WHITE CAKES
COFFEE

Menu III

RASPBERRY SHERBET WITH PHILADELPHIA ICE CREAM IN CENTER
COFFEE ICE CREAM WITH VANILLA MOUSSE AND NUTS IN CENTER
ANGEL CAKES FROSTED ALL OVER
PLAIN SPONGE CAKES
LADY FINGERS
TINY COCOANUT CAKES
TINY NUT CAKES WITH CHOCOLATE FROSTING

PUNCH   COFFEE

Served for $1.00 a Plate

Wedding Supper

FRESH SALMON IN ASPIC JELLY
CHICKEN AND MUSHROOM CROQUETTES
FANCY ROLLS
VANILLA PARFAIT
WHITE FRUIT CAKE   WEDDING CAKE
COFFEE   FRUIT PUNCH

Figuring Cost of Afternoon Tea Menu

From previous lessons and experience you should have data as to the cost of sandwiches and little cakes. In estimating the cost of a menu, use cards, ruled as in Lesson II.

Have one card for each sandwich, each cake, for beverages, with their different accompaniments, and for nuts, olives, bonbons, et cetera.

Then copy the totals from each card onto another card as follows, using cost and selling price of foods. It will be wise to make out a card, very carefully, for each menu that you propose to serve.

AFTERNOON TEA MENU—SAMPLE CARD

(For 40)

		Selling Price	Cost
Marmalade and Jam Sandwiches..	5 doz.	$1.20 doz. $6.00	$2.00
Nut and Butter Sandwiches.......	5 doz.	1.20 doz. 6.00	1.60
Little Chocolate Cakes	5 doz.	.75 doz. 3.75	1.45
Salted Almonds	2½ lbs.	1.50 lb. 3.75	2.72
Tea	½ lb.	1.00 lb. .50	.50
Orange Sugar	1 lb.	.50 lb. .50	.50
Lemons	½ doz.	.30 doz. .15	.15
Cream, thin	1 pint	.40 pint .40	.40
Cups and Saucers.................	3⅓ doz.	.50 doz. 1.70	1.50
Teaspoons	3⅓ doz.	.01 each .40	.35
Napkins (cloth)	3⅓ doz.	.05 each 2.00	1.50
Waitresses	2	.40 hour .80	.80
Transportation	5 mi.		
2 hours, including return		3.00 an hr. 6.00	6.00
Supervision, etc.		5.00	
		$36.95	$19.47

Catering for a Large Party

Catering for a large party may not be beyond your possibilities. The following description of a successful dancing party will show a supper which was supervised by a young woman of little experience. It was largely prepared in her own home.

This is an extract from her letter:

"The dance hall was finished in ivory and old rose. We had festoons of paper vines and wistaria from each light globe and entirely around the room direct from the ceiling; in the space between each window were huge shower bouquets of real roses, four dozen to the bouquet, and at each drape at the windows and doors were like bouquets of roses; at opposite ends of the room were tall floor lamps and at opposite sides were tall candle stands of fifteen cathedral candles; tall stands with bird cages were in various corners. The punch table was in one corner and also decorated with roses.

"The supper room was decorated the same way; a huge bouquet of roses formed the center piece, and festoons of roses and tulle decorated the tablecloth. Everything was served in silver dishes.

There were thirteen cakes, half white frosting, half pink; they were 8 inches wide by 12 inches long, one layer, nearly 2 inches thick; these were served in whole cakes, one of each color, cut 21 squares to a cake, in a large silver tray, just the size needed. There were 1,000 sandwiches, 500 made of ham, ground in a meat grinder and mixed with sweet pickle and mayonnaise, the other 500 made of cream cheese, stuffed olives, pimiento, celery and mayonnaise. These were served on silver plates. Ten pounds of pecans and almonds mixed were salted after being cooked in olive oil. These were served in a large tall silver bowl. Coffee was served from a silver urn placed at one end of the table.

"Pink mints and long slender candy sticks, and individual ice creams in the shape of a full blown rose completed the refreshments for a party of 200."

REFERENCE BOOKS

Lessons in Cooking, Through Preparation of Meals, Robinson and Hammel, $2.50.

Boston Cooking School Cook Book, Fannie Merritt Farmer, $2.50.

New Book of Cookery, Fannie Merritt Farmer, $2.50.

Company Cooking and Correct Table Service, Alice Bradley, $0.15.

Table Service, Lucy G. Allen, $1.75.

Paul Richards' Pastry Book, $2.50.

Mrs. A. B. Marshall's Larger Cookery Book of Extra Recipes, Marshall's School of Cookery, London, England.

The Ideal Cookery Book, M. A. Fairclough.

Recipes and Menus for Fifty, Frances Lowe Smith, $2.00.

More Recipes for Fifty, Frances Lowe Smith, $2.00.

New Day Drinks, Alice Bradley, California Fruit Growers Ass'n, Los Angeles, Cal., free.

Salads, Sandwiches and Chafing Dish Dainties, Janet M. Hill, $2.00.

QUESTIONS IN COOKING FOR PROFIT
VI
Catering for Social Occasions

Estimate the cost of serving Menu II (Buffet Service), page 125, to 50 persons, as follows, giving all data:

1. Recipes for 50 people for each dish.
2. Estimate time required for preparation of each dish.
3. Cost of preparation at 50 cents an hour.
4. Total of each dish, and its selling price.
5. Market order and cost of food material required for the menu, at your local prices.
6. Estimate cost of china, silver and linen for 50 from tables on pages 102 and 128.
7. Wages for 2 men and 1 maid as paid where you are now located.
8. Total cost of overhead if work were done in your own kitchen.
9. Cost of truck or taxi for transporting everything 2 miles.
10. Any other costs that you may think of.
11. Possible profit for yourself.

COOKING FOR PROFIT

VII

LUNCHEON SERVICE FOR ONE; BOUILLON COURSE

COOKING FOR PROFIT

PART VII

CATERING FOR SPECIAL LUNCHEONS AND SUPPERS

ADVERTISING; TABLE DECORATIONS; MENUS; FRUIT COCKTAILS;
SOUPS; FISH COURSE; ENTRÉES; MAIN COURSE; VEGETABLES;
SALADS; DESSERTS; CHILDREN'S PARTIES; MENUS FOR SPECIAL
AND HOLIDAY PARTIES

MANY women who have had experience in cooking and serving company meals in their own or in other people's kitchens, find profit in preparing meals for special occasions at the home of the person who is entertaining.

If to a knowledge of cooking is added artistic ability that can be displayed in planning and arranging decorations, favors and menus in accordance with special occasions, a woman will find few unengaged days during the whole season.

The best way to advertise such a business is probably to send out an announcement card something like the following to women who entertain frequently.

Almost no capital is needed in order to start such a business, but a very practical knowledge of all kinds of good cookery is essential. When no entertaining is being done, you can go once or twice a week to a few people and cook enough food to last several days.

131

Catering for Luncheon and Supper Parties

You will probably be called on the phone and asked if you are free on a certain date. On replying that you are

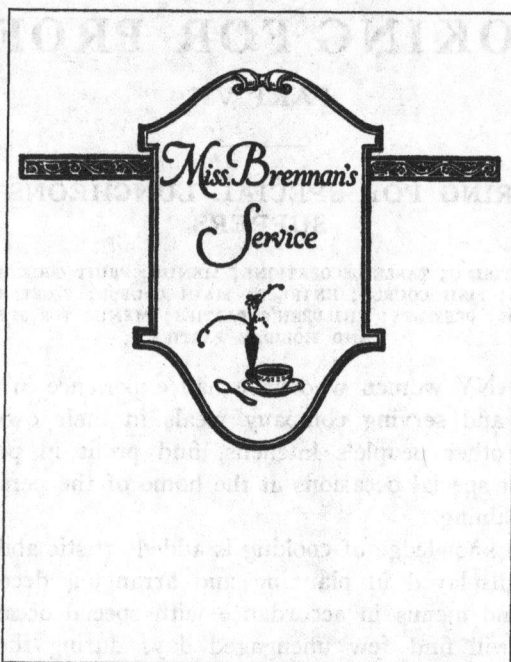

FIRST PAGE OF AN ADVERTISING CARD

free, a time will be set for you to go to the home of the hostess and discuss with her the menu she is to have.

You must be able tactfully to make suggestions, or graciously to follow her ideas as to the number and kind of courses, the style of decorations, and other details. For her selection you may have a list of dishes, and combinations for each course that will be served.

After the menu is planned, a complete list of all the supplies required for the meal should be carefully made out. It will be well to go into the kitchen of the hostess

COPY OF AN ADVERTISING CARD

and see what supplies are on hand, and if she has all the equipment necessary for preparing the meal as outlined.

Most women find it necessary to take with them measuring cups and spoons, one or two sharp knives, special cutters and beaters and molds.

The marketing may be done by the hostess or the person who prepares the meal.

The price charged depends upon the number of persons to be served and ranges from five dollars a meal up, according to the elaborateness of the meal and the number served. It is all clear profit as all supplies are charged to the hostess.

TABLE DECORATIONS

The decorations for the table usually include a centerpiece which should be low enough or high enough not to obstruct the view across the table. This may be of flowers of appropriate colors, or tiny dressed figures suitable to the occasion.

A Jack Horner Pie of crêpe paper, containing favors, is frequently used as a centerpiece. If it is in the form of a huge turkey it is appropriate for Thanksgiving.

A lovely and enormous white crêpe paper rose is appropriate for an engagement or a bridal luncheon.

A stunning gray battleship of paper with tiny figures in uniform would grace the table at a luncheon for a navy man.

A chimney of crêpe paper colored to represent bricks, with a paper Santa Claus mounted on cardboard, and holding on his back a brown paper bag from which protrude the family's presents, would be the delight of any Christmas party.

There are yellow tulip pies, and rose pies of all shades to celebrate the luncheon given to the returning college girl.

All these centerpieces contain hidden favors which are attached to different colored ribbons leading to the seat of each guest.

Other decorations may consist of appropriate place cards, individual favors, a small basket of fresh flowers, a small box of candy or a single but very beautiful flower at each place.

It will be to your advantage to visit or otherwise keep in touch with favor shops in large cities. Study the suggestions found in magazines and originate or modify ideas. Keep a scrap book and note book.

CANDLE STICKS

Candles are not used for a luncheon but may be part of the supper decorations.

Where sufficient candles are used they make the only light provided.

POINTS FOR THE CATERER TO REMEMBER

Take the greatest care of the hostess' possessions.
Show consideration for other help in the house.
Work in harmony with the help.
Do not demand too much of the help.
Be neat in appearance.
Be agreeable in demeanor.

WAITRESSES

The woman who prepares the meal is not expected to serve, but she may be asked to engage the waiters or waitresses, having one maid for each six guests.

LUNCHEON MENUS

A luncheon menu may consist of five or six courses.

1. A fruit course or shell fish or fish cocktail.
2. A bouillon or cream soup with croutons, crackers or rolls.
3. A fish or entrée course if desired.
4. A main dish in individual services with two vegetables.
5. A salad with a cheese accompaniment or a sandwich.
6. Dessert, nuts, bonbons and coffee.

For special holidays and other occasions, the color scheme of centerpiece and favors, and the decorations of many of the dishes can be such as to suggest the special emblem for that day. With slight changes most menus suggested in this chapter can be adapted to every-day affairs or for a different holiday.

SUPPER MENUS

A supper menu may be similar to that for a buffet luncheon or a spread as suggested in Part VI, page 110. Ordinarily the guests will be seated at the table rather than be served while standing.

Be sure the foods you select are obtainable at the time the meal is to be served.

Do not repeat *flavors* or *foods* in a menu!

For instance, do not serve tomato soup and tomato in the salad.

Let each course be a contrast in color to the one that precedes or follows it, unless you are carrying out a special color scheme.

THE FRUIT COURSE

The fruit course may be of one fruit, a mixture of fruits, or one or several fruit juices. The fruit selected or its garnish may be of a color that matches the color scheme selected for the table decorations.

HOW TO SERVE THE FRUIT COURSE

This course may be on the table when the guests enter the dining room. The fruit should be thoroughly chilled and attractively garnished.

The fruit may be served in

1. Single glasses similar to a champagne glass.
2. In a double cocktail glass, the inside glass being surrounded with crushed ice.
3. In the skin of the fruit, as grapefruit, orange or cantaloupe.

4. Sections of fruit or perfect whole berries, arranged on a small flat plate with a mound of powdered sugar in the center.

COCKTAILS

A cocktail glass is served on a small plate covered with a doily with the spoon on the right-hand side of the plate.

Fruit cocktails, made of fruit juices or fruit, are best sweetened with a syrup made of equal parts of sugar and water cooked 3 minutes.

A crabmeat, lobster, or a scallop cocktail may be served in place of fruit. The arrangement is the same, substituting an oyster fork for the spoon if the cocktail is served in a glass. Other arrangements for fish cocktails will be given in the next lesson.

Fruit Cocktail Suggestions

(Those with unequal proportions of fruits)

NAME	METHOD
APPLE COCKTAIL	Apple strips covered with applju or sweet cider, packed in ice and salt until mixture is mushy. Served with maraschino cherries cut in strips and whipped cream.
FROZEN ORANGES WHOLE	Oranges packed in ice and salt until very cold. Served cut in halves with powdered sugar.
GRAPEFRUIT AND STRAW-BERRY COCKTAIL I	Sections of grapefruit cut in thin slices, with slices of strawberries; garnish of sprigs of mint, and sauce of honey and lemon juice.
ROMAN GRAPEFRUIT	Grapefruit pulp seasoned with salt, Roman punch and sugar and chilled. Garnished with whipped cream flavored with sugar and Roman punch, and with maraschino cherries.

STRAWBERRY COCKTAIL I

Large strawberries cut in quarters. Served with a preserved marron cut in small pieces, sprinkled with syrup from bottle of marrons and served very cold.

STRAWBERRY COCKTAIL II

Unhulled strawberries and grapefruit sections arranged on plate and a sauce of maraschino cordial, powdered sugar and salt put in center glass and garnish of sprig of mint.

STRAWBERRY COCKTAIL III

Combination of grapefruit juice, fresh strawberry juice, lemon juice, honey, sugar and White Rock. Serve very cold.

WINTER FRUIT COCKTAIL

Grapefruit pulp, orange pulp, and banana cut in small pieces, with Malaga grapes and walnuts. Serve very cold.

CASSABA MELON

Sections of melon served very cold.

PINEAPPLE COCKTAIL

Portions of fresh pineapple, covered with syrup of sugar, water, orange juice and grapefruit juice and colored pink.

BUTTERFLY COCKTAIL

A slice of pineapple cut in two and rounded edges placed together. Decorated with bits of candied cherry, plum, angelica and pistachio nuts for wing spots and lines. Body made of whipped cream, and ornamented with paprika and cress.

(Fruit Cocktails containing about even proportions of fruit)

FRUIT CUP

Mixture of white grapes, pineapple, oranges and strawberries in equal proportions. Season with sugar, salt, orange juice and pineapple syrup. Pack in ice and salt until barely frozen, and serve at once.

CASSABA COCKTAIL

Pulp of Cassaba melon mixed with an equal amount of Tokay grapes. Flavor with maraschino syrup and salt.

WHITE CHERRY COCKTAIL

Mixture of white cherries, pineapple and grapefruit. Served with dressing made of maraschino syrup, pineapple syrup, cherry syrup, lemon juice and salt.

CANNED FRUIT COCKTAIL — Equal parts of sliced bananas, canned pears and canned peaches. Served with sauce of pineapple syrup, sugar and orange juice.

GRAPEFRUIT AND STRAW- BERRY COCKTAIL II — Grapefruit pulp, sliced strawberries and sliced kumquats piled in grapefruit baskets. Served with sauce of mashed strawberries and sugar.

PREPARATION OF FRUIT FOR THE FRUIT COURSE

Special care must always be taken to prepare fruit neatly and attractively when served at a company luncheon.

FRUIT	METHOD
GRAPEFRUIT	Cut the grapefruit across the sections in half. Loosen the pulp around the inside by cutting between the pulp and the skin, then loosen each section by cutting between the pulp and the membrane.
	Loosen the membrane underneath at the center of the fruit with a grapefruit knife or a pair of scissors, and lift it out entirely leaving the fruit in its shell in its original shape. Garnish or decorate each half, or take out the sections of fruit, cut in two and use in a fruit cocktail.
TO REMOVE PULP FROM ORANGES AND GRAPE- FRUIT	Pare the fruit with a sharp knife, removing every particle of the thin inside membrane with the peel. This will leave the pulp exposed. Hold the fruit over a plate, so that any juice which may drop will be saved. Insert the point of the knife at the stem end of the fruit close to the membrane that divides the sections. Carefully work the knife in, separating the membrane from the section. Then carefully separate the section of fruit from the membrane on its other side; remove the whole section, complete in shape, and entirely free from membrane. Repeat until all the sections are removed.

APPLES	Pare, cut in cubes or strips and cover with lemon juice or with 1 quart of cold water to which 1 teaspoon of salt has been added, until ready to use.
BANANAS	Remove skins, scrape and cut in pieces just before they are to be used.
WHITE GRAPES	Remove skins and seeds using a small sharp vegetable knife.
STRAWBERRIES	Dip strawberries one at a time in cold water and remove hulls if desired.
MELONS	Chill thoroughly, cut in sections and serve, or cut pulp in uniform pieces.
PINEAPPLE	Use fresh or canned pineapple. Cut in cylinders or cubes.
ALLIGATOR PEARS	Cut in two, remove stones and serve thoroughly chilled or cut in pieces of uniform size.
PEACHES	Dip for a moment in boiling water to loosen the skin, and remove skin with a silver knife; use as soon as chilled.

Soups

A clear bouillon or a cream soup may be served at a luncheon. The bouillon may be hot or jellied.

The bouillon cup and saucer are placed on the service plate, handles directly parallel to the edge of the table.

Fruit juice sweetened, slightly thickened and chilled is sometimes served and takes the place both of a cocktail and a soup.

Foundation Soup Recipes

The foundation of a bouillon is a beef, chicken or fish stock cleared with whites of eggs and always strained through double cheesecloth.

Many cream soups are a combination of thin white sauce, strained vegetable pulp and meat or vegetable stock.

Recipes can be found in almost any good cook book.

Suggestions for Luncheon Bouillons

Beef Bouillon.

Clam Bouillon with or without whipped cream and a dash of paprika.

Chicken Bouillon with or without whipped cream.

Tomato Bouillon with or without oysters.

Luncheon Cream Soups

Any cream of vegetable soup such as the following is suitable to serve at a luncheon.

Artichoke soup
Purée of Rice and Chicken Stock
Andalusian Soup, (tomato soup with macaroni or tapioca)
Cream of Brussels Sprouts
Beetroot Soup
Cream of Peanut Butter Soup
Cream of Sorrel Soup
Cream of Lettuce Soup
Purée Parisienne (Cream of potato)
Bisque of Scallops
Scallop and Mushroom Soup
Bisque of Clams
Cauliflower Soup
Cream of Oyster Plant Soup
Cream of Corn and Tomato Soup
Pimiento Bisque
Cream of Chestnut Soup
Cream of Almond Soup
Cream of Watercress Soup
Bisque of Oysters

Soup Accompaniments

An accompaniment to the soup course may be on each bread and butter plate or may be passed after the soup is served:

Crisp Crackers—Crackers spread with butter and delicately crisped
  in the oven.
Imperial Sticks—Strips of buttered bread toasted in the oven
Souffléd Crackers—Crackers soaked in ice water and baked until
  puffed and brown
Popped Corn
Pulled Bread
Bread Sticks
Parmesan Cheese Sticks
Croutons—small cubes of bread toasted in oven or fried
Oyster Crackers
Brown Bread and Butter
Toasted Triangles of Bread
Mock Almonds—thin toast the size and shape of almonds

Celery, radishes, or olives are usually served after the
soup has been placed.

Fish Course

A delicate fish course is sometimes served preceding the
meat course at luncheon, or it may take the place of the
meat course or the entrée.

This may be arranged in the kitchen on individual plates,
or fish plates may be placed in front of each guest and
the fish attractively garnished may be served on a platter
or a fish plate.

Fish should always be very fresh, and served, if possible,
free from skin and bone. Fish may be fried, steamed or
baked and should be served with a nice sauce.

Consult the markets as to the best fish to serve, and
cook books for attractive methods of serving.

Sliced tomatoes or cucumbers served in some attractive
manner and dressed with French dressing are a good accompaniment for the fish course.

Luncheon Entrées

An entrée, which is a made dish, may take the place of
the fish course, or may be used for the main course at a

luncheon. The hot dishes suggested in Lesson VI may be used or any of the following. Many other suggestions will be found in good cook books. A delicately flavored sauce is an important part of most entrées. A delicate vegetable with a rich sauce is sometimes served as an entrée.

A Few Pleasing Entrées

Eggs, hard cooked or poached, in individual dishes with a rich sauce. These or other egg dishes may be used as the first course at a luncheon.
Stuffed Mushroom Caps
Shrimps and Mushrooms with a good sauce
Scallops creamed or fried
Oyster and Shrimp Newburg
Lobster in a cream sauce, served in pastry boats or patty cases
Chicken and Mushroom Timbales
Chicken, Ham or Fish Mousse—(Raw meat combined with heavy cream and egg whites and steamed or baked).
Sweetbread and Mushroom Patties
Devilled Crabs
Sweetbreads in Ramekins

Main Course

Where a substantial fish course or entrée has been served no other meat course is necessary, but the following meats may follow or be used in place of the fish or entrée courses mentioned above. They should be attractively served. One or more vegetables often are used for garnish.

A Few Delicious Luncheon Meats

Veal Cutlets, with or without thin slices of ham
Beef Tenderloin, broiled, with mushrooms
Sweetbreads, braised, with French chestnuts and mushroom sauce
Sweetbreads with French peas.
Sweetbreads and hard cooked eggs in sauce, served in pastry cases
Lamb Chops stuffed with mushrooms or horseradish dressing
Lamb Chops, breaded, mushroom or truffle sauce.
Kernels or Tournedos of Lamb (the lean part of chops), broiled with currant mint sauce, bacon, savory potatoes, or mint jelly

Lamb Chops with mashed potato roses, broiled ham, artichoke
    bottoms and mushroom caps.
Fried Chicken
Roast Incubator Chickens
Chicken Breasts stuffed with mushrooms, cream sauce.
Chicken baked in cream
Guinea chicken breasts, broiled or baked, with ham in thin slices,
    and brown sauce
Pigeon Pie
Squabs en Casserole

Potatoes

Potatoes served at a luncheon should be attractive in
appearance and taste, such as:

Mashed potatoes, beaten until light or forced through pastry bag
    and rose tube
Mashed potatoes with cheese, or chopped parsley or pimiento
Mashed potatoes covered with whipped cream and with grated
    cheese or bread crumbs and baked
Mashed potatoes shaped like apples or pears and baked
Creamed potatoes sprinkled with parsley
Creamed potatoes covered with buttered crumbs and baked
Creamed potatoes with grated cheese or chopped green pepper or
    pimientos
Potatoes baked and stuffed
Potato balls
Potatoes fried—as French fried, shredded, balls, curls, etc.
Potato croquettes
Sweet potatoes, creamed
Sweet potatoes candied
Sweet potatoes with orange sections, bananas, prunes, white grapes
    or cooked apple sections
Sweet potatoes mashed

Luncheon Vegetables

The tender and less common vegetables should be used
for special luncheon and dinner menus. They should be
very carefully prepared and served as attractively as possible.

Suggestions

French artichokes with Hollandaise or Mousselaine Sauce
Artichoke Bottoms with peas, mushrooms or other vegetables
Asparagus on toast with butter or a rich sauce

Brussels Sprouts with white sauce
Brussels Sprouts with celery
Carrots and Peas
Carrot Timbales
Cauliflower with white sauce and cheese
Cauliflower with Hollandaise or Mousselaine Sauce
Celery creamed or braised
Corn fritters
Corn Soufflé
Egg Plant Timbales or Scallop
French Endive braised with melted butter
Leeks on Toast
New Lima Beans
Mushrooms creamed or stuffed
Oyster plant creamed
Stuffed Peppers
String Beans
Green Peas
Spinach with egg
Spinach Soufflé
Spinach Timbales
Tomatoes baked or sautéd with a sauce
Tomatoes stuffed
Mixed vegetables en casserole

Rolls to Serve with a Luncheon

These should be fresh, small and delicately brown.

Butterfly Rolls
Cream Bread Fingers
Luncheon Rolls, heart or flag shape for special occasions
Parker House Rolls
Salad or Dinner Rolls
Clover Leaf or Shamrock Biscuit
Sweet French Rolls
Crossett Rolls

Luncheon Salads

A luncheon salad may be more substantial than that served for a dinner. It may be arranged on individual plates, or on a large dish and passed that each guest may help herself.

Salads suggested in Lesson VI and made of many other fruits and vegetables alone or in combination may be served at a luncheon. Mayonnaise dressing, plain or combined with cream, chili sauce, et cetera, may be served.

Do not serve a fruit salad if a first course of fruit has been served. It is not necessary to serve a dessert if a fresh fruit salad, or one that has been jellied or frozen has been served with a cream or mayonnaise dressing.

Salad Accompaniments

Whatever is offered should be something to bring out, rather than to overpower, the flavor and seasonings of the salad.

Cheese croquettes—served with salad greens simply dressed
Cheese balls—served with salad greens simply dressed
Crackers, thin, unsweetened, buttered, sprinkled with mild paprika, and heated. Served with fruit salads.
Simple sandwiches
Baking powder biscuits, fresh and hot
Cheese straws
Graham bread and butter

Desserts

For suggestions for ice cream, cakes, bonbons, et cetera, consult previous lessons in this course, and standard cook books. Let your ingenuity suggest special decorations for the holidays.

Color and arrangement of whipped cream, frosting, candied fruits, tiny candies, nuts, et cetera, may be made to be typical of the special day, as green for St. Patrick, red for St. Valentine, and patriotic holidays, heart shapes for St. Valentine and engagement luncheons, and so on.

Bonbons, mints and other candies, the color in keeping with the decorations, may be on the table during the luncheon and passed after the dessert. Salted nuts may be on the table in individual dishes or in two large dishes.

The coffee may be brought in after the dessert or may be served in the drawing room.

Decorations for Finger Bowls

Finger bowls, one-fourth full of tepid water, which are brought in after the fruit course, or with the dessert plates, may be garnished with a few petals from the same flowers that are used in the decoration of the table. A few drops of rose or violet water are sometimes added.

Children's Parties

For children's parties the dishes selected should be *suitable to the age of the child*. It is a great mistake to serve to children such combinations of food as may make them ill afterward.

If the children's party is also a birthday party, special pains should be taken to provide a birthday cake with favors inside and with the right number of candles blazing on the cake.

Birthday cake boards, round, plain or decorated, with space for the cake in the center and holes for candles around the edge, may be purchased at many kitchen furnishing and other shops.

Animal crackers dipped in sugar syrup which has been cooked to the crack, and then attached to small crackers, make an attractive table decoration when formed into a procession marching around the table just inside of the plates.

Individual ice creams in animal shapes are always attractive. Toys representing stories with which the children are familiar are an effective table decoration. Toy balloons hanging from the doors, windows and chandeliers of the dining room make a pretty effect. Bonbons containing toy hats of paper may be at each plate.

If possible, have something for each child to take home. An individual basket of candy, a balloon, a toy of some

kind, or a small musical instrument will all give much
pleasure to the small guest.

Entertainment for Children's Parties

It is not easy to give a successful children's party. Many
children demand a good deal of entertaining. Practically
every moment of the afternoon should be planned beforehand so games will follow each other smoothly and with
sufficient variety to prevent restlessness and consequent
loss of interest.

There are Mother Goose Parties, and Fairy Story Parties,
May Parties, Doll Shows, and many other kinds of parties
which appeal especially to the young members of the neighborhood.

Most of the women's magazines issue booklets giving
suggestions for children's parties and delightful books are
suggested at the end of this chapter.

"When is the party going to commence?" You should remember that to a child the *party* means refreshments, and
not spend too much time on entertainment before the supper
is served.

MENUS FOR SPECIAL OCCASIONS

St. Valentine Spread

MENU I

TOMATO BISQUE
CREAMED SWEETBREADS IN HEART-SHAPED TIMBALE CASES
HAM MOUSSE IN HEART SHAPES
SANDWICHES IN HEART SHAPES SPREAD WITH PIMIENTO BUTTER
ICE CREAM TARTE
(4 meringue hearts put together with pink ice cream between)
WHITE FRUIT CAKE   (heart shaped) COOKIES
LOGANBERRY PUNCH

St. Valentine Luncheon

MENU II

SHRIMP COCKTAIL
CLAM BOULLION WITH WHIPPED CREAM
FILLETS OF HALIBUT   PAPRIKA SAUCE
LUNCHEON ROLLS (heart shape)
CHICKEN BREASTS WITH BROILED HAM, CREAM SAUCE AND MUSHROOMS
MASHED POTATO APPLES
GRAPEFRUIT SALAD   TOASTED BUTTER THINS
STRAWBERRY ICE CREAM   MARSHMALLOW SAUCE
HEART-SHAPED WAFERS, PINK FROSTING   MINT HEARTS

Washington's Birthday Spread

MENU No. I

GRAPEFRUIT WITH CHERRIES
FRIED CHICKEN   CORN FRITTERS   SALAD ROLLS
CHAUFROID OF SALMON
LAYER SANDWICHES WITH RED AND GREEN PEPPERS AND MAYONNAISE
BISQUE ICE CREAM   PEANUT DROPS
HATCHET-SHAPED COOKIES   FRUIT PUNCH

MENU No. II

TOMATO BOUILLON
CHICKEN CROQUETTES WITH PEAS   CHERRY SALAD
LAYER SANDWICHES   CHOCOLATE CAKES
APRICOT BOMBE   FROSTED CAKE WITH CHERRIES
OAT WAFERS   STUFFED FIGS

St. Patrick's Day Luncheons

MENU I

OYSTER COCKTAIL
GREEN PEA SOUP   CRISP CRACKERS
HALIBUT WITH PARSLEY SAUCE   SHAMROCK BISCUIT
TOURNADOS OF BEEF   POTATO CROQUETTES, CORK SHAPE
SPINACH TIMBALES
SHAMROCK SALAD OF PINEAPPLE SLICES WITH GREEN PEPPER STUFFED
WITH CHEESE AND SLICED
CHEESE CAKES
VANILLA ICE CREAM WITH GREEN COCOANUT AND MARSHMALLOW SAUCE
ROLLED GREEN WAFERS
CAFÈ NOIR

Menu II

SHAMROCK CANAPÉS (tiny cream cakes in groups of three
filled with sardine butter)
SPINACH SOUP   IMPERIAL STICKS
MOLDED HALIBUT, NORMANDY SAUCE TINTED GREEN   COLE SLAW
KERNELS OF PORK   SAVORY POTATOES   STUFFED ONIONS
MALAGA SALAD
PISTACHIO ICE CREAM, PEACH SAUCE
FROSTED CAKES WITH PISTACHIO NUTS
COFFEE

Easter Luncheons

Menu I

GRAPEFRUIT AND ORANGE COCKTAIL
CREAM OF CHICKEN SOUP WITH EGG YOLKS
BAKED SHAD ROE   SANDWICHES
ASPARAGUS HOLLANDAISE
STUFFED LAMB CHOPS   NEW POTATOES   GREEN PEAS
FRESH MINT SHERBET
BUTTERFLY SALAD
ICE CREAM IN EGG-SHAPED MERINGUES
SMALL CAKES, JONQUIL DECORATIONS
COFFEE

Menu II

STRAWBERRY COCKTAIL
SOUFFLÉ OF SHAD ROE
BROILED CHICKEN WITH ASPARAGUS TIPS   POTATO ROSES
DANDELION SALAD
MAPLE MOUSSE   BUTTERFLY CAKE
COFFEE

Fourth of July Luncheons

Menu I

JELLIED TOMATO BOUILLON
SALMON   GREEN PEAS   MASHED POTATO
WATERMELON SALAD   LUNCHEON ROLLS
STRAWBERRY ICE CREAM OR STRAWBERRY MANHATTAN PUDDING
RED PUNCH

Menu II

ICED CANTALOUPE
SCALLOPED LOBSTER
JELLIED VEAL   HORSERADISH SAUCE
FINGER ROLLS   RIBBON SANDWICHES WITH PIMIENTO BUTTER
ORANGE ICE CREAM WITH CRUSHED STRAWBERRIES
NUT WAFERS   LITTLE POUND CAKES
PINK LEMONADE

MENU III

MARASCHINO COCKTAIL
PLANKED SALMON   POTATOES   PEAS
CHIFFONADE SALAD
RADISH SANDWICHES
STRAWBERRY AND MARSHMALLOW BOMBE   WAFERS
COFFEE

Hallowe'en Parties

MENU I

FRUIT COCKTAIL IN APPLE CUPS
BOUILLON
BROILED BONED CHICKEN WITH SPAGHETTI, TOMATO SAUCE
AND GREEN PEPPERS
ROLLS
GRAPEFRUIT SPONGE SALAD MOLDED IN THE SHAPE OF APPLES,
CREAM CHEESE LEAVES, FRENCH DRESSING
ICE CREAM, APPLE SHAPES, SPRINKLED WITH GRATED SWEET
CHOCOLATE AND SERVED WITH WHIPPED CREAM
LITTLE CAKES   CAFÉ NOIR

MENU II

DEVILLED OYSTERS, BROWN BREAD SANDWICHES
APPLE AND CELERY SALAD
FRENCH AND CHOCOLATE ICE CREAM
ORANGE CAKE WITH ORANGE FILLING AND FROSTING
CHOCOLATE COOKIES, BLACK CAT SHAPE
SUGARED POPCORN
COCOA

Christmas Luncheon

TOMATO SOUP
CRAB MEAT A LA KING   POTATOES FONDANT
STRING BEANS AND CELERY IN CREAM
CHRISTMAS SCONES
CHICKEN SALAD   CHEESE BALLS
TOASTED CRACKERS
ORANGE MOUSSE
CAKES DECORATED WITH HOLLYBERRIES AND GREEN LEAVES
COFFEE

All Done in Green

MINT COCKTAIL
GRILLED FRESH FISH WITH WATERCRESS BUTTER
PEPPERS AND CUCUMBER JELLY
ASPARAGUS VINAIGRETTE
HARLEQUIN PUDDING   CAKES
GREEN GAGE BONBONS
COFFEE

Thanksgiving Supper

CREAM OF CORN SOUP WITH POPPED CORN
SAUTÉD OYSTERS ON TOAST WITH CELERY SAUCE
TURKEY SALAD   ROLLS
FROZEN PUDDING
FRUIT CAKE
NUTS   RAISINS
BLACK COFFEE

Card Party Luncheon

CHICKEN SOUP GARNISHED WITH HEARTS AND DIAMONDS
OF PIMIENTO, SPADES AND CLUBS OF TRUFFLE
HAM MOUSSE, BAKED IN HEART SHAPED MOLDS SERVED ON BED
OF SPINACH   ALLEMANDE SAUCE
BAKING POWDER BISCUITS SHAPED WITH CARD CUTTERS
GINGERALE JELLY SALAD
LAYER SANDWICHES
CHOCOLATE ICE CREAM AND RASPBERRY SHERBET
HEART AND DIAMOND COOKIES SPREAD WITH
RED CONFECTIONERS' FROSTING
SPADE AND CLUB COOKIES SPREAD WITH SWEET CHOCOLATE
SALTED NUTS   BONBONS
COFFEE

A Butterfly Luncheon

BUTTERFLY COCKTAIL
TOMATO BOUILLON
BUTTERFLY SHAPED CROUTONS
MOLDED FISH
NORMANDY SAUCE
POTATO BUTTERFLIES   PEAS
VEAL CUTLET WITH PEANUT BUTTER SAUCE
CAULIFLOWER   MACARONI MOLD
BUTTERFLY ROLLS
BUTTERFLY SALAD   CHEESE CRACKERS
RASPBERRY BOMBE GARNISHED WITH
CANDY BUTTERFLIES AND SPUN SUGAR
BUTTERFLY CAKE
BONBONS   COFFEE

A Jonquil Luncheon

CLAM BOUILLON OR CREAM SOUP WITH JONQUIL GARNISH
MADE FROM ROYAL CUSTARD
FISH MOLDED IN OVAL SHAPE WITH ALMOND SAUCE AND GARNISH
OF EGG YOLK, CRESS AND ROMAINE
STUFFED PORK OR LAMB CHOPS DIPPED IN EGG
AND CRUMBS AND SAUTÉD
UNTIL A GOLDEN BROWN
MASHED POTATO MADE YELLOW WITH EGG YOLKS
YELLOW BANTAM CORN CUT FROM THE EAR
APPLE FRITTERS WITH LEMON SAUCE, OR MINT AND ORANGE JELLY CUT
IN FANCY SHAPES, OR CUBES OF YELLOW JELLY WITH
BORDER OF GREEN
TURNOVER ROLLS FILLED WITH ORANGE MARMALADE
ORANGE AND GRAPEFRUIT SALAD   CHEESE STRAWS
MOLD OF LEMON SHERBET AND FRENCH ICE CREAM
IN FORM OF A JONQUIL
A YELLOW AND WHITE CAKE DECORATED WITH JONQUILS
DEMI-TASSE   GREEN AND YELLOW BONBONS   ALMONDS

Menus for Birthday Parties

MENU I

(For Child Under Five Years)

BREAD AND BUTTER SANDWICHES IN FANCY SHAPES
MILK TO DRINK
JUNKET COLORED PINK, WITH WHIPPED
CREAM ROSE ON TOP
SPONGE CAKE SPRINKLED WITH POWDERED SUGAR
ON BOARD WITH BIRTHDAY CANDLES

MENU II

(For the Child Six and Seven Years)

ROUND BREAD AND JELLY SANDWICHES
PEANUT BUTTER SANDWICHES CUT IN FANCY SHAPES
COCOA
ORANGE ICE CREAM, PINK AND WHITE
ANIMAL CRACKERS
BIRTHDAY SPONGE CAKE WITH THIN ICING
CARAWAY CANDIES AND CANDLES

Menu III

(Noon-Time Party for Children)

CREAM OF CORN AND TOMATO SOUP
BREAD STICKS
EGGS IN RAMEKINS   LETTUCE SANDWICHES
ORANGE MARSHMALLOW PUDDING
MOONSHINE CAKE
LOLLY POPS IN CREPE PAPER COSTUMES

Menu IV

(For the Child Eight to Ten Years)

EGGS MARGUERITE   LETTUCE SANDWICHES
BREAD AND BUTTER SANDWICHES   COCOA
JUNKET ICE CREAM AND CRUSHED
STRAWBERRIES
ANGEL CAKE, ORNAMENTAL ICING
ASSORTED MINTS

Menu V

(For the Teens)

LOBSTER SALAD IN DINNER ROLLS, OR CHICKEN SALAD
IN ECLAIR CASES
LAYER SANDWICHES
CHOCOLATE ICE CREAM   MARSHMALLOW MINT SAUCE
BIRTHDAY FRUIT CAKE   BONBONS
KISSES

REFERENCE BOOKS

Catering for Special Occasions, Fannie Merritt Farmer.
New Dinners (Calendar), Elizabeth O. Hiller.
Company Cooking and Correct Table Service, Alice Bradley.
Lessons in Cooking, Robinson and Hammel.
Boston Cooking School Cook Book, Fannie Merritt Farmer.
New Book of Cookery, Fannie Merritt Farmer.
Table Service, Lucy G. Allen.
The New Hostess of Today, Linda Hull Larned.
The R. Wallace Book, Winifred S. Fales.
The Children's Party Book, Woman's Home Companion.
Book of Games and Parties for All Occasions, Theresa Hunt
    Wolcott.
The Children's Book of Games and Parties, Carolyn Sherwin
    Bailey.
Children's Games and Children's Parties, Gladys Beattie Crozier.
What Shall We Do Now? Dorothy Canfield.
Games for Everybody, May C. Hofmann.
The Book of Games, Mary White.
Indoor Games for Children, Gladys Beattie Crozier.

QUESTIONS ON COOKING FOR PROFIT

VII

CATERING FOR SPECIAL LUNCHEONS AND SUPPERS

1. Write out three luncheon menus of dishes with which you are familiar.

2. Write out a menu for a spring luncheon with roses for decoration, suggesting ways of carrying out the color scheme for each course and in the decorations.

3. Write out a menu for a company luncheon that you yourself have prepared.

4. Make a complete list of all supplies, utensils, table equipment, decorations, etc., required for one of these luncheon menus, served for six ladies.

5. Give plan for a child's party, and give order for refreshments for twelve children, as you might present it to a patron. State age of children planned for.

COOKING FOR PROFIT

VIII

TABLE SET FOR FORMAL DINNER

COOKING FOR PROFIT

COOKING FOR PROFIT

PART VIII

CATERING FOR DINNER PARTIES

TABLE SERVICE AND SERVING; CANAPES AND OTHER FIRST
COURSES; SOUPS; FISH; ENTREES; MEAT COURSE AND ACCOM-
PANIMENTS; DINNER SALADS; DESSERTS; HOW MUCH TO PRE-
PARE; COSTS; TYPICAL MENUS

THERE are many opportunities for women to go
into a patron's home and prepare dinners for parties of from two to twenty people. The price charged
is proportionate to the number served. It should not be less
than $5.00 and may be $10.00 to $15.00 and is all clear
profit as suggested in Lesson VII.

Many people find it more convenient to entertain guests
at a tea room or hotel than in their own homes, therefore
the manager of such a business needs to be familiar with
the service of a formal meal as well as the preparation of
each course.

It has become very common for a host or hostess to
telephone or write ahead to such a place ordering a steak
or chicken dinner to be served at a definite hour for a
definite number of guests. If a formal dinner is to be
served at a tea room or hotel, a private room is desirable
but this is not required for the informal dinner party.

A dinner or luncheon at which there are more than twelve

guests may be called a banquet. This is usually a more formal meal than a dinner and may be followed by speeches. Special decorations and music may be provided and at the large hotels more than two thousand guests are sometimes served.

TABLE SERVICE AND SERVING

For formal luncheons and formal dinners the service is practically the same and is known as modified Russian service. No food, save nuts and bonbons, is on the table, but everything is served from the kitchen and passed to or placed before the guests. In a private home one waitress cannot satisfactorily serve more than five or six people, therefore two waitresses will be needed for most formal meals. At hotels one waiter or waitress is provided for every eight guests. When the work is very well systematized two cooks can serve ten waiters and each waiter can serve ten guests.

A formal dinner table is laid first with a silence cloth, covered with a tablecloth, which should hang not less than nine inches on all sides.

A formal luncheon table should be laid with a luncheon set, consisting of a centerpiece and doilies, all of the same pattern, or with a luncheon cloth. The luncheon cloth should reach just to the edge of the table or hang six to seven inches below it. If the bare table is used the centerpiece is laid so that the thread of the linen runs with the grain of the wood of the table.

Place the table decoration in the center, having it low or high enough not to obstruct the view across the table. Candlesticks and bonbon dishes are placed symmetrically about the decoration. The covers are marked by placing handsome service plates one inch from the edge of the

table, having them directly opposite each other. The centers of the service plates should be twenty-four to thirty inches apart. The silver should be placed in the order in which it is to be used, beginning on the outside so that it will be used toward the plate. The knife or knives are placed at the right of the plate, half an inch from the edge of the table with cutting edge toward the plate. Place soup or bouillon spoon with the bowl facing up at the right of knife, teaspoon for fruit cocktail, or fork for oysters or clams, at the right of soup spoon. The forks are placed at the left, tines turned upward, one-half inch from the edge of the table. Do not place more than three forks. If more are required, they should be placed with their respective courses.

Goblets for dinner or tumblers for luncheon are placed at the tip of the knives. They are filled two-thirds full before the meal is announced. They may be replenished at right of guest without lifting them from the table. Place filled individual nut dishes in front of the service plate, place cards either in front or back of nut dishes.

The napkin, in size from twenty-four to twenty-eight inches, is placed at the left of forks, folded square; however, if covers are close, they may be folded again to save space. If the napkin is monogrammed, it is placed so the monogram may be easily read by the person at the table. A luncheon napkin may be folded in three-cornered shape. If napkin has an embroidered letter, it should be placed with the point of the napkin toward the plate. If there is no initial, place the long edge of the napkin parallel with the fork.

Butter is not served at a formal dinner, or a very formal luncheon, but is used at informal meals. A bread and butter plate is placed above the service plate and a little to the left with the butter spreader across the upper right

hand side with the blade turned toward the center of the plate. If no butter is served the knife is not used but the plate may be used for radishes, olives, bread, etc. The plate may be omitted and small baskets, as favors, filled with candies, may be placed above the forks.

Salts and peppers are placed between each two covers. If an open salt cellar is used, place the salt spoon across the top or on the doily beside it.

After the meal is announced and guests are seated the head waitress starts with the hostess and serves to the right, including the host; the assisting waitress starts with the lady guest of honor at the right of the host and serves to the right.

Everything except beverages and extra silver are placed by the waitress from the left of the guest. A napkin squarely folded, or a serviette, should be used under all dishes of food to be passed.

FORMAL DINNER SERVICE

FIRST COURSE: A formal dinner menu generally consists of a beginning such as canapé, oysters or clams on the half shell, or a fruit cocktail, and this first course is on the table when the guests come to the dining room.

OTHER COURSES: The first course is removed from the table by the waitress with the left hand from the left of each person before the soup is placed. The soup is served next from the pantry in filled soup plates and with the left hand placed on the service plate. One waitress then passes the crackers and the other follows with the olives and celery, etc.

The service plates, and soup plates with silver are then replaced by the warm plates for fish or entrée. If the plate is empty, it is placed with the right hand; if filled,

with the left hand to avoid accident. If empty plates are placed, the fish or entrée is passed by the head waitress from the left on a platter held on a folded napkin in the waitress's left hand and balanced with the right. The serving silver should be so placed that guests can easily serve themselves.

When this course is finished, the fish or entrée plates with silver are removed with the left hand, and the empty warm meat plates placed immediately with the right hand.

The head waitress serves the meat (previously carved), beginning with the hostess, to everyone at the table, and the second waitress follows with the first vegetable. The head waitress then passes the second vegetable and the second waitress follows with the rolls. Serving silver should be on the platter and vegetable dishes.

At a banquet or informal meal the meat and vegetable may be on the plates when they are placed, or the main dish nicely garnished may be carved and put on plates by the host and passed by the waitress.

The next course may be an entrée but is usually a salad. It may be served on the plate, or empty plates may be placed and the salad passed by the head waitress on a platter with serving silver, the assisting waitress following with the accompaniment of dressing, crackers, cheese balls, etc.

After the salad, plates and silver are removed, the bread and butter plates if used, and the salt and pepper shakers.

The table is then crumbed, using a plate and folded napkin, forefinger placed in fold, three fingers on outside of napkin.

DESSERT. Dessert plates are next placed with the left hand. The silver may be on the dishes or may be brought in by one of the waitresses on a folded napkin and placed at the right. If the dessert is not on the plates, the mold, already cut, is passed with serving silver in place. Small cakes are then passed and finger bowls placed on a small plate covered with a doily are placed on table above the ice cream dish a little to the left. The bonbon dishes are then taken from the table by each waitress, passed to guests, and placed again on opposite ends of the table.

Coffee is served in the drawing room or at the table; the cups two-thirds full are placed on a doily covered tray, with the spoons placed on saucers so that handles run parallel to handles of the cups. This tray is passed by one waitress. The other waitress follows, serving cream and sugar on a doily covered tray, the handle of tongs beside bowl running parallel with the handle of the pitcher. If the coffee is served at the table she places the cup at the right of each guest.

The same method is used in serving a larger number of people, whether at the same table or at several tables. There must be enough people in the kitchen to place the food on the serving plates or platters, and great care must be taken that hot things are served hot, and cold things, cold, and everything as daintily and attractively as possible.

CANAPES AND OTHER FIRST COURSES

The first course of a formal dinner may be a canapé, shell fish in some form, a half grapefruit, a fruit cocktail or assorted hors d'oeuvres. A canapé is a piece of bread cut one-fourth inch thick, delicately toasted and spread with butter highly seasoned with one or more of the following ingredients:

Anchovy essence or paste.
Lemon juice.
Sardine paste.

Chopped olives, pickles, capers, and parsley.

Mustard or

Table sauce.

Upon the savory butter is usually arranged in an orderly manner caviar or small pieces of shell fish, canned fish or smoked fish and the top is garnished with hard cooked eggs, capers, pickles, olives or pimiento as the fancy dictates. The effect of the whole should be a dainty picture as it rests on a small fancy plate on the service plate.

Oysters on the half shell are a popular first course, served on a bed of crushed ice in a soup plate on the service plate. A small glass of cocktail sauce may be in the center of the plate. Lemon cut in quarters and a bit of parsley is used as a garnish.

Little neck clams on the half shell, pieces of lobster or crab meat or whole shrimps on heart leaves of lettuce or parboiled scallops on a small scallop shell may be served on ice instead of oysters, or the fish, covered with cocktail sauce, may be served in a glass surrounded with crushed ice.

Cocktail sauces may be purchased ready mixed or the following may be used:

Cocktail Sauce

Mix
1 teaspoon salt
¼ teaspoon pepper
1 teaspoon chopped parsley
1 teaspoon chives, finely cut
½ teaspoon salad oil
6 drops tabasco sauce
½ teaspoon dry mustard
2 tablespoons vinegar and
8 tablespoons tomato catsup.

Hors D'Oeuvre

A plate of Hors D'Oeuvres may contain for each person
½ cold stuffed egg on a leaf of lettuce
1 sardine

1 narrow strip of toast with anchovy fillets or anchovy butter
1 olive
1 radish
A bit of crab or lobster meat on a lettuce leaf with Russian
   Dressing
A cornucopia of thinly sliced smoked salmon with or without a
   bit of cavier in the center
A slice of Italian sausage
A small stalk of celery raw or braised, with a savory stuffing in
   the groove
⅛ of a lemon and a sprig of parsley as a garnish.

A fruit cocktil may be served instead of a fish cocktail. Suggestions for these are given in lesson VII. A dinner roll, or small crackers are a suitable accompaniment for this course.

SOUPS

A soup is always served at a formal dinner. It may be a clear soup, like a consommé with a garnish of dainty bits of vegetable, royal custard cut in fancy shapes, macaroni or other paste in small pieces, bits of chicken or delicate quenelles. An oyster, clam, lobster, or vegetable bisque may be served instead of the consommé especially if a canapé takes the place of an oyster course. Mock turtle, green turtle or any nice soup not too rich or thick may be used. For informal meals cream soups are popular.

Accompaniments may be bread sticks, delicately toasted strips or triangles of toast, small rolls or crackers.

FISH

A fish course or an entrée may follow the soup course. Both used to be considered necessary but now both are frequently omitted. It should be of a color and flavor in contrast with the soup. The fish should be so prepared that it can be easily taken from the platter or it may be served in the kitchen directly onto the fish plates. It should be as far as possible free from bones, surrounded or covered with a rich, well flavored sauce, and garnished with lemon or parsley, with fancy potatoes, cucumbers, tomatoes. etc.

A few suggested fish dishes, recipes for which may be found in most cook books, are

Baked stuffed smelts with Bernaise Sauce
Smelts à la Langtry with Aurora Sauce
Baked fillets of halibut or flounder with Hollandaise, Tartare, Lobster, Cheese or Mushroom sauce
Molded fish, Normandy sauce
Fried fillets of halibut or flounder or fried smelts, scallops or lobster with Sauce Tartare
Terrapin
Lobster or oyster patties
Crab Meat Mornay
Halibut Veronique (with white grapes)
Stuffed turbans of flounder
Fillets of sole with oysters or clams, white sauce and cheese
Baked shad, roe sauce

In recipes which call for wine, lemon juice to flavor or a little Worcestershire sauce and white or fish stock may be used instead.

ENTREES—CROQUETTES

The entrée should be a contrast in flavor and color to the courses that precede and follow it and may consist of a patty case, vol au vent, or timbale case containing creamed sweetbreads or mushrooms, or it may be an egg or mushroom croquette, timbale or soufflé, braised sweetbreads, an egg dish, or a fancy vegetable such as mushrooms under glass or asparagus Mousselaine.

Sometimes a sweet entrée is served, for example a fritter or rice with fruit, but this generally accompanies the meat course and is not often served by itself.

Mushroom Croquettes

Chop
1 lb. fresh mushrooms (there should be 4 cups), add
2 tablespoons butter
1 teaspoon salt
1 teaspoon chopped onion
1 teaspoon chopped parsley
A few grains pepper, and
2 tablespoons stock. Stir and cook five minutes, add

2 egg yolks slightly beaten, and
1 cup soft bread crumbs; spread on a plate and when cold shape
 like large mushroom caps and stems, an equal number of
 each. Dip in
Crumbs
Egg and
Crumbs again, and fry in
Deep Fat. Put caps on stems and arrange on platter covered with
 a doiley.

MEAT COURSE

The meat course at a dinner is almost always a roast or
poultry or game in some form. It is usually carved in the
kitchen and should be attractively placed on the platter or
serving plate. Among the most suitable meats are

Roast Beef	Roast turkey
Larded fillet of beef	Roast chicken
Beef steak	Boned chicken stuffed and roasted
Planked steak	Broiled chicken
Saddle of lamb	Planked boned chicken
Crown of lamb	Roast duckling
Roast leg of lamb	Broiled duckling
Saddle of veal	Roast squab
Stuffed cushion of veal	Broiled squab

Planked Steak

10 potatoes, boil, pare and mash. Add
⅛ cup butter
6 egg yolks slightly beaten
1½ teaspoons salt, and
Milk to moisten. Beat until very light. Grease a plank to keep
 it from burning, put on a border of the potato, using pastry
 bag and tube, and put in hot oven until lightly browned. Wipe
2½ lb. Porterhouse steak and remove superfluous fat; the bone
 may or may not be removed, as preferred. Heat and grease
 a heavy frying pan; when hissing hot, put in steak, turn very
 often until seared on both sides, then occasionally until steak
 is cooked. Cream
¼ cup butter, add
1 tablespoon pimiento, chopped
1 tablespoon parsley, chopped
1 teaspoon onion juice. Place steak in center of plank, spread
 with creamed butter and arrange
8 small onions, glazed

1 small bunch cooked asparagus
¾ cup cooked carrot balls
¾ cup cooked turnip cones
1 cup cooked peas and
1 cup cooked string beans on the plank between the steak and
    potato border. Put in oven for a moment to be sure that
    everything is very hot; pour
Hollandaise Sauce over the asparagus, place plank in holder and
    send to the table immediately.

Stuffed peppers, stuffed tomatoes, stuffed onions, pimientos stuffed with eggplant, flowerets of cauliflower or spinach timbals may be used on a planked steak.

A planked steak should be brought to the dining room before it is carved and may, after being shown, be served by the host or by the waiter. It should serve four people.

VEGETABLES

The potatoes and vegetables suggested for luncheons in Lesson VII may also be used at dinners.

An especially nice vegetable like mushrooms, fresh asparagus or French artichokes may be served as a course by itself, following the meat course.

A sherbet or water ice is sometimes served with a roast at a hotel or a very formal dinner or banquet. It should be one that goes especially well with the meat, as cranberry ice with chicken or turkey, or mint sherbet with lamb.

ACCOMPANIMENTS FOR MEAT

Such accompaniments and sauces as belong with certain meats should be served with them. For example, with

Roast Beef—Yorkshire pudding
          Horseradish sauce
          Mushroom sauce

Beef Steak—Maitre d'Hotel butter
          Mushroom sauce
          Oyster blanket
          Hollandaise sauce with variations
          Sautéd bananas

Roast Lamb—Mint sauce   Lamb Chops—Currant jelly
           Mint jelly
           Currant mint jelly
           Mint sherbet

Chicken and Fowl—Cranberry jelly
                Cranberry sauce
                Frozen cranberries
                Mushroom sauce
                Oyster sauce
                Celery
                Spiced figs

Duck—Celery   Goose—Apple sauce
       Green salad   Celery
       Orange salad
       Orange marmalade

DINNER SALADS

Many of the salads suggested as luncheon salads may be served for dinner. Most people, however, prefer a simple green salad with a well flavored French dressing. For the salad may be used

Lettuce separated as usual or
California or Iceland lettuce cut in halves or quarters
Romaine heads cut in halves
French endive

Standard French Dressing

    Put in small jar
½ teaspoon salt
¼ teaspoon pepper or paprika
4 tablespoons salad oil
2 tablespoons vinegar or lemon juice or grapefruit juice. Shake well just before serving.

French Dressing may be varied in many ways as follows:

Tabasco French Dressing

    To French Dressing add
5 drops tabasco sauce
1 teaspoon powdered sugar

Savory French Dressing

To French Dressing add
⅔ teaspoon mustard
2 teaspoons Worcestershire sauce and
⅛ teaspoon onion juice, secured by scraping the cut edge of an onion with a silver teaspoon.

Chutney Dressing

To French Dressing add
⅔ cups chutney sauce.

Martinique French Dressing

To French Dressing add
½ teaspoon finely chopped parsley and
½ tablespoon finely chopped green pepper

Parisian French Dressing

To French Dressing add
½ tablespoon finely chopped onion
1 tablespoon finely chopped parsley and
6 tiny peppers taken from a bottle of pepper sauce. Do not chop or eat these peppers, because they are exceedingly hot

Chiffonade Dressing

To French Dressing add
½ tablespoon salad oil
1 tablespoon finely chopped parsley
1 tablespoon chopped pimiento
½ teaspoon chopped shallot or onion
1 hard cooked egg chopped, and
⅛ teaspoon paprika

Indian Dressing

To French Dressing add
1 hard cooked egg yolk rubbed through a strainer
½ tablespoon red pepper, finely chopped
½ tablespoon green pepper, finely chopped
½ tablespoon pickled beets, finely chopped, and
½ teaspoon chopped parsley.

Belmont Dressing

To French Dressing add
2 tablespoons small tomato cubes,
½ tablespoon capers, and
Worcestershire sauce or mushroom catsup to taste.

Russian French Dressing

To French Dressing made with only 1 tablespoon vinegar, add
2 tablespoons chili sauce
1 teaspoon chopped chives, and
Few grains cayenne.

Porto Rico Dressing

Make French Dressing, using 3 tablespoons lemon juice instead
of vinegar, and add
1 tablespoon chopped olives and
½ tablespoon tomato catsup.

Thousand Island French Dressing

Make French Dressing, omitting vinegar, and add
Juice ¼ lemon
Juice ¼ orange
½ teaspoon onion juice
½ tablespoon finely chopped parsley
4 sliced olives
½ teaspoon Worcestershire sauce, and
⅛ teaspoon mustard

DESSERTS

A frozen dessert is most frequently served at a formal dinner or a banquet. Suggestions may be found in Lesson VI, in many cook books and on hotel menus. Individual molded ices in a nest of spun sugar are always popular and in good taste.

Small cakes, macaroons, lady fingers, or pieces of pound, sponge, or angel cake should be served with the ice cream.

Directions for making coffee are found in Lesson VI. It is served clear in small cups. Cream and loaf sugar are passed with it.

Directions for making bonbons and salted nuts are found in Lesson V.

How Much to Prepare

A famous chef explaining his system of preparing and serving banquets said that before each banquet he or his assistant conducted a demonstration. He showed the size of portion and how it should be dished up, so as to be most attractive and most economical. In this way he gauged the quantity for each person and then multiplied by the number to be served. You should work on a guarantee of so many covers and prepare enough food for that number of people. In that way everyone is served and very little is left over.

The allowance may be as follows:

> 1 gallon soup—17 guests
> 1 gallon vegetables—40 guests
> 1 gallon sauce—80 guests
> ¼ lb. fish—each guest
> 1 duckling—6 guests

Some other quantities are given on page 99.

If you are asked to plan a meal for a definite number of people at a definite price it is wise to make out a tentative menu and then make a list of the ingredients of the dishes you must serve, not forgetting coffee, cream, sugar, bread, butter, main dish, etc.; after each article put in the amount required, figuring from what you know. For instance if you use the amounts for four people when your list is complete divide by four and multiply by the number to be served. Put the cost of each article in a column after the amount required. When you have found the cost of most of the things you must have, add the totals and find out how much you have left for extras or whether the menu must be changed one way or another to be within the price quoted.

ESTIMATING COST OF SERVING A DINNER OR BANQUET

In estimating the price to charge for a special dinner or banquet it is necessary to know

When it is to be given

Where it is to be given

For how many it is to be given

Cost of food stuff not counting value of left-overs that may be used at another meal

Cost of flowers and other decorations

Cost of printing if menus are used

Cost of rental, if any, for dishes, silver, chairs, etc.

Cost of transportation if meal is not served where it is prepared

Time required for preparation

Number and cost of help required, estimated by time necessary for preparation and serving that particular meal.

Cost of overhead, rent, heat, light, laundry, etc., for the time the rooms are used.

DIRECTIONS TO HELP

Before the preparation and serving of the meal most careful directions must be given to the cooks, servers and waitresses as to the

Menu itself

Recipes selected

Manner of serving

Kinds and number of dishes; china, silver, and glass to be used; those that should be hot and the ones that must be chilled

Arrangement of tables, serving tables, decorations and every other detail that will make the meal pass off like clock work.

The following menus are typical of informal dinners at home or at a public dining room.

INFORMAL DINNER MENU I

CREAM OF CORN SOUP
CRACKERS
BROILED CHICKEN
FRENCH FRIED POTATOES
STRING BEANS
BREAD AND BUTTER
LETTUCE SALAD
FRENCH DRESSING
ICE CREAM
CAKE   COFFEE

$1.50 each.

INFORMAL DINNER MENU II

CREAM OF CELERY SOUP
CROUTONS
BROILED STEAK
DELMONICO POTATOES
PEAS
BREAD AND BUTTER
LETTUCE SALAD—RUSSIAN DRESSING
ICE CREAM   CAKE
COFFEE

$1.50 each.

INFORMAL DINNER MENU III

CLAM BISQUE
PLANKED STEAK
GARNISHED WITH DUCHESS POTATOES, CARROTS,
STRING BEANS, STUFFED TOMATOES OR PEPPERS
CAULIFLOWER AND MUSHROOMS
BREAD AND BUTTER
ICE CREAM   CAKE
COFFEE

$2.00 each.

The following menus are typical of meals that may be served as formal dinners or banquets to any number of people. The prices are those charged at a first class hotel:

FORMAL DINNER MENU I

HALF GRAPEFRUIT
(With garnish of strawberries or cherries and angelica)
SALTED NUTS
RADISHES   OLIVES
TOMATO BOUILLON
ROLLS
FILLET OF HALIBUT WITH LOBSTER SAUCE
POTATOES PERSILLADE

ROAST DUCKLING, PAN GRAVY
ORANGE MARMALADE   SWEET POTATOES, CANDIED
STRING BEANS OR PEAS
HEARTS OF ROMAINE
CHEESE DRESSING
VANILLA AND STRAWBERRY ICE CREAM   FANCY CAKE   COFFEE

$3.00 each.

Formal Dinner Menu II

OYSTER COCKTAIL, MIGNONETTE
OLIVES   RADISHES   SALTED NUTS
CONSOMMÉ
ROLLS
BOILED SALMON   HOLLANDAISE SAUCE   NEW PEAS
BROILED CHICKEN ON TOAST
POTATO CROQUETTE   ASPARAGUS POLONAISE
STUFFED TOMATO SALAD
FRUIT FANCY ICES   ASSORTED CAKES   DEMI TASSE

$4.00 each.

Formal Dinner Menu III

HORS D'OEUVRE
MOCK TURTLE SOUP WITH EGG GARNISH
ROLLS
BROOK TROUT MEUNIERE
JULIENNE POTATOES
CUCUMBERS   FRENCH DRESSING
SWEETBREAD PATTY WITH FRESH MUSHROOMS
ROAST JUMBO SQUAB ON CANAPÉ   GUAVA JELLY
POTATO DUCHESSE   STUFFED GREEN PEPPER
NEW ASPARAGUS ON TOAST
FRUIT SALAD   CREAM MAYONNAISE DRESSING
CHEESE CRACKERS
FANCY ICES   FANCY CAKE   COFFEE

$5.00 each.

Simple Banquet Menus

At a simple banquet or dinner there may be served only
a first course of fruit, a main dish of meat, potato and a
vegetable or salad, rolls, ice cream, cake and coffee.

Menu I

GRAPEFRUIT
COLD HAM   SCALLOPED OYSTERS
MASHED POTATO   SQUASH
ROLLS
HARLEQUIN ICE CREAM   CAKE
COFFEE

Menu II
CANTALOUP
MEAT LOAF
CREAMED POTATOES
LETTUCE AND TOMATOES WITH FRENCH DRESSING
VANILLA ICE CREAM   CHOCOLATE CAKE
COFFEE

Menu III
Even the fruit course may be omitted
SLICED BRAISED BEEF
MASHED POTATO   COLE SLAW
ROLLS
ASSORTED PIES   COFFEE

Menu IV
CHICKEN PIE CONTAINING POTATO
GREEN PEAS
ROLLS   SWEET PICKLES
STRAWBERRY SHORTCAKE
COFFEE

Thanksgiving or Company Dinners

Menu I
OYSTERS ON THE HALF SHELL
SQUASH SOUP   POPPED CORN
ROAST STUFFED TURKEY   BROWN GRAVY
SWEET POTATOES   BOILED ONIONS
TURNIP CROQUETTES   CRANBERRY CONSERVE
LETTUCE   CHIFFONADE DRESSING
VANILLA ICE CREAM
MINCE PIE   PUMPKIN PIE
NUTS AND RAISINS   ASSORTED FRUIT
CAFÉ NOIR

Menu II
CELERY WITH CAVIARE
OYSTER SOUP   OLIVES   OYSTER CRACKERS
ROAST TURKEY   GIBLET STUFFING
POTATO AND SPINACH CROQUETTES
GLAZED SILVER SKINS   SQUASH SOUFFLE
FROZEN CRANBERRIES
FRUIT SALAD   BROWN BREAD SANDWICHES
NEW ENGLAND THANKSGIVING PUDDING
MOUSSELAINE SAUCE
VANILLA ICE CREAM   LOGANBERRY SAUCE
ASSORTED NUTS   BONBONS
TOASTED CRACKERS   CHEESE
CAFÉ NOIR

QUESTIONS ON COOKING FOR PROFIT
VIII
CATERING FOR DINNER PARTIES

1. Draw a diagram of one cover of a table set for the $5.00 dinner on page 174.
2. Plan a dinner of four courses for 100 people for a club, lodge or school, at 75 cents a plate for food material. Give all data.
3. Give menu different from those suggested for a dinner party for 12 guests where money is no object.
4. Draw a simple diagram of a canapé indicating each ingredient of the make-up.
5. If convenient, prepare and serve a planked steak dinner and tell us or question us about it.

REFERENCE BOOKS

Company Cooking and Correct Table Service. Alice Bradley, price 25c.
Table Service, by Lucy Allen, price $1.75.
Up-to-Date Waitress, by Janet M. Hill, price $1.75.
Lake Placid Club Table Servis, Lake Placid Club, N. Y., price 25c.
Catering for Special Occasions, by Fannie M. Farmer, price $1.50.
Boston Cooking School Cook Book, by Fannie M. Farmer, price $2.50.
New Book of Cookery, by Fannie M. Farmer, price $2.50.
The Dinner Calendar, by Fannie M. Farmer.
The St. Francis Cook Book, Hotel Monthly, price $5.00.
The New Hostess of Today, by Linda Hull Larned, price $1.75.
Lessons in Cooking, by Robinson and Hammel, price $2.50.

COOKING FOR PROFIT
IX

CLASS ROOM IN MISS FARMER'S SCHOOL OF. COOKERY, BOSTON
Efficient Arrangement of Kitchen Utensils Shown

COOKING FOR PROFIT

PART IX

GUEST HOUSE MANAGEMENT

TYPES—HOMES, CAMPS, HOTELS, ETC.; NAMES; HOW TO PLAN
MEALS, FOOD VALUE, BALANCED MENUS, WHEN TO SERVE
WHAT; THREE MEALS A DAY, LEFT-OVERS, MENU LISTS, THE
MENU BOOK, THE COOK'S MENU BOOK, VARIETY IN MEALS;
HOW TO BUY, THE ORDER BOOK; STORE ROOM; KITCHEN EQUIP-
MENT; SERVICE; OVERHEAD COSTS; COST OF MEALS; NUMBER
NECESSARY FOR PROFIT; HOTEL COSTS, RENTING ROOMS; SAVING
EXPENSE; HOTEL POSITION.

IF YOU have had special training or have successfully
planned and cooked the meals for a large family you
may use your knowledge in managing a so-called
boarding house or if you have had hotel or other catering
experience you may take charge of a small hotel. In some
places you may do all or part of the cooking or you may
supervise and direct without doing any cooking at all.
Whether you cook or not the more knowledge you have
of cooking, of food values, of dietetics, of household engineering, of bookkeeping, sanitation, bacteriology and allied
subjects the more successful you will be.

A guest house or hotel may be for
    Small children
    School boys
    School girls

Men
>   Students
>   Sedentary workers
>   Manual workers

Women
>   Students
>   Teachers and office workers
>   Shop and factory employees
>   Mothers with small children
>   Women of leisure
>   Tired-out women
>   Elderly women

Families

NAMES

Common usage has made the terms boarding house and boarder unattractive. You do not wish to "run a boarding house" or "keep boarders," but many people cannot have their own homes and must be "paying guests." The term "guest house" has been introduced here as a substitute. The word hotel usually implies bellboy service, considerable style and pretension and transient guests. You may call your establishment an inn, tavern, home, camp, club, lodge, guest house, or the like. It is desirable to have a name such as the Lincoln Tavern, Shirley Inn, Harvard Camp, Hilldale Farm, Oakhaven, Elmhurst, Hadley Guest House, Women's City Club, Longfellow Hall, West House, Student's Union, Hemlock Manor, Two Acres, The Gables, Lake View Lodge, or the like.

Your house may be located in the
>   City
>   Country
>   Seashore
>   Mountains

It may be open
>   All the year round
>   During the schoolyear only
>   During the Summer only
>   During the Winter only

Choose for your guests the class of people you can most acceptably feed or house or those for whom no provision is being made.

HOMES AND CAMPS

A home for nervous, tired women should meet a need in some towns. Well balanced attractive meals and breakfast in bed if desired, would be the popular feature. An inn which cares for children while their parents are away is a boon to mothers who must work. It provides special children's meals, and a nurse or kindergartner to supervise their play, their naps, and their out-of-door activities.

The students' home for boys or girls or for young men or women should be an attractive place with a home atmosphere, an abundance of well cooked food and a person at the head who understands the food needs of growing children and can "mother" and chaperone the young people when they require it.

The summer camp should serve real country cream, plenty of rich milk and fresh fruit, berries and vegetables and not too much meat. Houses in districts that are famous for some particular kind of food should endeavor to feature it on their menus.

INSTITUTIONS

An institution is usually a home where some particular type of person is cared for and where special needs must be met. The officers' table of an institution is like that of a high class guest house. In the dining rooms for inmates and help, less expensive foods are used, but the meals should be carefully planned and as attractive as possible.

THE HOTEL

To be successful in the hotel business one should work up from a minor position until familiar with all departments of the hotel. In addition to the guests who stay in the house, most hotels must cater to outsiders who come in for occasional meals and the manager must be prepared to serve special luncheons, dinners and banquets for private parties, clubs and other organizations.

In most hotels, chefs are employed who are in charge of the kitchen and the kitchen force but a small hotel may have a woman cook and in some instances she may be the wife of the proprietor or even the owner of the hotel.

Hotel meals differ from family meals in that there may be a choice of two or more dishes for each course. Menu cards are provided which may be printed on a small press owned and operated in the hotel or they may be printed forms filled in each day on the typewriter or with pen and ink or they may be printed outside and sent in daily. There may be a regular à la carte menu with a special menu attached each day. Many people get tired reading a long menu; it is better to have few things and have them deliciously cooked and the menu changed daily than to have more dishes and a sameness about it each day. You may make a collection of menu cards, as you go about, and on your own cards embody the good points and eliminate the bad points as you see them.

Planning Meals

Hotel menus are more or less standardized all over the world. What one gets in one city is very like what one finds on the menu card on the other side of the continent. The hotel that provides different and especially fine food is likely to build up a reputation that will mean profit for the dining room, and cause people to come from near and far for your special dishes. One hundred miles is not too long a distance to motor for an especially good dinner or a week-end party.

QUALITY OF FOOD

No matter how delightfully situated your hotel or guest house or how artistically and beautifully furnished, people will not crowd your doors if the food is not first class. Quality of food is of far more importance than is sometimes realized although cleanliness and service should receive equal consideration. The greatest attention must be paid to every detail, every source of waste, every wish of the patrons if one is to make a profit.

HOW TO PLAN MEALS

Since the planning of meals is a most important duty of the manager of a guest house, a small hotel, a college, school or institution dining room, it is well to make a special study of the best methods to follow.

There are many excellent books to study in order that you may know how to best meet the needs of the particular group of people who will live with you. You will find that the character of your menus should be determined by

the age of your guests
their sex
their occupation
the amount they pay
their inherited tastes
their food habits
their likes and dislikes
the time of day that meals are served
the ability of the cook
the amount of help in the kitchen
the location of your house, whether in town or country
the season of the year
the nature of your equipment
the method of service whether
with waitresses
family style, the hostess serving
cafeteria style.

All these things will make a difference in the type of meal you are to serve. For instance if the guests are women of leisure who are paying a large amount of money for their meals they will require an entirely different food and service from hard working men, or school boys or girls who can pay very little, but the fundamental principle of balanced meals should hold good in any case.

NEEDS OF THE BODY

A well planned meal should supply:

Fuel foods to furnish heat and energy for the activities of the body; these are foods rich in starch, sugar, and fat.

Building foods to supply material for the growth and repair of body tissue; these are the protein foods, meat, fish, eggs, milk, cheese, beans, etc.;

Foods containing mineral salts and vitamines and which furnish bulk or "roughage" that so regulate the vital processes as to conserve health; these are vegetables, fruits, milk and whole grains.

In general all natural foods are building foods, as they all contain *some* protein and mineral salts, and all foods can serve as *fuel*. The extra refined foods like granulated sugar, corn starch, lard, lard substitutes and salad oils are fuel foods *only*. Fats have $2\frac{1}{4}$ times the fuel value of starch, sugar or protein per ounce or pound.

The "food unit" is the calorie, which indicates the fuel value, and the number of calories required depends on the age, weight, and especially the physical activity of the person in question. Three to four thousand calories per day are needed by the hard working man and active school boys. Men at sedentary occupations, women and girls require less —2,000 to 3,000 calories. The appetite is a good guide as to the amount of food that people require, and a sufficient amount of the right kinds of food must be supplied to fill the *demands* of the appetite of the guests but not to stuff them to repletion.

What Constitutes a Well Balanced Menu

In general the daily menus for each person should be composed of

> generous amounts of fruit and vegetables
>
> ⅔ pint or more of milk per day per person
>
> usually not more than ¼ to ½ pound of meat or other protein food
>
> a sufficient amount of starch, sugar and fat to supply the required number of calories and to make the meals palatable.

It is a common mistake to use too large amounts of cereal products, sugar and meat with too small amounts of fruit and vegetables and milk.

The above foodstuffs, fruit, vegetables, milk, meat and fish or meat substitutes, bread and butter and sweets must be so combined as to make palatable and appetizing and interesting meals that do not become monotonous and that serve to keep your people in good health with plenty of pep, vitality and force.

When to Serve What

Fruit should be served two or three times a day, for instance at breakfast and at one of the other meals either in or for dessert, in a fruit salad, as a cocktail, as a preserve or as spiced fruit with meat.

The *vegetables* should include from one-half to three-fourths of a pound or more of potatoes which may be served at dinner and may also be used at the other meals if desired; one green and one root vegetable at dinner and one or two vegetables at luncheon or supper.

The *meat* that is served may be used chiefly at dinner. There may be leftovers that can be served at breakfast or luncheon, but it should not often be necessary to buy meat for luncheon as meat substitutes may be used at this meal. If you buy meat for breakfast it may be bacon, dried beef, fish, ham or sausages. Steaks and chops are not necessary, although you may have to serve them under some conditions.

Eggs may be used as freely as the price allows, for breakfast or luncheon and in cooking.

Milk to drink, top milk, thin cream and whipped cream served with cereals and desserts, and skimmed milk used in soups, sauces and desserts will use up the amount of milk suggested.

Bread in some form should be served at every meal and there is enough variety with rolls, muffins, griddle cakes, toasts and waffles to prevent monotony.

Cereals, preferably the coarse kinds which supply vitamines and mineral salts not present in white bread, should be used freely.

Fats—ten ounces of butter or less per week per person for the table, oil for salad dressings, margarine and other fats used in cooking will supply all the fat needed in the diet. All fats that accumulate from cooking meat, soup, stock, etc., should be used in cooking or saved for soap.

Sugar will be used in desserts and on the table and will average from one to one and one-half pounds a week per person.

Coffee may make or mar the reputation of your house. You must have good coffee with good cream for breakfast unless your guests are children. Have it good under *all* circumstances! If the coffee is poor the whole house will suffer. Have hot milk available for those who like it in their coffee and cereal coffee, tea, cocoa, or milk for those who do not take coffee.

THREE MEALS A DAY
BREAKFAST

The first meal of the day should be planned to suit the season of the year as far as possible. It should consist of

SEASONABLE FRUIT, RAW OR COOKED
A CHOICE BETWEEN COOKED AND READY-TO-EAT CEREAL
BREAD IN SOME FORM
EGGS, BACON, FISH OR A MADE-OVER DISH
COFFEE OR OTHER BEVERAGE

DINNER

Dinner may consist of soup or chowder followed by the main meat course which may be steak, roast, smoked meat, corned meat, casserole of meat or fish of some kind. Whether or not you serve a choice of meats will depend on the number of people you are serving. It may be profitable to have two kinds of meat or meat and fish from which they can choose. When serving fish as a main dish it is wise to have meat on hand for those who do not care for fish. With a small number of guests who do not pay a large amount for board it will not be wise to offer much choice. With meat serve gravy, potatoes and at least one hot vegetable. A relish, such as pickle, jelly, apple sauce, and the like is a pleasing addition.

Serve some sort of salad daily either at this meal or at luncheon or supper or both so that the people will get some uncooked green; serve such desserts as your guests like, as well as those that are best for them. With some people a cold or frozen dessert is almost necessary, with other groups you may have to serve pie almost every day or simple milk puddings or fruit. There may be a choice of two or three desserts each day.

Bread or rolls should be provided and coffee or tea or both. Such extras as are suggested in Part VIII may be added at your discretion.

The time of serving dinner is determined by custom or the habits, age or occupation of your guests. It may be served at noon but is more commonly served from six to eight o'clock in the evening.

The first course and the last course should be especially

pleasing; the first to create an appetite and pleasure in the
meal; the last that guests may carry away a good impression.

LUNCHEON OR SUPPER

The third meal of the day may be served at noon and be
called luncheon or served at night and be called supper.
This will depend, of course, on when dinner is served. In
some houses guests do not come home at noon and a third
meal need not be prepared except for the help. At luncheon
or supper the food is used which is left over necessarily
from some dinner dishes, although left-over meat may sometimes be used for another dinner in another form. There
may be a soup or chowder, one or more hot dishes, vegetables, rolls, biscuit or muffins, salad, dessert and a beverage.
Among the main dishes from which one may choose are

Croquettes
Scalloped dishes
Stuffed peppers
Beans baked and in other ways
Cheese dishes
Fish in various ways
Egg dishes
Salads of egg, meat, or fish

The luncheon dessert may be of fruit, fresh or cooked,
cake, pudding, pie, fruit salad with wafers, custards, etc.

The following are typical of the table d'hote meals at a
hotel where there is a choice of dishes:

BREAKFAST, 85 CENTS

GRAPEFRUIT OR STEWED FRESH PLUMS
CREAM OF WHEAT, OATMEAL AND CREAM OR GRAPE NUTS
FRIED OR BOILED EGGS

OR

PAN FISH WITH BROWN BUTTER

OR

HONEYCOMB TRIPE IN CREAM
HOT ROLLS OR TOAST
MILK. COFFEE OR TEA

LUNCHEON, $1.50

CONSOMME WITH VERMICELLI
OR
CHICKEN MULLIGATAWNEY
SHIRRED EGGS WITH KIDNEYS
OR
RAVIOLI NICOSE
OR
FISH SALAD, HAVANAISE
FRENCH PASTRY
OR
APPLE ROLL
COFFEE OR TEA

(This menu would be better if one or more vegetables were added.)

DINNER, $2.25

CONSOMME NINO OR POTAGE LAMBALLE
CASSEROLETTE OF SEA FOOD, POULETTE
LEG OF LAMB, POELE
OR
SWEETBREAD PATTY, FINANCIERE
OR
ROAST IMPORTED PARTRIDGE, BREAD SAUCE
BRAIDES CELERY KNOB   POTATOES FONDANT
CHICORY SALAD
TUTTI FRUITTI ICE CREAM   CHOCOLATE SAUCE
AND DUNDAE CAKE
DEMI TASSE

This is not reverting to the old-style, American plan, for the reason that the little word "or" prevents a wicked waste of food that unlimited selection entailed.

LEFT-OVERS

The use of left-overs is most important as it is one of the things that will help to make your guest house a financial success. It is a good practice for the manager each morning soon after breakfast to look over the contents of the refrigerators, the fresh fruit and vegetable store closet and cake and bread boxes and to plan for the immediate use of any supplies that will not keep well. Soups, salads, croquettes, and other made dishes, crumb cakes and cookies will suggest themselves to the person of imagination who is familiar with the recipes for a large number of dishes. Foods should be used so intelligently that neither guests nor help will realize that they are being served with left-overs, but nothing except food left on guests' plates should be wasted. After some experience meals may be planned so that there will not be great amounts of left-overs to be used up, but no good foodstuff should be allowed to spoil or be thrown away.

MENU LISTS

The planning of meals is very greatly simplified by having lists of dishes from which to select, not like an index in the back of a cook book, but such dishes as meet the needs of your particular family, those you can afford to serve, and dishes that your people like.

Lists for different occasions have been given in previous lessons and many dishes if not whole lists may be used in these guest house lists which should have as headings

1 Breakfast fruit
2 Breakfast cereals
3 Breads for breakfast
4 Breads for luncheon
5 Breakfast eggs and other main dishes for breakfast
6 Clear soups
7 Cream soups
8 Chowders
9 Soup accompaniments
10 Beef
11 Lamb
12 Pork and ham
13 Veal
14 Poultry
15 Fish
16 Meat sundries
17 Meat substitutes
18 Relishes for main course
19 Made over dishes with meat
20 Made over dishes with eggs
21 Made over dishes with fish
22 Cheese dishes
23 Macaroni and other starchy dishes
24 Hot sandwiches
25 Potatoes
26 Sweet potatoes
27 Spring and summer vegetables
28 Fall and winter vegetables
29 Vegetable dishes for luncheon
30 Salads with protein (meat, fish, cheese, etc.)
31 Salads with vegetables
32 Salads with fruit
33 Dressings for lettuce, etc.
34 Sweet entrees (fritters, etc.)
35 Puddings
36 Pudding sauces
37 Frozen desserts
38 Cold desserts
39 Pies
40 Winter fruit desserts (canned preserved, etc.)
41 Summer fruit desserts
42 Cakes
43 Cookies

It is wise also to have lists of dishes that can be made from left-overs, for example

DISHES WITH SOUR CREAM

Salad dressing
Muffins
Luncheon cake
Ice cream (if cream is not very sour)
Griddle cakes
Waffles
To moisten Cottage Cheese, etc.

DISHES WITH LEFT-OVER CEREAL

Cereal muffins
Oatmeal bread
Oatmeal soup
Rice and cheese
Rice custard
Rice and tomato
Stuffing for peppers
Croquettes
Fried hominy
Tomato soup with macaroni

Have one or more pages in a large note book, or a large card or sheet of paper, for each list. Have columns on the right of the list for each month; figures indicate the day of the month on which the dish is served. At left of the list of dishes, use as many headings as you like, such as page of Cook Book where recipe is found, number of people served by the recipe, the amount of food stuff to be used for it, as pounds of cereal or meat, number of times to increase the recipe for your family or amount for one serving; there may be a column for the cost or the food value or the selling price of the dish.

With these lists at hand it is not a difficult task to plan menus for a week or a month in advance with very little repetition.

YOUR MENU BOOK

For your menus have a note book of about the size that stenographers use and a page dated for each day with

PAGE OF MENU BOOK

Sunday, March 6th

BREAKFAST

LUNCHEON

DINNER

spaces headed breakfast, luncheon or dinner, and dinner or supper.

PLANNING DINNER MENUS

From your list select first and enter in your menu book the dinner meat or fish that you will serve on the first day for which you are planning ahead, then the second day and so on. When you have entered roast lamb for example in your menu book, place in the column for that month on your list the day of the month on which you are to serve it so that when you have finished your menus, on the list of lamb dishes for instance, the column under each month will show the dates on which was served roast lamb, lamb chops, lamb chartreuse, lamb stew, and any other lamb dish.

When the meats have been entered for the week's dinners, enter the potatoes and vegetables that go best with

SAMPLE PAGE FROM MISS BRADLEY'S LISTS

PAGE IN COOK BOOK	LAMB	JAN.	FEB.	MAR.	APR.	MAY	JUNE	JULY	AUG.	SEPT.	OCT.	NOV.	DEC.
4	Mutton duck						.					...	...
5	Salmi of lamb							12	30		27	...	...
6	Scotch broth											..	..
	Roast leg lamb			7		24		11				..	5
	Lamb chops					5				8	31	.	...
	Stuffed chops		29				...					.	...
	Breaded chops											.	...
	Fricassee of flank		25					24		9		..	...
	Lamb stew			9			29	22	31			.	...
	Fillets of lamb	3							5	.			
	Chopped with green peppers	4				25							8
	Cold roast lamb			8								22	..
	Rice and lamb Chartreuse			11							2		..
	En casserole				7						22		..
	Braised leg				6								
	With currant jelly sauce				8								
	A la mode					23					26		
	Boiled lamb						7	.					
	With caper sauce							.					
	Braised breast						28						6
	Rechauffe						8						
	Lamb and macaroni scallop						9						
	Casserole of lamb and rice												
	Curry lamb with rice						13						7
	Hot pot, lamb and barley						15						
	Roast shoulder lamb								29		21	..	
	Croquettes with peas										24		...

them in your menu book, placing after each in your lists the day of the month on which you use it.

PLANNING OTHER MEALS

Next you can plan your lunches or suppers using up left overs if you can anticipate what they are going to be. If you cannot tell ahead leave the place open and decide about it later. Next enter the breakfast fruit for the week or month, then the cereals, then the luncheon and dinner desserts and salads using fruit in one or the other meal, both if you like but not the same fruit that you serve for breakfast. Desserts need not be repeated in two months. Next enter the luncheon breads and plan the breakfast breads at the same time to prevent duplication and also, so that you may perhaps use the same dough you make luncheon rolls from, with a change of shape or flavor, for the breakfast buns. From your lists continue until every meal is complete, with relishes, pudding sauces, etc.

CONTRAST AND HARMONY IN MEALS

The courses and dishes in a meal should be varied in their character as hot and cold, soft and crisp, dark and light. Avoid colors that clash, as beets and tomatoes; too much water, as clear soup and jelly at the same meal. Use sauces with tasteless and colorless foods. Do not use the same food more than once during the day if it is a food of distinctive flavor.

Plan special meals for special occasions as birthdays and holidays. Use seasonable foods abundantly in their season, using your lists of "special dishes to be served at different seasons of the year." With these lists it is possible to secure great variety in menus with little effort. Add to your lists such new dishes as your people will like and cross off those that are not popular.

VARIETY IN MEALS

Variety with a big V is of the greatest importance when you are catering for the same group of people day after day. It is no wiser to serve a thing that they like too often than to serve something that is not very popular. Do not have a definite day for special dishes even though it be chicken and ice cream or corned beef and canned peaches. Surprises are of great value in maintaining interest in your table and pleasure in your meals. You cannot please all the people all the time, but if good wholesome food and well balanced meals are provided the health of your guests will be better than if rich and indigestible though popular dishes are supplied too abundantly.

The most carefully planned menus will not be satisfactory unless food is attractively served, unless it looks well, and tastes good. Careful cooking is of great importance as well as correct seasoning. To men serve generous portions and hearty foods. Women and girls as a rule prefer more fruit and salads, smaller amounts and greater variety.

If possible do not serve a second time foods that are universally unpopular and of which the portions were left on the plates and wasted. Cross these dishes off your list or prepare them differently. Do not make it necessary for people to eat things they do not like.

THE COOK'S MENU BOOK

A menu book should hang in the kitchen where it may be consulted by the cooks at any time. This need not be the book in which you make out menus for a week or more in advance as those menus frequently have to be changed to use up left-overs or because certain foods come into market or are not in market or fail to arrive in time to be used. The menus for the cook should be posted if possible two days before they are to be served as some dishes need to be started twenty-four hours or more in advance of a meal.

HOW TO BUY

If menus are planned a month in advance and you know approximately how many meals you will serve, an order for groceries and non-perishable supplies can be given for the entire month with little or no need for ordering goods of that type for another thirty days. Naturally this saves much time and worry. All supplies must be checked up as soon as they arrive and be put away where they will be safe from theft, mice, and spoilage. It is efficient to have to do this for groceries only once a month.

Canned goods should be bought by the case and may be ordered in the spring for a year ahead to be delivered as needed. No. 10 cans of most fruits and some vegetables are satisfactory for large families. It is a help to consult a wholesale grocers' catalogue and price list when making out the grocery order. Keep a variety of seasonings on hand to vary the flavor of your dishes; buy cherries, ange-lica, nuts, etc., for garnishing. Buying in original packages saves expense if the stuff can be used before it spoils.

Order perishable supplies twice a week, or oftener, and a day before needing them. With good refrigerators most foods will keep well several days. It is a good policy to deal at the same markets regularly. If dealers know that you depend on them for most of your buying they will take particular pains to send you the quality of supplies that you need and, if they issue them, will mail you weekly price lists. Try to buy in sufficiently large quantities to secure wholesale prices. Vegetables and fruits are cheaper in original packages, but the amount you should buy will depend on the number of people you are feeding, your storage space and distance from the market.

Eggs may be purchased in April. Your dealer will store them and deliver as required or you can put them down in water glass.

Butter for the year may be purchased in June and kept in storage. Be sure always to serve *good* butter. If you cannot secure or cannot afford good butter, use a good margarine which is better than poor butter.

The amounts to be ordered of food stuffs depend on so many things that it is impossible to give any special quan-tities. The number of guests, their food requirements, storage space, etc., make each person's order different from every other. After the first few orders it is not difficult to plan your orders so that you will have enough, yet no waste. Keep accurate record of all supplies that are ordered and the price.

The sample page of my order book, used when prices were lower than they are now, shows how a book may be kept. Between 150 and 200 people were being fed. The names indicate dealer so bills can be easily checked up.

SAMPLE PAGE OF MISS BRADLEY'S ORDER BOOK

90 qts.	Milk.........................	.08	7	20
4 qts.	Cream........................	.45	1	80
2 cases	Eggs—Williams—60 dozen............	.33	19	80
100 lbs.	Butter—Gray.....................	34	34	00
1	Cheese—Weston—31½ lbs.........	.20	6	30
6	Yeast cakes.....................			12
12	Loaves bread—Dunton...............		1	20
1 can	Saltines—Cobb—7 lbs...........	.13		91
1 can	Butterthins—Cobb—10 lbs.........	.13	1	30
1 can	Vanilla creams—Cobb—7½ lbs........	.18	1	35
1 can	Fluted cocoanut—Cobb—12 lbs........	.11	1	32
1 can	Gingersnaps—Cobb—11 lbs............	.08		88
150 lbs.	Chicken—Weston....................	.20	30	00
4 strips	Bacon—Dunton—49½ lbs..............	.21	10	40
52½ lbs.	Corned beef—Weston..............	.12	6	30
1	Round beef, Argentine—83 lbs.........	.13	10	79
5	Lambs—214 lbs....................	.18	38	52
27 lbs.	Dried beef.........................	.38	10	26
50 lbs.	Frankfurters......................	.14	7	00
100 lbs.	Mackerel...........................	.06½	6	50
3 crates	(45) Cantaloups....................		6	00
1 bunch	Bananas—Puffer...................		2	15
2 crates	Plums..........................		4	00
1 crate	(32 boxes) Blackberries................		5	76
5 qts.	Blueberries..................	12		60
2 crates	(64 boxes) Currants................	.05	3	20
6	Watermelon..........................		2	10
1 bushel	Beets—Puffer.....................		1	25
1 barrel	Cabbage—Puffer...................		1	00
2 barrels	Potatoes—Puffer...................		8	00
1 bushel	Cucumbers—Puffer.................		1	50
1 bushel	Green beans—Puffer................		1	00
1 basket	Peppers—Puffer....................			40
1 bushel	Sweet potatoes.....................		2	25
1 peck	Parsley—Puffer....................			20
25 heads	Lettuce—Mosher....................		1	00
4 bushels	Beet greens—Mosher................		2	80

Storerooms

A storeroom should be light and well ventilated with an abundance of shelves of the correct width and height to hold the things that will be put on them. For instance, shelves for canned goods may be wide enough to hold two or three cans deep and two cans high with no waste space. Shelves for extracts, seasonings, etc., may be narrow. Never place one thing in front of another different thing. It is inefficient to have to move things to find something that is wanted. Have covered receptacles, moisture and mouse proof, for bulk cereals, tea and coffee. Have a refrigerator that is well constructed and large enough for your needs.

Kitchen Equipment

It is impossible to give here a complete list of the kitchen equipment required for a boarding house or a hotel. There are large firms whose business it is to supply everything necessary from cellar to garret. It will be best for you to visit as many establishments as you can, send for catalogs and, knowing how much money you wish to invest, decide for yourself how best to spend it. The equipment required differs with the number and class of people to be fed. One hundred to two hundred people can be fed with simple meals with a large double range, a bake oven with four or five shelves, cook's tables with rack overhead for utensils, large boilers of tin, copper or enamelware, large roasting pans that fit range ovens, agate pans for baking puddings, apples, etc., of size to fit bake oven shelves, food chopper, bread mixer, bread slicer and such other utensils as are found in home kitchens, but of larger size or in larger numbers. For a larger number of people it will be necessary to install a steam table, steam kettle for vegetables, soups, etc., power ice cream freezer, power mixing machine, dish washer, bain marie, broiler, vegetable parer, meat slicer.

SERVICE

The method of service makes a difference in the amount that you must charge for meals and the amount of profit that you will make. You may have waitresses and the serving done as explained in Lesson VIII. In a small guest house the hostess may sit at the table, do the carving and serving and have a waitress to take the filled plates to each guest. In a large establishment or institution, cafeteria style may be employed. This method of serving will be fully explained in Lesson XII. It is more economical for the proprietor if food is put on the individual plates than if platters and serving dishes are passed or put on the table, where guests may help themselves to as much as they wish.

Where people pay by the week a second order of the main dish and vegetable should be allowed and all the bread and butter that anyone wishes. Fruit, soup, salad, and dessert courses may well be limited to one serving each. In a hotel, people are expected to pay for extra orders of anything.

OVERHEAD COSTS

The overhead expense of running the guest house or hotel may be estimated as suggested in Lesson I. It is usually possible to separate the cost of serving meals and the cost of rooms. It is absolutely essential that you know the overhead cost of doing business in order that you may know whether you are making or losing money.

The price charged for meals must cover

1 Rent of kitchen
2 Rent of dining room
3 Rent of hall or public parlor

4 All or part of rent of laundry, if table linen is laundered in the house
5 Rent of rooms occupied by cooks and kitchen help and all or part of rent of rooms of proprietor, waitresses, cashier, book-keeper, or such other help as live in the house and give all or part of their time to the food service
6 Interest and depreciation, on value of furnishings and equipment in all the above rooms
7 Renewal and replacement of equipment
8 Cost of cleaning, painting, renovating, etc.
9 Light used in lighting above rooms
10 Fuel used in heating above rooms
11 Fuel used in cooking
12 Ice
13 Soap and cleaning materials
14 Proportionate part of telephone expense
15 Wages of help
16 Salary of at least $25.00 a week for proprietor
17 Cost of laundering all linen used in dining room and kitchen
18 Laundering maids' and cooks' uniforms, unless they pay for them themselves
19 Water and other taxes, license fees, insurance, garbage collection, etc.
20 Advertising and other expense peculiar to your situation
21 Cost of food served to kitchen and dining room employees

COST OF MEALS PER DAY AND PER WEEK

The cost of raw food stuffs, sufficient for one day for one person varies from fifty cents to two dollars or more. It is necessary to keep accurate account of all food purchased; it is worth while to make an inventory of supplies on hand at the beginning of each month and their value. To cost of food purchased during the month, add the cost of supplies on hand the first day of the month and subtract value of supplies on hand the last day of the month. The result will show the cost of food for the month. You should charge up at its selling price food stuffs that you raise, can, etc. A record should be kept of the number of meals served each day to paying guests and to help and other non-paying people. Divide the total amount spent for food by the number of meals served to get the cost of food per meal per person. Multiply per capita cost of food by the

number of meals served to each guest each day or each week
to learn the cost of raw food material per day or per week.
Add to this the overhead cost of feeding guests per day or
per week to learn the amount that must be taken in.

NUMBER NECESSARY FOR PROFIT

You should have enough paying guests to guarantee all
the above expenses. To find the number necessary, divide
the overhead and operating expense by the number of
people that you serve or can easily accommodate. Add to
this the cost of food material per person. This is what
your guests must pay for table board before there will be
any profit for yourself more than the salary suggested
above. People sometimes say "But no one will pay that
much for board." If that is true you must reduce the cost
of food or overhead expenses or both, or secure more paying guests without increasing your overhead expenses, or
consider that you are working hard for less money than
you would get if you rented your furnished house and
went to work for some one else.

WHAT IT COSTS TO RUN A HOTEL

The cost of raw food material will probably be more
than fifty per cent of the total cost of doing business, although one hotel man writes: "There are few rules for
pricing food, but you may divide the price paid by seventy-
five guests into four parts allowing
        ¼ for food cost
        ¼ for overhead expense
        ¼ for service
and the remaining fourth might be your profit."

FIGURING COSTS

Your figuring may give some such results as this:

Value of equipment, furnishings, etc.—$1,000.00.
Interest at 5½% for one year..............$ 55.00
Depreciation at 20% for one year.......... 200.00

Total for one year....................$255.00
Total for one month.................... $ 21.25
Rent, kitchen, etc., 1 mo. 35.00
Fuel for cooking and hot water........... 10.00
Fuel for heating 14.00
Lights 3.00
Water 50
Ice 5.00
Telephone 3.50
Soap, cleaning materials 1.50
Laundry 15.00

Total Running Expenses for one month—30
    days 109.75

Wages kitchen assistant, 1 mo. ....$ 50.00
Wages 3 waitresses, 1 mo. 120.00
Salary yourself, 1 mo., at least........... 100.00
Food for 5 (help) at $4.00 a week, 1 mo...... 93.00

Total for service, 1 mo. 363.00
Total for overhead, 1 mo. (30 days)........ $494.00
Total for overhead, 1 day..................   16.44
Total for overhead, 1 week (7 days)........   115.08

With 24 boarders, overhead one week, each
    boarder ....$ 4.80
Food for 1 boarder, 1 week.................   6.00

Total Cost for 1 boarder, 1 week........... $ 10.80

If each boarder pays, 1 week, $12.00—
Estimated profit per week per person.........   1.20
Estimated profit per week for 24 boarders....   28.80

If only fifteen boarders are served the loss will be $1.67 per week
per person or $25.05; all the salary of the manager. Learn to esti-
mate every week or so just where you stand financially so that you
will make a profit instead of losing money or just barely paying
expenses.

In a hotel the number of guests varies greatly. A sufficiently
large staff must be kept to care for the average or the largest
probable number of guests, therefore prices charged must be higher
than in a guest house.

The average price paid for meals in eight hotels where tens of thousands of meals are served daily was figured as follows:

	Table d'Hote	A la carte
Breakfast	$0.85	$1.42
Lunch	1.38	1.80
Dinner	2.08	3.79

RENTING ROOMS

The cost of the rooms that you rent should be figured as above and added to the cost of food service. When you know all these actual or probable costs you are in a position to make your price for "meals and room by the day or week." This price must be based on the actual cost as figured above, plus enough more to give you a reasonable income proportionate to the size of your business and the amount invested in it. Prices charged by other people who give the same service in the same locality will help to determine the price that you will charge.

Many people because they have linen, china, silver and a house, and are good cooks think they can make a profit from paying guests. They decide that they will charge for board what they think people will pay, and do not reckon at all what it is going to cost them. If you cannot charge the amount as estimated above and enough more to really pay you for being in business with its responsibility and its risks there is no sense in having boarders because you won't make anything on it. There may be some conditions under which it may be wise to work for just your bare living, but these are unusual. You must charge enough.

KITCHEN HELP

The number and duties of the employees where many people are fed depends on the number to be cooked for, the character of the meals and the price paid. One meat cook, an assistant or vegetable cook and a pastry cook can prepare the food if it is not elaborate for from twenty to two hundred people or more. A kitchen man and a kitchen woman will be needed to prepare vegetables, freeze ice cream, wash pots, and keep the kitchen clean. One waitress can serve six to twelve people at a time. Waitresses may wash all the china and silver used in the dining room and do all the cleaning of that room and of the serving room. Where much help is kept a separate dining room is reserved for them and special meals are prepared by a special cook. In many states women can not be employed for more than forty-eight hours a week. Hours of work therefore must be carefully planned with a half day off every week and part time on Sundays, and menus so planned that they can be carried out when the cook or her assistant are away.

It is a great assistance in managing help to have the hours and duties of each person posted with regular time specified for each thing that has to be done daily and days for such things as are done less often.

SAVING EXPENSE

Where the price paid for board is not large every possible means of reducing expense must be resorted to, except curtailing the food supply to the extent that people actually are undernourished. Cheap cuts of meat, the least expensive cereals, vegetables and fruits, are just as nutritious as the expensive and out of season foods. With care they can be made palatable and attractive. Dishes that are easily prepared lessen the number of cooks necessary.

In many college boarding houses no tablecloths or doilies are used, save a centrepiece on each table. In a summer camp, paper napkins may be used and bare or oilcloth covered tables. Meals may be given in payment for work done in the dining room. Many other suggestions and economies will occur to the woman of experience. The woman who has had none should start in a small way or gain experience by working under a good manager before attempting a business of her own.

WELL-PAID POSITIONS

There are many excellent positions in institutions and hotels, open to women with training and ability. These pay good salaries and do not involve any money investment or as much care as when one is owner and proprietor of a business. Among these positions are those of

Employment manager
Dietitian
Steward
Cafeteria manager
Manager of service in dining room
Storeroom manager
Storeroom assistants
Cook
Pastry cook
Vegetable cook
Salad maker
Coffee woman
Toast woman
Cereal woman

Many women as well as men find employment in the resort hotels, going south in the winter and to a summer hotel for the summer.

There is much pleasure and satisfaction in so feeding people day after day that they enjoy their meals and remain in good health and spirits and stay or return to you year after year.

REFERENCE BOOKS

Boston Cooking School Cook Book by F. M. Farmer, $2.50
New Book of Cookery by F. M. Farmer, $2.50
Recipes and Menus for Fifty by F. L. Smith, $2.00
More Recipes for Fifty by F. L. Smith, $2.00
Feeding the Family by M. S. Rose, $2 40
The American Home Diet by Simmonds and McCollum, $3.50
Hotel St. Francis Cook Book by V. Hirtzler, $5 00
Lessons in Cooking through Preparation of Meals by Robinson & Hammel, $2.50
Household Engineering by C. Frederick, $2.50
Low Cost Cooking by Florence Nesbitt, $1.00
Marketing and Housework Manual by S. A. Donham, $2.00
Low Cost Menus for June and July by A. Bradley, $0.20
Food Values and Economical Menus by A. Bradley, $0.25
Wheatless and Meatless Menus and Recipes by A. Bradley, $0 25
Free Hand Cooking, Am. School of Home Economics, $0.10
Food Values, Am. School of Home Economics, $0.10
Ten-Cent Meals, Am. School of Home Economics, $0.10
The Up-to-Date Home; Labor Saving Appliances, A. S. H. E., $0.10
American Cookery, Boston, $1.50 a year
Hotel Monthly, Chicago, $1.00 a year

QUESTIONS ON COOKING FOR PROFIT

IX

Guest House Management

1. What type of guest house are you most familiar with or interested in?
2. Write out seasonable menus for a week for a guest house where twenty people are served with two meals a day and pay $12.00 a week and ten are served with lunch at $5.00 a week. Plan to make use of left-overs.
3. Estimate the amount that can be spent in this guest house for overhead and operating expense and still leave a profit.
4. Write out a grocery order for next month for twenty people.
5. Write meat, vegetable and fruit order for 50 people for 1 week.

COOKING FOR PROFIT

x

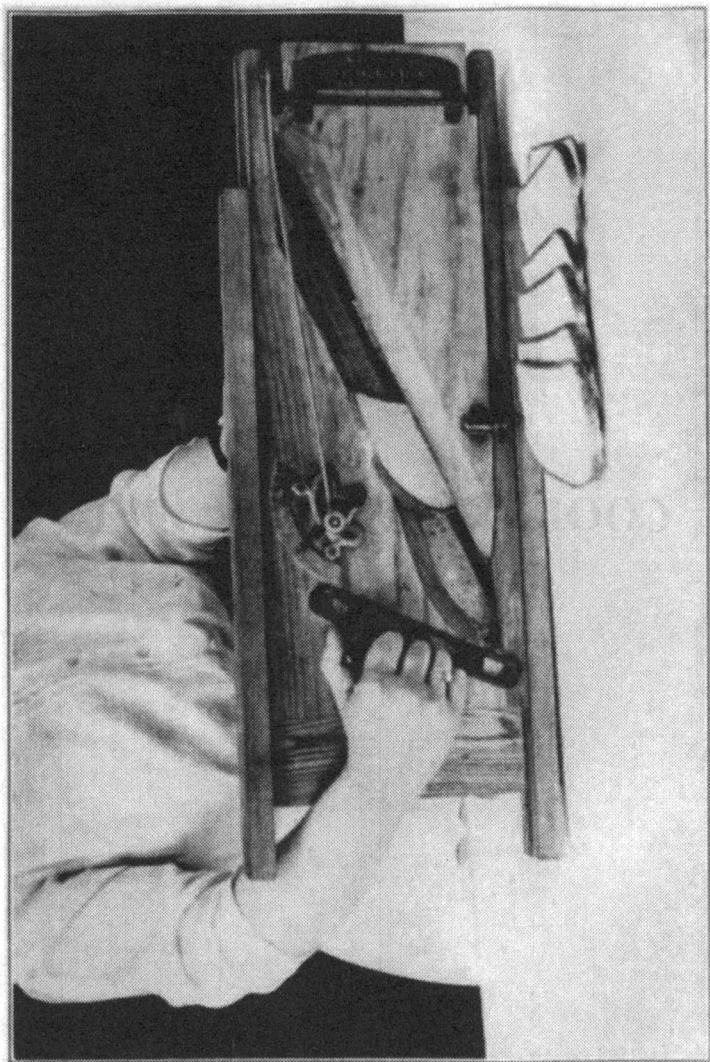

BREAD CUTTER USED FOR SANDWICHES

COOKING FOR PROFIT

PART X

SCHOOL, INDUSTRIAL AND COMMUNITY FOOD SERVICE

SCHOOL LUNCHES—MENUS, PRICES, ETC ; STORE AND FACTORY
LUNCH ROOMS—MENUS AND PRICES, MATRON'S DUTIES;
LUNCH ROOM EQUIPMENT; LUNCHEONETTES; COMMUNITY
KITCHENS—HELP REQUIRED, DELIVERING OF FOOD AT A DIS-
TANCE, MENUS; COMMUNITY CENTERS, RECIPES AND EXPENSES;
TRAVELING KITCHENS; HOW MUCH TO SERVE, DISPOSAL OF
LEFT-OVERS ; PRICES AND PROFIT; CAMP LUNCH ROOMS; PACK-
ING LUNCH BOXES; PLANNING MENUS; LIST OF DESSERTS

THERE are many opportunities open to the woman
who wishes to live at home and have comparatively
short hours of work elsewhere supervising or cooking one meal a day. Such a position may be found in
schools, stores or factories. In such places a hot lunch
at noon has proven its great superiority over the cold
lunch carried from home. The lunch room may provide
the entire lunch, or merely a soup, cocoa or other hot dish
to be eaten with other things brought from home.

In every such place the manager must be a woman
*(1) with a knowledge of food values; (2) the foods best
adapted to the needs of the people who are to be served;
(3) the foods that give the most nourishment for the least
money; (4) how to prepare simple, inexpensive and nutritious foods so that they will be attractive and appetizing;
(5) how to make combinations that will supply for little
money a well balanced meal; (6) how to develop in the
people fed, food habits that will be valuable to them in their
homes and all through their lives.*

205

It is essential that the manager of such a business keep in close touch with what is in market and its cost, know what supplies are on hand in the storeroom and refrigerator every day, the dishes that are most popular with the people fed, the overhead costs, and the amount of money taken in daily, or the sum available for food each day.

The thought of profit from cooking should not be considered in a school or factory lunch room, although many of them are self-sustaining and the manager should be able to keep them so. The employees are paid for their labor, except those who, because of their interest in the group that is being fed, are glad to give their services until such time as the project is well launched.

SCHOOL LUNCHES

In the New York City schools, lunches costing only a few pennies furnish between 400 and 500 food units (calories). In Boston, lunches are provided in 18 high schools by the Women's Educational and Industrial Union in co-operation with school authorities and health experts. All the food is prepared and cooked at the central kitchen, from which it is sent to the various schools. The food served in all the schools is the same in kind and quality. The head server, who is in charge at each school, makes a report of food sold and money received each day. The average cost of each student's lunch is from nine to eleven cents. Receipts from lunch counters pay for—

1 The charges for supervision, preparation and service of luncheons;
2 The expense for food;
3 Rent, light, heat, and overhead expenses at the central kitchen;
4 All movable equipment in the schools.

Each day the luncheon menu includes—

1 soup such as tomato, green pea, split pea, white or black bean which are nutritious and inexpensive. Four days out of the five it is a milk soup.

1 or 2 hot dishes, creamed or scalloped, such as spaghetti with tomato sauce, mashed potatoes with green peas, baked beans, corn pudding, a stew or hot roast beef sandwich. Meat is not served except in made up dishes where it flavors potato or rice or macaroni. Cheese and vegetables are much used. These dishes are baked in large round "milk" pans.

1 salad such as potato, egg, fruit or green vegetables. Most salads are made up at the schools, ingredients and dressing being sent out separately.

5 sandwiches

> 1 meat sandwich, varied daily.
>
> 1 cheese sandwich, varied by using factory or cream cheese with olives, pimiento, catsup, etc.
>
> 1 jam sandwich.
>
> 1 peanut butter sandwich.
>
> 1 lettuce and mayonnaise sandwich.
>
> These are made at the central kitchen, but material for the three latter sandwiches is kept on hand at each school for use when more sandwiches are required than were sent.
>
> Boys like heavy meat sandwiches thickly cut. Girls prefer jam, lettuce, and cream cheese sandwiches thinly cut and daintily served.

1 pudding such as rice, bread, blancmange, or jellies.

Every day there is served—

> baked custard
>
> ice cream
>
> plain cake or sweet wafers offered only in combination with milk or other plain food
>
> milk
>
> cocoa
>
> fruit such as apples, bananas, or stewed fruits of various kinds.

Sweet chocolate and plain candies are often for sale.

The dishes, except those specified, are not repeated oftener than once in ten days.

PRICES

The price is usually put at 2 to 2½ times the cost of food material. It is well to figure the cost of the different soups that will probably be served and then make an average price so that soup, whatever its ingredients, will cost the same per cup throughout the year or, if a change must be made, that such a change does not occur more than twice a year.

The same thing should be done for scalloped dishes, puddings, etc., in order that children may always know how much money they will need for certain types of dishes. Boys and girls may serve at the lunch counter and for their services be allowed 20 cents' worth of lunch.

In many schools the food prepared in the cooking class as the regular lesson is sold in the lunch room. This eliminates the cost of food material for the class, trains the pupils in buying and preparing good substantial every-day food, in family quantities, and gives all the children an opportunity to purchase at cost a nourishing and satisfying luncheon.

Employees who prepare and serve food in a school lunch room work usually from nine to four and are paid about 30 cents an hour. The manager, who may do a part of the cooking, should receive from $20.00 a week up.

STORE AND FACTORY LUNCH ROOMS

There are many opportunities in stores and factories for women who can serve efficiently as managers of lunch rooms where one meal a day is served to employees. The cafeteria plan is usually followed as in schools. This method will be discussed in Lesson XII. The hours are not very long and the pay is commensurate with the work done. The menus may be longer than those for the school lunch room and generally include a well planned meal of meat, potato, vegetable, bread and butter, dessert and coffee, as well as separately priced dishes like those suggested above. The manager plans the menus, does the buying, engages and supervises cooks and waitresses and keeps the books, so that she knows just how she stands financially every day.

MENUS AND PRICES

One large corporation, with branches in many places, has 75 standard menus, 40 for winter, 35 for summer, which are served in rotation. In this way employees may secure for the price usually charged for meat alone, meat or meat substitute, potato and bread and butter, which keeps them in better health than the lunches they might select for the same price if no combinations were offered.

In addition to the combination menu, a soup, salad, several desserts and beverages are also provided.

Specific cooking instructions accompany each menu, for the use of the cook, and a chart of food values showing the calories contained in each article, to help the patron order an adequate ration. Each branch has the same menu at the same time. All the buying is done from the central plant and supplies are sent daily to each lunch room in such amounts as are ordered by the matron in charge.

The Matron's Duties

In addition to sending in this daily requisition the matron's duties include the cooking of the food, selling it over the lunch counter, keeping track of income by means of a cash register and taking an inventory once a month; in fact, she is responsible for the entire management of that particular lunch room, including supervision of the woman who washes the dishes and a woman to assist in serving if more than 200 people are served there.

Equipment

Oftentimes the lunch room equipment is very simple, scarcely more than a stove, a work table and a counter with shelves underneath; when the enterprise has proven its value more elaborate equipment may be provided costing up to $10,000. Steam kettles, a steam table, a dish washing machine, dish warmer, coffee urns, a bake oven, bread and meat slicer, power mixer, ice cream freezer, vegetable paring machine, and vegetable masher are among the larger things that will be needed where many people are fed daily.

Many breads, desserts, cakes, etc., are purchased from concerns which specialize in making such things on a large scale, others go to the serving counter in the pans in which they are baked. There should be a large supply of these pans, either round or of a size about 11 by 19 inches, that fit into the steam table and keep food hot until the last portion is served.

LUNCHEONETTES IN STORES

In many stores that are equipped with soda fountains light lunches are being served to increasing numbers of patrons. Hot beverages, as chocolate, bouillon, coffee, etc., with sandwiches and cakes, cookies, doughnuts and pies, are first added to the list of fountain drinks and ices. The cakes and sandwiches may be prepared in one's home and delivered daily to the store or cooking equipment may be installed near the store and more dishes added to the menu as the demand increases.

All food served should be above the average in appearance and taste and no dishes should be listed unless there is a good demand for them, as the success of such a department depends on the call for large quantities of a limited number of articles. There may be a hot "special" each day, as Chicken Pie, Hot Roast Beef Sandwich, Baked Beans in individual pots, Scalloped Oysters, etc.

COMMUNITY KITCHENS

Community Kitchens have been opened in many places. Food is prepared in a central kitchen and delivered in special containers to the homes of families that subscribe for the service. The original investment may be very small or as much as $20,000. In order to make it self-sustaining it should feed 250 persons daily. It pays better if 500 persons can be daily supplied. In addition to the dinners that are furnished regularly a general catering business or food shop or both should be carried on. Such a station should be located on a popular street, with considerable traffic, in order to display to advantage in an attractive window its catering specialties. The location should also be central with a desirable class of homes radiating from it. There must be ample room in the building or house for cold-storage, kitchens with ranges, dish-washing machines and sterilizer for containers; pantries, and rooms for office staff. A garage is an important item as it saves rent outside. For delivering food for 250 persons four motor cars are required.

A station requires the following help:
Office Staff
Manager who makes out menus
Purchasing agent, who reports to manager on market conditions so that menus shall include seasonable food stuffs only and omit those which are scarce and high priced (the manager and purchasing agent may be combined in one person)
Kitchen director, chef, or cook
Pastry cook
2 packers in hot food department
1 packer of cold food
Dish, pan and container washers
4 delivery hands

DELIVERING FOOD AT A DISTANCE

A most important item for a community kitchen is the type of food container selected for transporting meals from the central kitchen to individual homes. One container on the market is composed of five parts; the base, the outer insulating sleeve or jacket, four insulated glass lined metal inserts and covers. In this container food can be kept hot for hours and the separate inserts may be used on the table in place of other platters and serving dishes. Another style has a high container insulated like a fireless cooker. It is heated with hot stones for an hour or two before being packed, then the stones are removed and aluminum pans holding hot soup, meat and two vegetables are packed in one upon another. Other containers hold the cold dessert and the salad in individual paper cups. Salad dressing, custard sauce, etc., are sent in small glass jars. Ice cream is packed in molds holding the required number of orders and sent out in buckets of ice and salt.

Menus may be sent out in the container one day. The number of portions required must be ordered before a certain hour the next day. The entire meal is delivered piping hot to be opened and served when the family has assembled. The following is a copy of a menu used in one well-to-do community:

DINNER

TOMATO BOUILLON OR CONSOMMÉ
ROAST SIRLOIN OF BEEF OR
ROAST LEG OF LAMB, MINT SAUCE
SCALLOPED POTATO OR RICE CROQUETTES
LIMA BEANS OR HARVARD BEETS
PEAR SALAD
APPLE PIE OR TAPIOCA CREAM

SUPPER

LAMB CHOP OR HALIBUT TIMBALES
POTATOES   SALAD   DESSERT
(AS GIVEN ON DINNER MENU)

To regular customers (those who subscribe to a dinner or supper book of twelve tickets) the price of the dinner is $1.00 a plate; supper 85 cents a plate; Sunday dinner $1.25 a plate.

In one city a kitchen has been established in the poorest section. Women who go out to work can send over for hot cooked cereal and rolls for their breakfasts, the children can go there from school for a nourishing ten cent luncheon and anybody may purchase a hot dish and dessert for supper.

COMMUNITY CENTERS

In a country town, each housekeeper may contribute to a community center any kind of cooked or canned food or fresh fruit or vegetables that she does not need for her own family. Different townswomen may take turns in tending the shop and there is therefore little overhead expense to be deducted from the profits from sales. Automobile tourists as well as townspeople and farmers' wives patronize such a shop. Accurate record should be kept of each article received and of every sale every day and settlement made weekly.

TEA ROOM AND COMMUNITY SHOP

PAID OUT

Manager's Salary	$1,423.31	
Assistants' Salary	414.50	
Rent	300.00	
Equipment	1,188.52	
Insurance	3.55	
Electricity, for lighting and cooking	418.60	
Telephone	29.26	
War Tax	54.95	
Fuel, wood and coal	105.58	
Total Overhead		$3,938.27
Groceries	1,364.24	
Ice	119.09	
Milk	390.57	
Other Food and General Expenses	796.86	
Food Total		2,670.76
Paid to Consignors		3,759.70
Total Disbursements		$10,368.73

RECEIVED

From Tea Room	7,906.42	
Interest	8.79	
Dues (25c—$25.00)	568.00	
Gifts	563.00	
Loan	950.00	
Benefits	825.54	
Total Received		$10,821.75
Total Disbursements		10,368.73
Balance on hand		$453.02

A paid manager and assistants may be necessary for such a community kitchen. The foregoing figures are those of a community shop and tea room for a period of fourteen months as reported by the manager.

TRAVELING KITCHEN

A traveling restaurant or kitchen has been successful in some places. A large automobile, fitted up with steam table for keeping food and dishes warm, a range for cooking "short orders" (steaks, chops, etc.), a refrigerator to keep meat, milk and fruits in prime condition, storage space for other foods, a cook and a driver complete the outfit which covers a regular route at a regular time every day.

HOW MUCH TO SERVE

The proprietor of a lunch room or community kitchen with a number of things on her menu but without definite knowledge of how many people are coming in to eat, or what these people are going to order, must depend on statistics in order to always have enough on hand to feed everyone. She should keep a daily record of the number of people who come in and the number of orders served of the dishes which are provided on different days. These records should be so compiled that after a little experience she will be able to tell approximately how many orders will be given for sandwiches or salads, how many patrons are going to order meat, and how many may prefer fish, what desserts will be most popular, and how many whole meals will be served.

You can multiply the number of chairs by the length of time for serving, allowing time for the quickest possible service, and this will give the maximum number which could be served. It is not likely that a new lunch room, unknown and unestablished, would serve to more than one-half its capacity the first few days. If the time of serving is 11 to 3, the number of chairs, 50, and the minimum time for service, 20 minutes, the capacity of the lunch room would be approximately 150 an hour or 600 people in the four hours.

Of course, not all of the 600 are going to select all the ready-to-serve items on the menu, so that considerable judgment has to be shown in providing larger quantities of some of the hot dishes, because of their general popularity, and their selling price. The public will more often select a dish with which they are familiar, particularly in a new establishment, and when the price is moderate, than one which is unknown to them. The location and class of patrons must also be considered in estimating the possible number to be served. If the lunch room caters largely to business people whose lunch hours are practically the same, the rush of trade will be greater during those hours, and the first and last hour will not be likely to even approach a maximum number of customers. This should be considered when estimating the number to be served, as the figures used, 600 for four hours, is the maximum number for the entire time. Where quick service is essential, a sufficient quantity of food should be prepared before the bulk of the trade is expected, but where it is possible, materials should be partially prepared, but not combined until ordered. This avoids waste and also makes it easier to use the left-overs, as the materials may be combined in different ways on successive days.

DISPOSAL OF LEFT-OVER FOOD

In schools where a simple lunch is served to the pupils at noon, it is possible to make a fairly accurate estimate of how much food to provide. Any left-over sandwiches, etc., may be sold at a very small cost to the poorer children, or given to the very needy or used the next day for toasted sandwiches.

Left-over cake may be made into cakes, cookies, and desserts. Melted ice cream can be utilized in bread puddings.

In estimating the first amounts that you may have to serve it is better to make your estimate too low than to plan too much and so have a lot of food wasted.

The portions served should be standardized as suggested in previous lessons. You must know how many portions can be served from one recipe and always secure that number. If one recipe fills fifteen pans and each pan contains forty portions, then 200 portions should be served from that recipe.

A well-known writer talked one day with the manager of a restaurant where the employees of a great factory are fed. "The place was losing money when I took it," the manager said. "Now we just break even, which is all we want to do. And there is the machine that made the difference." He pointed to a machine that cuts the portions of butter for each butter plate. "The difference between just enough butter and just a little too much was the difference between making expenses and making a loss."

In one kitchen where six legs of lamb had been required, careful carving by another person made five legs serve the same number of people equally well.

PRICES OF FOOD AND PROFIT

Lunch rooms, community kitchens, etc., are usually operated on a very small margin. The following figures were recently published in the Hotel Monthly.

"The business was a lunch room system—several places operated in different parts of a large city and supplied from a central commissary with the bulk of the foods. The gross receipts aggregated $2,000,000 a year. The distribution of these receipts in the operation was, approximately: Food, 55 cents; labor, 16 cents; rent and taxes, 5 cents; expenses and supplies, 4 cents; light, heat, power, fuel, ice, 4 cents;

laundry, 2 cents; furniture, 1½ cents; general overhead, including repairs, 4½ cents; depreciation, 2 cents. These items figure up 94 cents, leaving 6 cents on the dollar of receipts for profit.

"A business of this kind, where 'service' is a prime factor in its success, so that patrons will be encouraged to come to these places regularly, must be operated scientifically, and every point of expenditure watched closely; for the margin of the business is so small, and the gamble of the business is so great, that most careful and exacting management is demanded. When the average patron sees a busy lunch room, he is apt to think it a very profitable business. He does not see the expenses over and above the costs of food, which, in the above showing, are small as compared with the average lunch room in which the receipts are not so great.

"It is volume of business that enables the average lunch room and restaurant to give so much as it does for the money."

Summer Camp

The cooking for a summer camp is much the same as for a guest house. As most camps are for boys or girls a knowledge of the best foods for children is essential. Plenty of milk to drink and in soups, creamed dishes and puddings, an abundance of fruits and vegetables, small amounts of meat, good bread and butter, simple desserts, but each one different are most important. Have an abundance of cereal cooked in fireless cookers over night, varying these with the ready-to-eat cereals. They may be served for both breakfast and supper. If you have your own cows be sure that the cream comes to the table instead of being kept in the kitchen. More cereal is eaten if cream is supplied, even if it be thin cream, and an abundance of milk should also be available.

It is well to be careful in the use of onion for flavoring. It is distasteful to many people and should be used sparingly if at all. Casserole dishes will help make left-over dishes so popular that many will want the recipe to send home to mother.

Something for lunches should always be available. Simple cookies or crackers and milk to drink is sufficient. The younger children need it at ten o'clock in the morning and in the middle of the afternoon. The others all want something when they come in from bathing. The lunch should be sufficiently attractive so the children will not buy and eat too much candy.

Make up your menus with a few dishes only at each meal and enough of them, but different dishes every day.

Sometimes an extra helper in the kitchen need not be hired if the girls are allowed so much an hour to prepare the vegetables. This money can be turned into a fund for the needy at home or abroad. Four or more girls may be allowed part payment of their camp expenses to set the tables, wait on table, keep the main hall tidy and wash glass and silver. Remember that cleanliness in the kitchen and dining room and speedy service of meals are essential to success in catering for young people.

The housekeeper will be popular with the boys and girls and their counsellors if she shows a willingness to make special arrangements for birthdays, to plan Sunday night suppers so the young people can get them ready, and relieve the cook, ingenuity in serving fish so that it will be enjoyed and in using the berries that the children like to pick.

PACKING BOX LUNCHES

It is essential that she also know how to pack lunches for all day and over-night trips so that food will be appetizing and satisfying. Wrap every sandwich separately in wax paper. Do not use messy fillings in sandwiches. A meat sandwich, a peanut butter sandwich and a sweet sandwich make a good combination. Hard boiled eggs with salt and pepper or devilled eggs wrapped in wax paper and packed in an egg box are always popular. Turnovers instead of pies, cookies instead of soft cakes and firm fruit like oranges, apples, bananas and pears are good. A thin unpeeled slice of pineapple cut in quarters, wrapped in wax paper and accompanied by an envelope of sugar is very refreshing. A small cucumber pickle and olive should be added to each lunch.

Boxes of plain crackers, a jar of jam or marmalade, sardines and a package of cheese may be provided for an emergency, that is in case more people come than were provided for or in case the party is delayed by accident or weather in their return home. Coffee in a cheese cloth bag and a large kettle or boiler that can be used over an open fire may be sent out with the party.

Lunches are most easily served if packed in boxes holding lunch for not more than four people. A discarded quart berry box may be used for each person in the party and packed in a berry crate. For breakfast after an over-night trip bacon to be cooked over the coals may be provided. Corn meal seasoned with salt and pepper, a piece of salt pork and a frying pan should be taken if there is a possibility of there being fresh fish to fry. Potatoes and sweet corn to be cooked in the ashes and marshmallows to toast over the fire will make any meal interesting.

Where conveyances are going to the camping place a hot dish usually of stew may be sent in one compartment of a fireless cooker and a frozen dessert packed in ice and salt in the other compartment so that the campers will have a real meal on their arrival. It is sometimes convenient to send a salad nicely packed in glass jars or wooden containers. In such cases as these forks, spoons and paper plates should also be provided. Tin cups to hold coffee or other beverage may be strung on a rope or packed in a berry crate unless each camper has her own plate, cup and cutlery.

For real "Camping Out" a knowledge of how to build a fire in the open and the best kinds of food to cook thereon, is essential. An open oven and few utensils mean a different type of cooking than is usually done in the home. Practice in this branch of cookery will soon make one an expert.

A pleasant summer in an attractive location with almost no expense and adequate salary make catering for a summer camp a worth while job.

PLANNING MENUS

In all these types of catering the lists of dishes from which to build menus, arranged as suggested in Lesson IX will be of great assistance in securing variety. Surprises appeal to young people in school or camp or factory and make community and lunch room meals more interesting than when the same things are served over and over.

Lists of dishes to be made from left-overs are as useful as in a boarding house.

The following list of desserts shows how easy it may be to provide a different inexpensive dessert every day for several months especially if a frozen dessert is served instead of pudding once or twice a week, and pies are allowed in the dietary.

LIST OF DESSERTS SUITABLE FOR A LUNCH ROOM

BREAD PUDDINGS

Plain bread pudding
  with (one at a time) pudding sauces on page 222.

with brown bread and molasses
with candied cherries
with molasses, cinnamon and raisins
with raisins, currants or dates
Bread and butter pudding
Bread and butter pudding with marmalade.
Caramel bread pudding
Caramel bread pudding with nuts
Chocolate bread pudding
Chocolate bread pudding with nuts
Cocoanut orange pudding with meringue
Cracker custard pudding
Fruit Betty with apples
        with berries
        with peaches
        with rhubarb
Hot cabinet pudding
Maple bread pudding
Mock Indian pudding
Queen of puddings

CEREAL PUDDINGS

Apple tapioca
Apricot tapioca
Baked rice molded with caramelized sugar
Baked Indian pudding
Baked tapioca
Coffee tapioca
Chocolate rice pudding with meringue
Date tapioca
Lemon tapioca mould
Marshmallow tapioca
Newton tapioca
Rice puddings
    Poor man's
    with chocolate sauce
    with dates
    with raisins
Rhubarb tapioca
Tapioca cream

COTTAGE PUDDINGS

Castle pudding (individual cottage puddings)
Chocolate pudding, with whipped cream and chocolate sauce
Chocolate cottage pudding with marshmallow sauce
Cottage pudding, containing blueberries and with hot stewed blue-
    berries and hard sauce containing cream served with it
Cottage pudding with strawberry sauce
Dutch apple cake
Dutch peach cake
Dutch prune cake

Fruit in bottom of dish, cottage pudding on top, serve with fruit
      juice
Gingerbread split with marshmallows and whipped cream
Gingerbread with hot chocolate sauce
Gingerbread with maple sauce
Gingerbread with apple sauce in bottom of pan
One-egg cake in layers with blackberry filling or with peaches and
      hard sauce
Peach cobbler
Orange fluffs with orange sauce

SHORTCAKES

Apple shortcake
Apricot shortcake
Blackberry shortcake
Cranberry shortcake
Fresh currant shortcake
Pineapple shortcake with marshmallow sauce
Prune and apricot shortcake
Raspberry shortcake
Strawberry shortcake

STEAMED PUDDINGS

Apple roly-poly, steamed or baked
Blueberry pudding
Chocolate pudding
Cranberry pudding
Emergency pudding with fruit sauce
Ginger pudding
Plum pudding
St. James pudding

PUDDING SAUCES

Brown sugar sauce   Loganberry sauce
Cinnamon marshmallow sauce   Marshmallow sauce
Chocolate sauce, hot   Raisin sauce
Egg sauce   Sea Foam sauce
Floradora sauce   Vanilla sauce
Hard sauce   Whipped cream sauce
Lemon sauce   Yellow sauce

FRITTERS

Apple fritters   Orange fritters
Apricot fritters   Peach fritters
Banana fritters   Pear fritters
Cream fritters   Pineapple fritters

Cold Cornstarch Desserts

Chocolate cream pudding
Plain cornstarch pudding with fruit
    with cream
Rebecca pudding with custard
    with chocolate sauce
    with cream
    with whipped cream
Norwegian prune pudding
Maple nut pudding

Custard Desserts

Baked custard, plain
    caramel
    coffee
Coffee floating island
Cold Cabinet pudding
Coffee soufflé
Floating island, plain
    with sponge cake
    with bananas
    with oranges
    with peaches
Macaroon cream
Rice lemon custard
Soft chocolate custard with marshmallows

Jellied Desserts

Spanish cream with nuts
    with nuts and whipped cream
    with fruit
Bavarian cream
        Apricot
        Caramel
        Chocolate
        Coffee walnut
        Vanilla
        Pineapple
        Raspberry

Many other simple desserts may be added to this list. Serving them all, one or more at a time, before repeating any will give the variety so essential in group food service.

REFERENCE BOOKS

School Lunches, Farmer's Bulletin No. 712, issued by the Dept. of
   Agriculture at Washington, D. C.
Food for School Boys and Girls by Mrs. Rose—Teachers' College
   Bulletin, 10 cents.
The School Lunch in Philadelphia, by Emma Smedley, $3.00
Food for the Worker, by Stern and Spitz, $1.00
Camp Cookery, by Kephart
Feeding the Family, by Mrs. Rose, $2.40
Laboratory Manual of Dietetics, by Mrs. Rose, $1.50
Boston Cooking School Cook Book, by Miss Farmer, $2.50
New Book of Cookery, by Miss Farmer, $2.50
Recipes and Menus for Fifty, by Miss Smith, $2.00
School Cafeterias, published by Albert Pick & Co.
Feeding the School Child, published by Albert Pick & Co.
Hotel Monthly, November, 1921

QUESTIONS ON COOKING FOR PROFIT

X

School, Industrial and Community Food Service

1. Estimate cost for raw food material in one serving each
    for each type of dish given in the list on page 207 ; that
    is, one soup, one hot dish, etc.
2. Write lists of dishes for three days suitable for a lunch
    room for employees with prices that might be charged.
3. Describe a steam table. How much do they cost?
4. Make a list of several combinations of foods that will
    make palatable casserole dishes.
5. Suggest six ways to serve the fish that is least expensive
    or most common in your vicinity, so that people will
    not tire of it or even recognize it, if you are sometimes
    obliged to serve it oftener than you like.
6. Tell of any school, industrial or community lunch rooms
    which you have visited.

COOKING FOR PROFIT

XI

TEA ROOM IN AN OLD COLONIAL HOUSE
Designed and managed by one of Miss Bradley's pupils

COOKING FOR PROFIT

PART XI

TEA ROOM MANAGEMENT

SELECTING THE LOCATION AND NAME; DECORATIONS, FUR-
NISHINGS, EQUIPMENT AND PLANS; SOME THINGS TO AVOID;
TYPICAL MENUS FOR TOWN AND COUNTRY TEA ROOMS; TEA
ROOM SPECIALTIES; SUGGESTIONS AND RECIPES FOR BEVERAGES,
SANDWICHES, SALADS, HOT DISHES AND DESSERTS; COSTS, PRIC-
ING AND PROFITS.

INTEREST in opening tea rooms is wide spread, from the Atlantic to the Pacific. Some people apparently think that little is required save an attractively furnished room and a teapot or two, but we advise anybody to consider carefully, before investing the amount of money that must be spent, if even the simplest tea room is to be opened.

When you have started such a business, in order to be profitable, it may need to be developed along any of the avenues suggested in previous lessons and every bit of knowledge, information and experience that you have gathered will be no more than you can use, no matter how simply you begin.

The serving of afternoon tea, only, does not often prove a profitable undertaking. In connection with a tea room it is wise to conduct a gift shop or a cake shop, to sell home-made candy or preserves, operate a soda fountain, put up box lunches for motorists, to serve lunches and suppers or cater for dinner parties.

Many a tea house has become a little motor inn, serving

dainty yet satisfying meals, and with cool attractive bed-
rooms, and immaculate bathrooms for guests who spend the
night, and dressing-rooms for others.

From replies to many questionnaires sent out to the managers of successful tea rooms we list the following:

REQUISITES FOR A SUCCESSFUL TEA ROOM

Good location
Unusual or expressive name
Distinctive decorations and furnishings
Absolute cleanliness
Competent hostess or manager
Wisely chosen waitresses
Effective advertising
Food beyond criticism and correctly priced
Care in business management

LOCATION

A tea room must have a good location, usually on or near
a much traveled road and preferably on the first floor. In
the city, when selecting the location for a tea room, you might
do as the representatives of some chain stores do, stand on
the various corners of the busy streets and count the number
of people passing and note where the greatest number pass,
of the type of people who might patronize a tea room.

In the country you should note the number of machines
passing on the various roads, and whether there are good
tea rooms in the vicinity. It is of no use to have a beautiful
place if your tea room is on a road where few or no autos
travel. You should also note whether there are attractive
surroundings about the place you decide upon, whether it
has a pretty view at the back or at the front or in both
places, shade trees, and a house that can be made especially
attractive. A summer tea room may have an out-of-door
dining porch or lawn umbrellas over painted tables.

CHOOSING A NAME

A tea room should have an unusual or expressive name, one that fits the location or the house or can be illustrated on the sign board or carried out in the decorations and furnishings. For example:

THE RED SQUIRREL TEA ROOM may have a painted squirrel on the sign and should be located where at least an occasional squirrel is to be seen.

THE MAPLE TEA ROOM may be under a grove of Maple Trees and specialize in maple sugar products.

THE RAGGED ROBIN,

THE SUNFLOWER,

YE HOLLYHOCK TEA ROOM should each be surrounded by flowers of that name in the summer and show them in chintz, china or wall coverings in the winter.

CANARY COTTAGE TEA ROOM should be a yellow cottage with canaries in tall bird cages.

THE GREEN ARBOR TEA ROOM shows tables under rose arbors, that invite you to tarry.

PEGGY'S TEA ROOM, where Peggy in a crisp muslin gown is seen in the garden by passing motorists, is irresistible.

THE ROWLEY-POWLEY TEA ROOM is in the town of Rowley.

THE BI-A-CAKE TEA ROOM and THE GINGERBREAD TEA ROOM specialize in delicious and unusual cakes.

THE CROOKED STAIRS TEA ROOM suggests a quaint old house.

POLLY'S PLACE serves old time country dishes, sausages, doughnuts and English crumpets.

THE SWEETHEART has maple sugar or praline hearts as the specialty.

NOBSCOT MOUNTAIN ORCHARDS specializes in jams, jellies and other preserves.

The name of THE MARAMOR, a most attractive tea room, is made from the proprietor's name, and has a charming cake, candy and favor shop in connection with it.

It may be well to avoid the name "tea room" as done by

Ye Bradford Arms
The Lightship
The Seagull
Vanity Fair
Sign of the Apple Tree
Tea and Crumpet Room
Sign of the Cross Roads
The Five Sisters
The White Turkey
The Tea Shed
Janet's Tea Garden

These are all suggestive of location or decoration. Indian decorations are used in some Western tea rooms and articles made by the Indians are for sale in the gift shop at "The Sign of the Totem Pole."

DECORATIONS AND FURNISHINGS

The decorations and furnishings should be distinctive and dainty and such as appeal to women of taste. In many instances the name is shown in the decorations as parrots of different colors painted on the walls and furniture and shown in the cretonne and china for a Pretty Pol Tea Room. The Sunbeam is an old house with several rooms in which meals are served. Each room is different, has beautifully decorated walls and painted tables and chairs, with window draperies and china in colors that match or harmonize with the walls. Painted furniture seems just now more popular than any other kind. One hostess purchased painted mahogany so she would still have good furniture when the painted craze had died down.

Quaint holders for flowers, unusual prints on the walls, hand-made draperies and doilies, antique treasures of different kinds, local color in the shape of ocean or mountain or Indian curios all add interest and pleasure, distinction and charm, as do brightly colored quaint china, polished Russian samovars, Sheffield silver muffin dishes, burnished copper utensils, century old pewter, trays that are different.

Even though the furnishings are of the simplest, if everything is in good taste and immaculate, fresh flowers daily on each table will give the touch that is far more appealing than an expensive, inartistic or untidy room that does not show the daily presence and care of a "real lady."

ABSOLUTE CLEANLINESS

Absolute cleanliness should prevail in every part of the establishment. There should be no hesitancy in allowing guests to inspect the kitchen, refrigerator, or back yard if they wish. Waitresses may do the daily cleaning of the dining room but a strong person should clean the walls and scrub the floor every week or oftener. The table linen must be immaculate whether table cloths, runners, or doilies are used. Glass topped or polished tables may be adopted if desired. Linen or crepe or paper napkins may be provided as suits the fancy of the hostess and the desires of patrons.

COMPETENT HOSTESS OR MANAGER

The hostess should have a pleasing personality, be fond of people, have executive ability and a knowledge of cooking. She should endeavor to create a home-like atmosphere in a tea room, that makes it seem different from the ordinary restaurant but, if it is to be a profitable undertaking, *it must be run according to business principles*. Among the many duties of the hostess or manager will be to

Know, not merely guess, the financial standing of the tea room every day.

See that the dining room is well aired and kept at the proper temperature.

Arrange the flowers.

Be accessible to patrons at all times.

Look over supplies in ice box each morning and see that everything is on hand that may be required.

Plan menus for the next day and place orders.

Check up supplies as they come in.

Know that every dish that is served is properly prepared, correctly seasoned and daintily served.

Audit accounts daily and be sure that all food served has been paid for.

Supervise the cleanliness, duties and general deportment of all employees.

WISELY CHOSEN WAITRESSES

The waitresses should be quiet, refined, well groomed, and with good dispositions. Their costumes should be neat and, if feasible, in keeping with the color scheme and name. Places with old fashioned names and old fashioned furnishings should have waitresses in old fashioned costumes. Waitresses should learn to take orders accurately, fill them as quickly as possible, with care to avoid accidents of any kind. Waitresses must be trained to remember that the customer is always right. This principle must be followed. They should have no arguments with patrons about anything. Each one should have a definite number of tables and definite duties in regard to the cleaning and care of the room.

All other employees should also be selected carefully. They should be trained in your methods. Adjust yourself to them and their dispositions. Give them the work for which they are best fitted. Secure their cooperation. Make them feel that their work, no matter what it is, is an important contribution to the success of the tea room. Raise wages when business warrants it or have some profit-sharing plan.

EFFECTIVE ADVERTISING

Some advertising must be done. You may—

Send out notices of your opening.
Take small space in the Automobile Blue Book.
Take small space in newspapers or magazines.
Have cards and photographs in nearby hotels.
Have attractive signs, at intervals, for several miles, on the roads leading to your tea room.
Have post cards of your tea room for guests to send to their friends.
Have a special room or porch where chauffeurs may rest, wash, read, smoke or be served with luncheon. (They will advertise such a place to other chauffeurs.)
Pay special attention to the children's needs. Sometimes you may give them cookies or fruit to take with them for a lunch.
Above all have everything so satisfactory that your guests will advertise you far and wide.

FOOD BEYOND CRITICISM AND CORRECTLY PRICED

As has been suggested in previous lessons perfection of cooking and a knowledge of right purchasing, apportioning, and pricing food is the foundation of success in all forms of *Cooking for Profit,* and tea room management is no exception.

Care in Business Management

Carelessness in collecting pay for every order served may easily spell failure. It is a pretty custom to have bonbons or mints in paper cases served for each person, on the tray with the check or the change. A tea room, effectively advertised, should very soon after being opened pay its running expenses.

If a tea room is not extravagantly fitted up, the profits should pay off the cost of equipment in one season.

Main Requisite

The main requisite is good food well and quickly served, and in portions not too small. Tea room prices should be high enough to warrant the use of the best and freshest materials and the choicest recipes. The best for the purpose is the most economical in the end. Do not skimp on butter or eggs or cream. Get the home flavor into your dishes. They need not be too rich but *they cannot be too good.* The above characteristics in a tea room will cause guests to return again and again.

Some Things to Avoid in Your Tea Room

Poor entrance
Obscure hall
Narrow stairs
No advertising
Cheap pictures on wall
Noise in kitchen
Poor music
Untidiness and dirt
Unmatched or nicked china
Unclean dishes
Slow service
Too small orders

Too high prices
Wrong temperature for the room
Mussy, unattractive dishes
Poorly seasoned sandwiches and salad dressing
Salads and foods that should be cold, served warm
Soft butter balls or cubes
Stale cake
Carelessness in collecting money for food sold

EQUIPMENT

The cost of equipping a tea room varies from $1,500 to many thousands of dollars. Unless it is possible to start in a small way under very favorable conditions, the wise person will seek experience in a successful tea room before investing her own or other people's money in a venture that is by no means simple. In any case, tea rooms should be visited, prices of furnishings and equipment should be studied, carpenters, plumbers and decorators should be consulted and lists and prices should be made out over and over until you are satisfied that they are correct. Give space only to efficient equipment and use that to its maximum capacity. A tea room seating forty-eight people will require

Range
Kitchen Tables
Refrigerator
Stools
Cooking utensils. (List the cooking utensils you think you will need and secure from several dealers prices on all the articles you will require.)
12 tables
48 chairs
Cash register
Cashier's desk and chair
2 or more side tables
6 tray stands
12 trays, 15" by 24"
Water cooler
Manager's desk
2 or more boxes for silver
4 doz. 7-inch plates
4 doz. 6-inch plates
4 doz. 5-inch plates
4 doz. 4-inch plates
4 doz. cups and saucers
4 doz. sauce dishes
4 doz. oatmeals (soups)

3 doz. bouillon cups
1 doz. tea pots
6 chocolate pots
5 doz. water glasses
4 doz. iced tea glasses
3 doz. sherbet glasses
1 doz. vases or other flower holders
1 doz. cream pitchers
1 doz. sugar bowls
1 doz. each salts and peppers
1 doz. candlesticks
16 doz. napkins
3 doz. tablecloths or runner sets. (These may be of linen or crash or paper doilies and napkins may be used.)
½ doz. vinegar cruets
½ doz. oil cruets
½ doz. mustard jars
4 doz. knives
8 doz. forks
8 doz. teaspoons
4 doz. soup spoons
4 doz. butter spreaders

The foregoing list does not make allowance for breakage or theft and it would be desirable to purchase more of some things in the beginning.

Overhead Expenses

Before investing a cent of money you should figure what your overhead expenses are probably going to be and what your income is likely to be.

Decide tentatively on your specialties and, if you do not already know from your experience, learn how to apportion the foods you plan to serve before you open your tea room, know the cost and selling price of a definite amount of each thing, and the number of portions you must sell in a day in order to pay for the food material and the overhead expenses as estimated. A common method of determining the selling price of cooked food is to double the cost of the raw material. Can you get this price? At this rate can you probably sell enough to pay expenses? You may need to serve smaller portions of some dishes. On some dishes you should charge more than double the cost because of the time necessary for their preparation. Some may have to be sold at cost or less than cost. If you feel confident of a reasonable profit on your investment of money and time, then go ahead.

Make Plans of Kitchen and Dining Room

Before you equip your establishment make a kitchen plan and a dining room plan on paper and locate the places for mixing cake, making frostings, salads and dressings, slicing and spreading bread for sandwiches, making waffles, and whatever else you plan to serve. Locate drain boards for receiving, sorting and draining dishes. Locate shelves near the sink for clean dishes, near the work tables for supplies and equipment. Locate coffee and hot water urns, a steam table for hot dishes and a chipped ice tray for salads.

Draw in the lines of travel from refrigerator to work table, to range, to dining room, to sink, etc., etc. Shorten these lines in every possible way, on paper, before building your shelves or setting up refrigerator, sink, and stove, that all the work of your tea room may be accomplished in the most efficient manner with a place for everything that will be needed and room for all the help you propose to have.

Plan where the tea tables and service tables shall be placed; as well as shelves and drawers, window boxes, cashier's desk, etc. These should all be on your list of necessary equipment suggested above and should now be located on your paper plan. In the dining room you may care to plan for electric wall outlets so you can plug in table lamps, waffle irons, toasters, chafing dishes or percolators at each table. These add distinction to your service and are greatly appreciated as patrons are assured of having their food hot. If you had not thought before of the cost of this or that, add it to your list, learn the price of it and add to the probable cost of equipment.

WHAT TO SERVE

In a small tea room it is desirable to specialize in a very few things and have them so attractive and distinctive and delicious that there will be a constantly increasing demand for them. The dishes most frequently ordered in tea rooms are tea or other beverages, sandwiches, salads, cakes and ice creams.

There is danger of losing money when very many dishes are attempted at one time, because of wasted food or poor service, unless you have a great deal of help and a very large patronage, which you can hardly expect at first.

Learn how many sandwiches you should get from a loaf of bread and from a definite amount of butter and of different fillings, file the data and strive to maintain this standard. Know how many servings you should get from one quart of ice cream and ice cream sauces, and one pound nut meats and use the same measures every day. Serve a definite number of salads from one fowl, one can of pine-

apple, one quart mayonnaise dressing, etc., etc. (See pages
99, 100.) From a standard cake mixture cut always the
same number of pieces and make a definite number of little
cakes or cookies. Servings may be larger for men than for
women.

As soon as possible after you are started learn approximately how much food will be used in a day that there may
be no waste of perishable material. Keep a sufficient supply of non-perishable supplies on hand in a locked store
room of which you hold the key, so that you may not lose
time sending out unnecessarily and may know when things
are getting low. Be careful not to have in the refrigerator
too much and yet have sufficient of perishable things such
as lettuce, lemons, chicken and cream. Accurate record
should be kept of the number of orders served each day,
of the different dishes listed on the menu, so that you will
learn as soon as possible the probable number to provide
for.

TYPICAL TOWN AND COUNTRY MENUS

Tea 25c	Chocolate Fudge Cake 15c
Iced Drinks 25c	Cake 15c, 10c
Sandwiches 25c	Ice cream 30c
Buttered toast 15c	Marmalade 20c
Cinnamon toast 20c	Jam 20c
Hot breads 20c	

Rarebit on toast
Eclair
Tea, coffee or chocolate
———75 Cents———
Club Sandwich or Fruit Salad
French Pastry or Plain Ice Cream
Tea, Coffee or Chocolate
———95 Cents———
Baked Lobster Cardinal or Patties of Sweetbread with Mushrooms
French Pastry or Ice Cream
Coffee, Tea or Chocolate
———$1.35———
Tenderloin Steak Jardiniere or
Breast of Chicken with Mushroom au Paprika
French Pastry or Frozen Pudding
Coffee, Tea or Chocolate
———$1.50———

THE FOODS YOU SERVE

Beverages

Tea should be made as ordered in individual earthen pots. Tiny muslin bags holding just enough tea for one pot may be purchased by the thousand in six different varieties, orange pekoe being the favorite. Use freshly boiling water for each pot of tea. Many suggestions for accompaniments are given on page 103. Cups, saucers, tea spoons, sugar bowl, pitcher of cream and any desired garnish should accompany the tea. Make a point of never forgetting anything in serving an order. With each order for tea with toast or sandwiches a piece of candied grapefruit or orange peel or ginger may be served.

Coffee must be freshly made as often as necessary. Electric percolators may be used and taken to the table. Guests may then have their coffee of the strength most pleasing to them. Serve real cream and enough of it, and loaf sugar. In Lesson VI are suggestions for making and serving coffee.

Chocolate syrup for hot or iced chocolate may be kept on hand.

Chocolate Syrup

Melt
½ lb. unsweetened chocolate over boiling water, add
2⅔ cups sugar and
¼ teaspoon salt and stir until well mixed; then pour on gradually
3 cups boiling water, stir until smooth and boil five minutes.
Cool, turn into a jar and keep in ice box or cold place.

Hot Chocolate

Add 2 to 3 tablespoons chocolate syrup to one cup scalded milk. Serve with whipped cream.

Chocolate Milk Shake

Put two tablespoons chocolate syrup in tall glass and fill glass with ice cold milk. Shake thoroughly and serve very cold with whipped cream or ice cream.

A quickly prepared iced fruit drink is popular, for instance:

Mint Cup

Reserve tips and remove leaves from
4 bunches of mint and bruise with the fingers. Cook
2 cups sugar and
2 cups water five minutes, add mint leaves,
Juice 12 lemons, and
Green color paste to make a delicate shade, and let stand over
    night. When ready to serve strain, fill glass of cracked ice
    half full of syrup, and add
Gingerale to fill the glass. Garnish with reserved tips from sprigs
    of mint. Other fruit juices may be used in place of some
    of the lemon juice.

TOAST AND SANDWICHES

Bread is used in tea rooms for toast of different kinds, sandwiches with a great variety of fillings and in several shapes; for ribbon sandwiches, toasted sandwiches, club sandwiches, hot meat sandwiches and French toast sandwiches.

White bread may be purchased in long loaves that will cut into fifty-six slices. These are more practical than the homemade loaf. Graham bread, nut bread, Boston brown bread, and other fancy breads suggested in Lesson II may be used. A bread cutting machine will insure uniformity, and may be regulated so that bread may be cut thin enough for sandwiches or thick enough for toast.

Toast

Toast must be fresh and hot to be popular. It may be made in the kitchen or on an electric toaster, on a side table in the dining room, where guests may watch the process and know that they get it as soon as it is ready. Toast may be served plain with butter ball, or be buttered before it is served. Some fancy breads are delicious toasted. Individual jars of marmalade or jam, or small portions served on small dishes or butter plates, usually accompany plain toast.

Cinnamon Toast

Work until creamy
3 cups butter, add slowly
2 cups light brown sugar and
⅓ cup ground cinnamon. Keep in a cool place. Cut
Stale bread in one-fourth inch slices, remove crusts and toast on one side. Spread untoasted side generously with a portion of the cinnamon mixture, and place under gas flame until mixture is melted.

Making Sandwiches

Butter for sandwiches should always be creamed, that it may be quickly and easily spread. A small palette knife or spatula is desirable for spreading the filling. It is advisable to butter both slices of bread, regardless of what filling is used. Fillings should be prepared before the hours at which the tea room is open, or the ingredients for fillings may be made ready and kept in separate dishes ready to be put together at a moment's notice.

Crusts may or may not be removed. Sandwiches may be cut in squares, strips, oblongs, or triangles. Round or fancy cutters may be used but with considerable loss of material. Before the hour for opening the tea room, the sliced bread may be spread with butter, piled up and covered with a dry towel or cheesecloth and with a wet towel. Sandwich fillings can be put between the slices as orders are received.

Garnishes for a Plate of Sandwiches

Many sandwiches are more attractive if served with a garnish such as

Lettuce leaf holding manyonnaise dressing
Spray of cress
Fresh flower
Cube of firm jelly
Ball of cream cheese

Tiny cucumber pickle with croquette stab in one end
Ring of sweet pickled cucumber
Radish rose
Stalk of celery curled on one end.

Bread buttered for sandwiches and not used may be utilized next day for toasted sandwiches. In addition to the sandwich filling suggestions on page 107 we list the following combinations. They should be seasoned as needed with salt and cayenne and paprika, materials may be chopped or cut in pieces, and whatever will secure the best results should be done. You may make up your own names for these sandwiches.

Sandwich Fillings

Cream cheese, salad dressing, orange marmalade or jam
Cream cheese, mayonnaise dressing, chopped green pepper
Cream cheese, maraschino cherries, marshmallow cream
Cream cheese, chopped nuts, prepared mustard or French dressing
Cream cheese, grated pineapple
Cream cheese, peanut butter
Factory cheese, chopped nuts, salad dressing
Factory cheese, catsup or chili sauce
Factory cheese, cooked as welsh rarebit or chilaly
Lettuce and mayonnaise
Lettuce and Russian dressing
Lettuce and Chiffonade dressing
Chicken, celery, and salad dressing
Chicken, whipped cream and lemon juice
Chicken, ham, salad dressing
Ham, hard cooked egg, salad dressing
Cooked bacon, hard cooked egg, salad dressing
Sardine, hard cooked egg, salad dressing
Shrimps, hard cooked egg, salad dressing
Crab meat, grape fruit, celery, salad dressing
Green pepper or pimiento chopped and salad dressing
Pimiento, sliced, and salad dressing
Tomato sliced, and salad dressing
Cucumber sliced and salad dressing (Bread cut size of cucumber)
Marmalade and chopped nuts
Cooked prunes, chopped nuts and lemon juice
Raisins, nuts and mayonnaise dressing

Banana Sandwich

Spread
2 slices bread with
Creamed butter. On one slice spread
Raspberry jam, cover with
Slices of banana, sprinkle with
Lemon juice and cover with second slice of bread. Serve cut in
squares.

Fruit Salad Sandwich

To
1 tablespoon mayonnaise dressing add
1 tablespoon heavy cream beaten stiff. Spread on
2 slices bread. Cover one slice with thinly sliced
Strawberries or pineapple, and with the other piece of bread.
Garnish with
Watercress.

Orange Honey Sandwich

Spread
2 slices bread with
Creamed butter and
Orange honey. Put together and cut in fancy shapes.

Orange Honey

Mix
1 cup sugar
¼ cup water
¼ cup orange juice. Boil until syrup will spin a thread when
dropped from tip of spoon. Add
½ cup finely chopped orange peel from which all white portion
has been removed and
½ teaspoon vanilla. Again bring to boiling point and cool.

Rolled Sandwiches

Use very fresh bread. Cut in very thin slices, remove crusts,
spread with filling, roll up and serve two or three on a lettuce leaf. These are very dainty and not commonly served.
Many of the fillings suggested above, especially those with
cream cheese, may be used for rolled sandwiches. They
may be toasted. Chopped hard cooked egg or walnuts,
mayonnaise dressing and watercress leaves projecting from
each end are attractive or celery, nuts and mayonnaise and
a celery leaf in each end.

Ribbon Sandwiches

These sandwiches are described on page 108. Any desired fillings may be used. Serve one large slice cut diagonally or in three strips on a leaf of lettuce.

Nut Bread Sandwich

Use
2 slices nut bread (page 29) and
1 slice white bread with filling of
Chopped ham and
Raspberry jam. Cut in strips for serving.

Hub Sandwiches

Steam
Boston brown bread, and bake
White bread in half pound baking powder cans. Cut lengthwise in quarters, put 4 pieces together, making two loaves, alternating brown and white, with a filling of
Cream cheese,
Creamed butter and
Chopped pimolas. Chill, cut in slices and place a slice of pimola in center of each slice.

Kindergarten Sandwiches

Use
2 slices each light bread and dark bread; cut in fancy shapes, spread 1 slice of each with
Creamed butter. Cut a figure with a fancy cutter from the other 2 slices and place the dark figure in the opening in the white bread and the white figure in the opening in the dark bread. Put the two slices together and serve on
Lettuce.

Salad Eclair

Make
Cream cake mixture (page 50) and shape on tin sheet five inches long and 1 inch wide. Bake, split, line with
Lettuce leaf, fill with
Chicken salad or
Lobster or other salad, and serve.

Salad Roll

Split
Long rolls, remove soft centers, fill with
Chicken or other salad and serve on a
Lettuce leaf.

Sweet French Sandwiches

Roll

Puff paste (page 46) ⅛ inch in thickness and cut in strips 3 inches long and 1 inch wide. Bake, split and spread one-half with

Whipped cream sweetened and flavored, and other half with any good jelly. Put together in pairs. Other fillings may be used

Toasted Muffins

Split

English muffins, toast, and spread lightly with

Butter. Serve with

Orange marmalade.

The English Muffins that are purchased from a concern that makes a specialty of their manufacture are more satisfactory than any that can be made in a small tea room because of the type of oven used. However the following recipe may be satisfactory.

Raised Muffins

To

1 cup scalded milk add

1 cup boiling water

2 tablespoons butter,

¼ cup sugar and

1 teaspoon salt; when lukewarm, add

¼ yeast cake, and when dissolved,

1 egg well beaten, and

4 cups flour; beat thoroughly, cover, and let rise over night. In morning, fill buttered muffin rings two-thirds full; let rise until rings are full, and bake 30 minutes in hot oven.

Katy's Toasted Raisin Bread

Scald

3 cups milk, when luke warm add

1¼ tablespoons salt and

1 yeast cake dissolved in

⅛ cup lukewarm water. Add

5 cups flour, beat thoroughly and let rise until it begins to sink in the center. Add

2 cups brown sugar,

¾ cup butter or margarine,

2 eggs well beaten,

3 cups flour sifted with

1½ teaspoons mace, and

1½ tablespoons cinnamon; mix well and add
1 package raisins, and
1 cup currants, and
1 cup nut meats if desired. Add sufficient
Flour to make a soft dough. Let rise until light, shape in
  three loaves, let rise again, and bake in moderate oven fifty
  minutes. After twenty-four hours remove crusts, cut in
  thin slices and in finger shaped pieces. Brush with melted
  butter and toast in the oven until crisp and delicately
  brown.

Toasted Sandwiches

Hot sandwiches are popular in most tea rooms. Many of
the sandwiches listed above may be made and toasted first
on one side and then on the other, cut in two or three
diagonally and served immediately. The best method of
toasting is under the gas flame or on a flat electric toaster.
Baking in a hot oven or sautéing in the frying pan may be
substituted for toasting. The bread may be toasted on one
side and the filling then be put between untoasted sides.

Hot Cheese Sandwich

Cut
Stale bread in ¼ inch slices, remove crusts; cut
Mild cheese in slices same size as slices of bread, and sprinkle
  with
Salt and cayenne. Put a slice of cheese, between each two
  slices of bread and toast until cheese melts or bake in a hot
  oven until cheese melts and the bread is browned; or sauté
  in butter first on one side and then on the other until delicately browned.

Open Hot Cheese Sandwich

Split
English Muffins, toast them, cover each piece with
Grated cheese seasoned with
Salt and cayenne and put in oven until cheese begins to melt.
  Serve three pieces on a plate garnished with
Leaf of lettuce and an
Olive.

Toasted Cheese and Date Sandwich

Toast
Bread on one side only, spread untoasted side with
Butter and spread one slice with
Cream cheese moistened with
Milk and seasoned with
Salt and paprika. Cover with
3 dates, washed, stoned and cut in thin slices crosswise, sprinkle
    with
Finely chopped nuts, cover with another slice of toast, cut in
    two diagonally, and serve.

Florentine Sandwich Seminole

Arrange
Boned sardines on a slice of
Buttered toast, cover with
Thin slices of tomato and sprinkle with
Salt and pepper. Cover with another
Slice of toast and sprinkle generously with
Soft grated cheese seasoned with
Salt and
Cayenne and put in oven long enough to melt the cheese. Serve
    at once on
2 lettuce leaves with
Mayonnaise dressing on a small lettuce leaf on the side.

Porto Rico Sandwich

Spread
2 slices of toast with
Tried out bacon fat in place of butter. On one slice place
Very thin slices of American cheese, cover this with
Thin round slices of cucumber pickles and pickle with
Crisp bacon. Cover with other slice of toast; cut once diago-
    nally and serve on
Lettuce.

Egomato Toast

On an individual plate put a
Leaf of lettuce; on the lettuce a
Slice of toast which has been spread with a little
Hot bacon fat; over the toast put a large
Spoonful of hot, well seasoned stewed tomato. Cut a
Hard boiled egg in two, remove center, and mix with
Salad dressing. Return to egg cup, place one half egg in
    the center of the toast, garnish with remaining egg mixture
    forced through pastry bag and tube; place a

Small, short stalk of asparagus in the center of the egg, and garnish toast with
2 small strips of hot cooked bacon.

Cheese and Bacon Toast

Beat
1 egg, add as much
Grated cheese as the egg will take up and season with
Paprika and
Worcestershire sauce. Spread on
2 slices bread. On top of each slice lay
2 thin slices bacon and place under gas flame until bacon is crisp.

Toasted Mushroom Sandwich

Melt
3 tablespoons butter, add
¼ cup flour and
¾ cup thin cream. Bring to the boiling point and add to
1¼ pounds chopped mushrooms, sautéd. Season with
Salt,
Pepper and
Paprika. Spread between thin slices of
Bread; put together in pairs, and cut in finger shaped pieces.
Sauté in
Butter until browned on one side, turn and brown on the other side.

Club Sandwich

On a
Slice of toast place
Leaf of lettuce washed and dried, then lay
Thick slice of tomato on top and cover with
Mayonnaise dressing. Place another
Slice of toast above the tomato and on it arrange sliced
Chicken covered with
Crisp bacon. Place a third
Slice of toast over all, and garnish with large
Olives or
Sweet pickled cucumber rings and
Lettuce cups holding
Mayonnaise dressing.

How to Use a Cooked Chicken

Use sliced breast meat of chicken for club or sliced chicken sandwiches or chicken pies. Smaller pieces of chicken and dark meat may be used for chicken fricassee. Trimmings may be used for chicken a la King, scalloped chicken and potato, or hot chopped chicken sandwiches. White meat of chicken cut in dice is used for chicken salads.

French Toast Sandwiches

Cut
Bread in one-fourth inch slices, spread 1 slice with
Filling, cover with another slice, cut in four pieces, dip in a
  mixture of
½ cup milk
1 egg slightly beaten and
¼ teaspoon salt. Drain, place on hot buttered griddle and brown
  first on one side and then on the other.

French Marmalade Sandwich

Make French Toast Sandwiches with a filling of marmalade

Hot Hamburg Sandwich

Make French Toast Sandwiches with a filling of meat prepared as follows:
1 pound chopped beef mixed with
1 cup thin cream
1 teaspoon salt
½ teaspoon pepper and
½ teaspoon onion juice. Serve with
Hot brown sauce or
Hot tomato sauce.

Hot Sandwiches

Hot Chicken Sandwich

Cut
Cooked chicken in small pieces, heat with
Chicken gravy, slightly thickened. Pour over a
Slice of bread, put second slice on top and pour plain
Chicken gravy over all.

Hot Roast Beef Sandwich

Put slices of
Cold roast beef (kept warm in small amount of gravy under hood
  of steam table) between
2 slices of bread. Pour
Beef gravy over all.

QUICK HOT BREADS

Baking Powder Biscuits are quickly made if you keep on hand flour ready mixed with baking powder and salt. Each day the shortening may be mixed with the amount of flour you are likely to use. As orders come in milk may be added and biscuits should be ready to serve in 20 minutes. Serve with butter and

> Honey or
>
> Maple syrup or
>
> Marmalade or
>
> Jam, preserve or conserve

Baking Powder Biscuits may have one of the following mixtures spread on the dough and then be rolled up, cut off and baked:

> Butter and brown sugar
>
> Butter, sugar and cinnamon
>
> Butter and marmalade
>
> Butter, sugar, raisins and spice
>
> Butter, maple sugar and nuts
>
> Butter, sugar and orange juice and rind.

Popovers, served with

> Maple syrup
>
> Honey or
>
> Canned fruit—are a treat to many people.

WAFFLES AND GRIDDLE CAKES

Waffles are probably more popular than griddle cakes but the latter when light, hot and with crispy edges may well cause patrons to return for more.

Griddle Cakes with Maple Cream

> Sift together

1½ cups flour
2 teaspoons baking powder
½ teaspoon salt
3 tablespoons sugar. Add
3 egg yolks beaten until thick and lemon colored,
½ cup milk and
2 tablespoons melted butter. Fold in
3 egg whites, beaten until stiff and dry. Cook in large cakes in hot greased frying pan. Between each two cakes put maple cream, spread with maple cream and serve at once cut pie shape.

Waffles with maple syrup or honey are the specialty of many tea rooms.

Waffles

Sift together
1¼ cups flour
½ teaspoon salt
1 teaspoon sugar
½ teaspoon soda, add slowly
1 cup sour milk
¼ cup melted butter
3 egg yolks, well beaten, and fold in
3 egg whites beaten until dry. Cook on hot waffle iron.
    Serve with
Butter and
Honey or maple syrup.

SALADS

Tea rooms usually feature one or more salads on their menus. A tea room may specialize in a few particularly delicious salads or if the menu is changed daily a great number of salad combinations may be necessary. With afternoon tea, fruit salads are most popular. For luncheon or supper salads, chicken, lobster, egg and potato may be served.

Keep salad plates or bowls near the ice. Do not serve salads on plates hot from the dish pan! Have enough china so such a thing will never be necessary.

Enough lettuce should be washed before your tea room opens to supply the number of patrons you expect to serve. Put it in a large collander, over it lay pieces of ice wrapped in cheesecloth and keep in refrigerator or salad pan. Have your dressings made and kept very cold. Prepare and cut up the fruit, nuts, celery, chicken and all the other ingredients you may need and put in a cool place. Make up each salad as it is ordered.

Many times it is well to line a shallow bowl with lettuce and arrange the ingredients of the salad in individual piles, then cover with mayonnaise or with any other prepared dressing.

Small amounts of salad ingredients that are left over one day may be used for salad sandwiches the next day. Make every salad a picture so that it will appeal to the eye as well as the palate.

Lobster Salad

In a bowl lined with
Lettuce leaves make a pile each of pieces of
Lobster meat,
Tomato peeled and cut in eighths,
Celery cut in one inch strips,
Shredded lettuce leaves. Make a mound of
Mayonnaise dressing in the center.

Chicken Salad

In a bowl lined with
Lettuce leaves make one pile each of
Chicken cut in dice,
Celery or cucumber cut in dice and
Hard cooked egg chopped. Serve with
Mayonnaise dressing.

Fruit Salad

On a bed of
Lettuce leaves make one pile each
Grapefruit sections cut in pieces,
Orange sections cut in pieces,
Pineapple cut in dice
Celery cut in small pieces,
Nut meats cut in pieces or
Cheese balls rolled in chopped nuts. Place
Mayonnaise dressing in a lettuce cup in the center.

Other fruits that are in season may be used instead of those specified. Cooked meat, fish, eggs, vegetables, rice or macaroni, celery, cucumbers, fresh or canned fruit, nuts and cheese, alone or in combination can all be used for salads. Use your own ingenuity and you may secure some new and attractive salads. Maraschino cherries on fruit salads are popular, chopped pistachio nuts add character to many simple salads. The combinations suggested on page 115 may be used. A few more suggestions are given here:

Salad Combinations

Chicken with celery, hard cooked eggs, cabbage, cucumber, nuts, peas or tomatoes

Cooked lamb and green peas

Shrimps with cucumber

Salmon with cucumber and hard cooked egg

Tuna fish, celery and pickle

Cooked lima beans, onion, celery and pimiento

Cream cheese balls rolled in chopped parsley or
chopped nuts or
paprika

Cheese balls made of cheese mixed with
chopped nuts or
chopped pimiento or
chopped olives

Potato with hard cooked egg, pimiento, chives, cream dressing

Potato with hard cooked egg, grated carrot, pickle and chopped or shredded cabbage

Egg stuffed on slice of tomato on toast on lettuce

Cabbage and nuts

Tomatoes with cheese balls and cress

Tomato slices with cheese between

Tomato stuffed with pineapple and nuts

Vegetables in separate groups; peas, beet dice, carrot dice, potato dice, string beans, shredded cabbage, cauliflower, celery, cucumber

Apple, celery and cocoanut

Banana rolled in peanuts with orange slices

Banana, raisins and chopped nuts

Orange sections, strawberries or cherries and cheese balls rolled in chopped nuts

Grapefruit, celery and green pepper

Grapefruit and orange sections, green or red pepper strips

Grapefruit and orange sections, with date strips, served star shape

Grapefruit, orange sections, pineapple, marshmallows and nuts

Grapefruit and orange sections, white grapes, cheese balls, with nuts

Pear, celery and maraschino cherry

Pineapple, celery and mint

Pineapple with celery, nuts, and maraschino cherries

Pineapple with slices of green pepper stuffed with cheese

Pineapple slice with half banana standing upright in center, maraschino cherry on top

Pineapple with grapefruit and maraschino cherries

Casaba melon sections with orange or grapefruit

Watermelon balls and cheese

Alligator pear alone or in combination with acid fruits

HOT DISHES

Most tea rooms specialize in one or more hot dishes making it possible for patrons to secure a real meal at odd hours. A "Rabbit Den" in which Welch Rarebits were the chief attraction proved popular in one town. Chicken fried or chicken á la King have made the reputation of some tea rooms as have broiled live lobster or fresh crab meat Newburg, or planked white fish. Tea rooms that serve lunches and suppers may have one or more different hot dishes on the menu each day. The following dishes are taken from a variety of menu cards.

Broiled chicken with waffles
Baked beans in individual pots
Corned beef hash (with poached egg)
Chicken croquettes with peas
Halibut croquettes
Fish cake with poached egg
Fried ham and eggs
Filet of sole with tomato sauce
Omelette aux fines herbes
Stuffed green peppers, sauce epicure
Chicken pie with potato crust
Rice croquettes with cheese sauce
Chicken and ham pie
Chicken pie with macaroni
Hot potato salad and bacon
Chicken liver sauté with bacon and creamed potatoes
Fresh shrimp patty
Boiled salmon, egg sauce, new potatoes, green peas
Broiled lamb chops, currant jelly, creamed potato, scalloped egg plant
Chops with lettuce salad
Shattuck halibut, cabbage salad, parsley potatoes
Fried oysters with bacon
Fresh spinach and poached eggs on toast
Chili con carne with rice
Creamed chopped beef on toast
Fried chicken, Maryland style, corn fritters, and glacé sweet potatoes
Veal cutlet, scalloped tomatoes, baked potato
Small steak, creamed cauliflower, French fried potatoes
Lamb chop, string beans, mashed potatoes
Egg croquettes, tomato sauce
Stuffed eggs on toast á la King
Oyster pie
French omelets

Broiled oysters wrapped in bacon on toast with brown sauce
Purée of tomato
Beef bouillon
Cream of celery soup
Cream of cauliflower soup
Chicken soup with barley
Purée of split peas
Scotch barley broth
Bean chowder
Cream of corn soup

Creamed Dishes

White sauce is quickly and easily made. It may be seasoned with celery salt, onion juice, chopped peppers, lemon
juice, parsley or table sauce. Egg yolks may be added to
the sauce, if desired. In it may be served with

Slices of toast
Cheese, eggs and seasonings
Cold cooked potatoes, diced, and grated cheese
Shrimps and peas
Shrimps and cooked rice and chili sauce for flavor
Oysters and celery
Salmon and celery
Chicken strips or cubes
Chicken and potato cubes
Chicken and mushrooms
Chicken and celery
Chicken and ripe olives
Chicken, mushrooms and pimiento strips
Chicken and pimiento strips
Chicken, pimiento strips and cooked macaroni or spaghetti
Chicken and green pepper strips
Chicken and oysters
Chicken and ham dice
Sweetbreads diced and mushrooms
Fresh honeycomb tripe and small boiled onions
Lobster dice
Flaked cooked fish and hard cooked eggs
Sardines flaked and hard cooked eggs
Asparagus tips and hard cooked eggs
Chicken and hard cooked eggs
Cooked rice, curry and hard cooked eggs
Shell fish with cooked rice and curry
Crab meat and red or green pepper
Shad roe and celery
Cooked sweet potato cubes
Roast fresh pork
Cooked veal

Any of these dishes may be served from individual chafing dishes or casseroles, on toast or in patty cases. With simple creamed things, a relish will be appreciated as spiced figs with creamed chicken, watermelon pickle with creamed fresh pork, sliced tomatoes with cheese dishes, chutney with curried dishes.

Cheese may be served as

    Welch rarebit

    English monkey

    Cheese toast

    Cheese and tomato rarebit

    Cheese and scrambled eggs

    Cheese dreams

    Cheese sandwiches

CAKES

The most popular cakes in most tea rooms are those with soft fluffy frostings, such as

Dark chocolate cake with marshmallow filling and white frosting with bitter chocolate on top

White cake with chocolate frosting

Yellow cake with chocolate frosting, and filling containing nuts and candied fruit

Very thin cookies, macaroons, sponge cake and angel food cake also have their appeal.

Any of the cakes and frostings noted in lesson IV may be used. Select your specialties perhaps from pages 66 to 73 and maintain your standard without fail. Never serve cake that is more than two days old.

Use for Stale Cakes

Cakes may be sold at cost at the end of the second day, or stale cake, crumbs and ends of cake that result from cutting cake in fancy shapes, may be used for pudding; or, rubbed through a coarse sieve or when dry, forced through the food chopper, the crumbs may be substituted for half the flour in hermits, spice cakes and Boston brown bread.

PASTRY

French pastries on pages 46 and 47 are very popular in some tea rooms. Summer tea rooms had better not attempt to make puff paste as it is difficult to handle in hot weather.

ICE CREAM DISHES

Ice cream, served in different ways and with different sauces, may be made or purchased. Buy it, the best quality you can secure, if your facilities for making it are not first class. Sherbets and water ices are more popular than poor ice cream. Most people like sauces of some kind with ice cream. A Thermos bottle may be used to keep chocolate, butterscotch, and similar sauces, hot. Ice cream sandwiches or shortcakes are popular.

Ice Cream Shortcake with
Butterscotch Sauce

Place a slice of white cake on the serving dish, cover with a slice of ice cream, with another slice of cake, pour butterscotch sauce (page 122) over all and sprinkle with chopped nuts.

Ice Cream Shortcake with
Fresh Strawberries

Use strawberry ice cream between two slices of white or angel cake and cover with fresh strawberries crushed and sweetened.

Ice Cream Shortcake
With Fudge Sauce

Use chocolate ice cream between two slices cake and cover with fudge sauce.

Other popular ices are:

Chocolate Peppermint Sundae

Chocolate ice cream served with marshmallow sauce, flavored with oil of peppermint.

Fudge Marshmallow Sundae

Ice cream covered with marshmallow sauce and then with fudge sauce.

Luxury Eclairs

Eclairs filled with ice cream and with hot fudge sauce or fresh strawberry sauce poured over.

Meringue Glacé

Two meringues with center removed, ice cream between and a few crushed strawberries, or maraschino cherries, over the ice cream.

MENUS

For luncheon, dinner, and party menus for a tea room many suggestions will be found in preceding lessons and it does not seem necessary to discuss them here. Prices must be carefully made and the dishes selected as specialties must be so standardized that they will always taste the same whether the patrons come in every week or do not return for several months.

Before and after opening your own place, or acting as manager for some one else, visit as many successful tea rooms as you can. Notice the dishes that are most frequently called for. Note the points that could be improved and then work hard in your own place and success should attend you.

REFERENCE BOOKS

Standard Cook Books
Journal of Home Economics, April 1920—Baltimore, Md.
Hotel Monthly Magazine—Chicago, Illinois.
American Cookery Magazine—Boston, Mass.
Tea Rooms—Albert Pick & Co., Chicago.
The Lunch Room as a Money Maker—Patterson Pub. Co., $2.00.
  Woman's Home Companion, Jan., 1921—Crowell Publishing Co.

QUESTIONS ON COOKING FOR PROFIT

XI

TEA ROOM MANAGEMENT

1. Estimate the cost of raw materials for the afternoon tea menu priced at 95 cents on page 235.

2. How much help is necessary in a tea room seating 48 people? Specify the duties of each person.

3. If you are thinking of opening a tea room secure data as to

    (a) Rent of a desirable house or space

    (b) Cost of decorating same

    (c) Cost of large equipment for kitchen and dining room of the size you have in mind.

    (d) Cost of small equipment for dining room only as listed on page 232.

COOKING FOR PROFIT

XII

CAFETERIA INTERIOR SHOWING ATTRACTIVE TABLES AND CHAIRS

COOKING FOR PROFIT

PART XII

CAFETERIA AND LUNCH ROOM MANAGEMENT

By

MARION E. HOPKINS

Field Secretary for Cafeterias
National Y. W. C. A.

EQUIPMENT, ARRANGEMENT AND COST; HOW TO USE AND CARE FOR
STEAM TABLE AND COFFEE URNS; HELP REQUIRED; DUTIES OF HELP;
STORE ROOM MANAGEMENT; INCOME NECESSARY FOR PROFIT; TYPICAL
MENUS.

THE small cafeteria is beginning to vie with the tea room in popularity as a channel through which a clever woman may turn her culinary ability into profit. Such cafeterias may be found in many small cities where the average restaurant manager has not learned the art of supplying "home-cooked" food; they also exist in tucked away corners of large cities where the "something different" which they supply brings them their necessary quota of patronage. The reasons which have been given for the popularity of cafeteria service are:

The saving of money to the customer since the reduced cost of operating expenses makes possible the charging of moderate prices and also an absence of tips.

The saving of time to the customer.

The stimulation of the appetite by the tempting display of dishes.

Larger profits are possible to the cafeteria owner than to the tea room owner as a larger volume of business can be taken care of for the same overhead expense.

257

Counter service is a more specialized task than waitress service, therefore the training and oversight of employees is simpler in the cafeteria than in the tea room or lunch room. Waitresses usually must price the customer's check in lunch rooms, a responsibility which never falls to the counter server.

The careful selection of attractive furnishings and color schemes in the most modern cafeterias, adds to these points of advantage, a "tea-room atmosphere" which is an improvement over the bare and unattractive room which is usually associated with the name.

Considerable noise is frequently eliminated and the rather unsightly view of the passing "line" by erecting, a few feet in front of the counter, a well designed screen. In some few cafeterias the counter occupies a distinct room from the dining room but this is not often possible.

ARRANGEMENT AND EQUIPMENT

Equipment firms will make, without charge, blue prints of recommended floor plans showing the location of all fixtures, but the cafeteria manager should, however, know the principles of operation which govern their location and have a sufficient knowledge of equipment to select that best suited to her purpose.

Except in large cafeterias where expensive subveyor service is possible it is best to have dining room and kitchen on the same floor. The counter should be at the rear of the dining room to provide for the formation of a "line" during busy hours. There should be two points of access from kitchen to dining room, one for the supply of food to the counter, one for the removal of soiled dishes from dining room. Care should be taken that the latter is at the opposite side of the room from that on which the customers approach the counter so that there is no possibility of the

line of customers coming in contact with employees re
ing soiled dishes.

THE SERVING COUNTER

The counter is usually placed four feet in front of the
partition wall between kitchen and dining room. A twelve
or fifteen inch service shelf, counter height, is usually built
on this wall, frequently with cupboards under. This leaves
three feet of working space for employees between shelf and
counter. When space is limited this may be shortened to
thirty inches. An inset should be made in the service shelf
directly behind the dessert and coffee counter for the placing
of a small refrigerator to hold milk, cream, butter and other
counter supplies which should be kept cold.

Standard counters are now built by all equipment firms.
They are thirty inches wide, thirty-six inches high and are
made with a sanitary base. They are built of wood, galvanized metal painted to match woodwork, vitrolite glass with
nickel trimming, and enamel baked on metal. Tops may be
of wood (heat and waterproof finish), monel metal or vitrolite glass. With a wood or glass top, metal protection under
the coffee urn must be supplied.

LOCALLY BUILT COUNTERS

It is possible to have a local carpenter build a counter, if
measurements are carefully made for the insets of salad
pan, steam table, coffee urn stand, ice cream cabinet. Wood
panelling should be used in preference to sheathing as the
many joints of the latter offer a harbor for vermin. Because
of the frequent warping of a wood facing in front of a
steam table this section of facing is frequently omitted and
the steam table front is set flush with the counter front.
The steam table front may then be finished in Russia iron
with nickel trimmings or, if of galvanized iron, may be
painted to match woodwork.

A double or triple bar nickel tray rail supported on nickel brackets should extend the length of the counter. This is one of the expensive fittings which is well worth its cost. One shelf for dish storage should extend under the counter.

Twenty feet may be considered a minimum length for the counter. A division which may increase proportionately with the length of the counter is

> Three feet for salad pan
> Two feet for bread and butter counter
> Six feet for steam table
> Three feet for dessert counter
> Two feet for coffee urn space
> Two feet for ice cream cabinet
> Two feet for checker's desk

Usually a tray and silver stand is provided before the customer reaches the counter. If it is necessary to use counter space for this purpose an additional three feet must be allowed and an allowance of two feet extra must be made if the checker is to serve also as cashier.

A glass display shelf twelve inches wide and set twelve inches above the counter usually extends over salad and bread counter and also over dessert counter.

The Salad Pan

An insulated salad pan is considered today as essential in a cafeteria as a steam table if cold foods are to be served cold as well as hot foods hot. The steam table follows the salad pan in the counter for several reasons.

1. By placing as late as possible in the counter there is the assurance that the hot foods will reach the table in as palatable a condition as possible.
2. Congestion in the line is avoided, for when the steam table comes first in order all customers stop at that point; with the salad counter first many stop at that point but others go on at once to the steam table.

3. The average customer selects the first attractive dish to meet his eye, therefore an early display encourages the purchase of healthful foods and at the same time brings a maximum profit to the cafeteria owner.

(I stress the first reason as strongly as the second.)

Usually bowls of lettuce and salad mixtures are placed in the salad pan and individual portions, served almost to order, are placed on the glass display shelf.

THE STEAM TABLE

The steam table should be built with a dish warmer and is in most cases fitted with gas connections. In large cafeterias and in those placed in institutional buildings or factories,

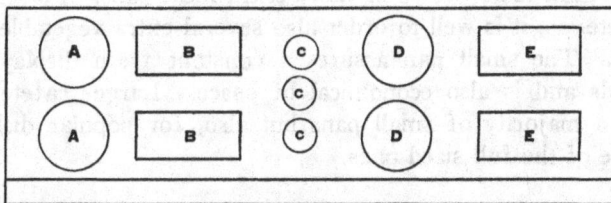

PLAN OF STEAM TABLE

A, Vegetable or Soup Inserts; B, Meat Pans; C, Gravy Inserts; D, Vegetable Inserts; E, Meat Pans

steam is frequently used for heating. The tops are made of monel metal, German silver, white enamel on iron, (named in the order of their preference). Copper is seldom used for this purpose today because of the difficulty of cleansing. Monel metal is strong, cleans easily and gives many years of wear. Nickel-plated copper is undesirable because with constant polishing the nickel wears off. White enamel meat pans and Hall china vegetable and gravy insets prove satisfactory. Retinned "copper pans" are in constant need of retinning and do not clean well. Aluminum discolors. Monel metal pans are sometimes used but are difficult to secure. The following plan is suggested for a small steam table

> 2 large vegetable insets (one for soup)
> 2 half size meat pans
> 3 round gravy insets
> 2 large vegetable insets
> 2 half size meat pans

A six inch carving board is on one side only. Entrée pans may replace the second set of vegetable pans as they display vegetables equally as well as meats. Macaroni and cheese and similar dishes are cooked in the pan in which they are displayed. For this reason it is well to order with the steam table twelve or more extra meat pans. For small cafeterias, it is well to order also several extra vegetable insets. The small pan assures a constant fresh display of foods and is also economical of space. Larger cafeterias use a majority of small pans but also, for popular dishes, some of the full sized ones.

The Coffee Urn

A six gallon combination coffee urn with large water jacket is recommended for this size counter. If this cannot be secured, an eight gallon hot water urn and a six gallon coffee urn should be provided. These may be set directly behind the counter or at right angles to it rather than upon it.

The ice cream cabinet is sometimes provided without charge by the firm supplying the ice cream. When this is the case it should be well fitted into the counter.

The health laws of some cities and states require glass protection of all foods displayed for sale. Special construction can be recommended by local glass dealers when this is true.

The Traffic Rail

A traffic rail to guide customers to checker is placed about three feet from the counter. This may be of pipe iron painted or of the more expensive cord and pedestal variety.

The Water Cooler

A water cooler with trays of glasses on shelves adjoining should be centrally located in the dining room. The type is best in which city water passes through coils in an ice chamber and does not come in contact with the ice.

Plumbing

In addition to kitchen plumbing water should be piped to water cooler, steam table and coffee urn, gas piped to steam table and coffee urn, drainage provided for water cooler, salad pan, steam table, coffee and ice cream cabinet.

Care of Steam Table and Coffee Urn

It is surprising how frequently the proper care is not taken of these two expensive pieces of equipment. The water pan of the steam table should be drained and thoroughly cleaned each day after the evening meal and left dry until time for its next use. A failure to do this causes the accumulation of rust in the bottom of the pan which in time causes holes in the metal. The smell of combined grease and rust in an uncleaned steam table water pan is unmistakable. It speaks of slovenly habits which mean poor business management. Coffee should never be left standing in an urn after a meal. It leaves a sediment in the jar which spoils the flavor of future coffee. The coffee should be drawn off and the jar washed after each use, with warm water with an occasional addition of soda. Poor coffee is more frequently caused by unclean jars than any other one thing. A fresh coffee bag should be used each week. It should be washed after use in cold water and hung to dry.

Kitchen, dish washing space, store rooms, employees' dressing rooms, and manager's office do not differ from those of tea rooms or small restaurants of similar size.

KITCHEN EQUIPMENT

A two section gas range with large ovens is sufficient for baking as well as other cooking for an attendance of less than two hundred and fifty. For more than this a pastry oven should be added. There should be a cook's table with a pot rack over it, bakers' table with metal bins, bread cutting table accessible to bread supply, salad preparation table accessible to sink and refrigerator. A standard large refrigerator should be provided as well as a small one behind the counter.

Three sinks are a minimum for dishwashing, pot washing, salad and vegetable preparation; the latter should be used for tray and glass washing during meal hours. They should be made of galvanized iron with metal drain boards. The one for dishes should be double with long galvanized tables adjoining for soiled and clean dishes.

LABOR SAVING MACHINERY

A Sterling Bread Slicer No. 50 and an Adjustable Butter Cutter are necessary items. A dishwashing machine, vegetable peeler, electric mixer may all be wisely added for numbers over 250.

STORE ROOM

A first shelf, barrel height, and others fifteen inches wide and fifteen inches apart have been found to hold two rows of No. 10 cans or three rows of No. 2 cans without waste of space. A small "day storage" space for the cook should be provided in the kitchen.

TRAYS, SILVER, GLASS

The following figures are based on a seating capacity of sixty.

90 Wearever Aluminum trays No. 348 (17¾"x11⅞")
8 doz. dessert spoons (soup)
10 doz. medium knives
10 doz. medium forks
15 doz. teaspoons
8 doz. soup bowls
10 doz. 7 inch plates
20 doz. 4 inch plates
10 doz. teacups
8 doz. saucers
20 doz. sauce dishes (vegetables, desserts)
8 doz. butter chips
20 doz. water tumblers
15 only salts, peppers, vinegar cruets
3 doz. individual teapots

A good grade of restaurant silver and hotel china with a rolled edge is recommended. Other glassware may be purchased for variety in counter display.

KITCHEN UTENSILS

This can best be selected by the manager. It is wise to leave a portion of this appropriation to be spent as needs arise. Aluminum ware proves economical in usage.

FURNITURE

Oblong tables are most economical of space, those thirty inches wide and forty-eight inches long prove most popular. Bentwood or rush bottom chairs are light and durable. Costumers are considered essential.

MENU

A menu board having white gummed letters on black cards is very satisfactory. It is well to have two of these boards, one placed where customers may study it before reaching the counter, and one back of the counter.

The small cafeteria need not offer a large variety of dishes daily but a variety from day to day. A cafeteria specializing on hot breads, fresh vegetables, moderately priced salads, and homemade desserts furnishes keen competition to the average "Meat and Potato Restaurant." One roast meat or fish, one made dish, as baked hash, stew, beef pie, one entrée, as baked beans, macaroni and cheese, Italian spaghetti, one starchy vegetable, and two green vegetables should suffice for the steam table. Salads will vary with the season; egg and fish salads as well as vegetable salads are popular sellers. Two kinds of pie, one cake, baked apple or fruit sauce and ice cream are sufficient desserts. Prices vary with localities. One hundred per cent over the cost of raw food is usually charged to provide for overhead expense and profit.

EMPLOYEES

Employees are needed for several distinct types of service

Cooking—Food production
Counter Service—Salesmanship
Checking, Cashiering, Bookkeeping—Clerical
Dining room work, dishwashing—Cleaning

A minimum number would be

1 cook
1 helper
2 dishwashers and cleaners
1 salad maker and server
1 steam table server
1 dessert and coffee server
1 checker, cashier and bookkeeper
2 dining room employees

A pastry cook would be the first addition. Some of these workers may be part time and the duties of some may overlap. Each community will determine the amount of wages to be paid. Fair wages, fair hours, and good working conditions are requisite for efficient loyal service.

Cost of Operating a Cafeteria

The first business problem is the amount of rent which can be afforded, a question dependent on possible average food checks and anticipated volume of business. Three to five per cent of gross receipts may be allowed for this item. A conservative estimate of receipts should be made to determine this. The second problem is the purchase of equipment. In consultation with equipment firms, lists should be made and estimates of cost secured and compared, before placing orders.

Business Equipment

Equipment for the transaction of business is as follows:
Standard duplicate order book
Bill and invoice file
Stock and issue cards
Requisition slips
Columnar record book, for attendance, receipts, expenses
Employees' record book, $2.50
Clarenback's Inventory Book and Stock Record, $2.50
A number of these supplies can be obtained from John Willy, Hotel Monthly, Chicago.

Checks should be issued from a check register (National Cash Register) the newest variety of which issues an itemized check with added total amount. The record of checks issued and their value in money should be compared with number of checks received and cash received by cashier after each meal.

STORE ROOM MANAGEMENT

The store room should be in charge of one person only. The buyer should give the store-room keeper, who also receives goods, a daily list of all purchases that they may be checked up accurately as they come in. Every purchase with Date, Rec'd from, Quantity, Unit of Cost, and Total Cost, should be entered on cards or in a record book, having a separate card or page for every kind of food stuffs.

Requisitions giving a list of materials which will be required the following day should be made out daily and signed by the head of each department, as the head cook, salad maker, coffee woman, pastry cook, head waitress, head cleaner, etc. These should be given to the person in charge of the store room each evening. Goods from the store room should be issued each morning, from these written requisitions. These requisitions should later be totalled and entered each on its individual card. Cards may be made out as follows. Note that twice as much space is allowed for foods delivered as foods received.

RECEIVED					DELIVERED				DELIVERED			
Date	Rec'd from	Quantity	Unit of Cost	Total Cost	Date	Quantity	Cost	Balance	Date	Quantity	Cost	Balance

The Perpetual Inventory

Balance in the last column is a record of stock on hand daily. This is obtained by deducting food issued from previous balance (on hand). This is called keeping a Perpetual Inventory. The perpetual inventory makes it unnecessary to take a monthly inventory, although it may be wise to check up the supplies, actually on hand at the end of each month, with the supplies as recorded on the cards, if there seems to be any question about their agreeing. An inventory is necessary for taking off the monthly trial balance and determining profit and loss.

The cards are also of great assistance in making out daily, weekly, or monthly orders for food stuffs. They are used for making the daily comparison of food stuffs issued, with dishes sold as indicated on the checks. This comparison will show whether the foods are being sold to good advantage or not. Waste or theft in the kitchen or dining room can be quickly detected. For example; 1 lb. of coffee makes 50 cups. If 4 lbs. of coffee were issued, more than 150 cups should appear on the sales checks. Canned goods, fresh and dried fruits, sugar used in desserts and on the tables, can be easily checked up from these Perpetual Inventory cards.

The Par Stock System

Sometimes a "par stock" is maintained in the kitchen of large establishments, i. e., so many pounds of flour, meal, sugar, potatoes, butter, etc.; so many cans of fruit, packages of cereal, etc.; sufficient for a little more than one day. At the end of the day requisitions are made out on the stock room to bring the kitchen stock "up to par." This order shows exactly what materials have been used during the day, which with overhead, gives cost and compared to receipts, the daily profit.

THE RECORD BOOK

The columnar record book should have headings of attendance, noon, night, etc., with similar headings for receipts and expenditures. Food, wages and salaries, rent, repairs, replacement and other expenses should all be listed. More expense headings may be used if desirable.

A daily overhead expense estimate may be determined by dividing monthly overhead expense of a past month by the number of operating days in a given month. The addition of this daily overhead estimate to actual expense for fresh supplies used and for store-room requisitions will give the total expense of operation for one day. This amount subtracted from receipts for the day will give daily profit or daily loss.

A good business manager ascertains and records this financial standing each day.

A fair percentage of monthly expenditure for commercial cafeterias has been found to be

Food	55% or	50%
Salaries and Wages	25%	25%
Rent	3% or	5%
Repairs and replacement	2%	2%
Other Expense	5%	5%
Profit	10% or	13%
Total	100%	100%

Ten per cent of gross receipts seems to be universally considered a good profit. Other percentages will vary with localities. A good business will repay the original investment the first year.

Usually an attendance of two hundred and fifty daily with an average check of forty cents is considered necessary for a profitable business but some successes have been made with smaller numbers.

LUNCH ROOMS

A lunch room or restaurant differs from a cafeteria in that the patron orders from a menu card or displayed menu, and food is brought from steam table, coffee urns, salad and dessert counters by waiters or waitresses. Prices are usually a little higher than in a cafeteria, to pay for this service, which will average about 10 cents a person served. Some lunch rooms are open 24 hours a day—never closed.

The preparation of foods, and number of employees in the kitchen differs but slightly, if at all, from that of cafeterias. The arrangement of steam-table, salad tray, coffee urn and ice cream containers is similar except that they are all placed on the kitchen side of the partition which separates the kitchen from the dining room, with a shelf in front of them and an opening over them where the waitresses can give and receive their orders. All the cold dishes as salads and desserts may be grouped together. Tray and traffic rails, of course, are not necessary. It is a convenient and attractive arrangement to have built-in screens in front of the kitchen partition and about three feet from it. On the kitchen side of this screen may be kept bread boxes on shelves at a convenient height filled with sliced bread in vertical piles, pans of iced butter cut for serving, and bread and butter plates. In this way one of the most frequently served foods is entirely eliminated from the kitchen service. The front of these screens may be fitted with large mirrors which give the impression of a larger dining room and more space. It is essential to have the window where the used dishes are left, at the extreme end of the room opposite from the serving tables. An electric dish washer is desirable where more than 150 people are fed daily.

Requisites for a successful lunch room are:

LOCATION—Where there is much passing—from 3% to 15% of passersby should come in.

APPEARANCE—White tiling, and nickel finish have a strong appeal.

CLEANLINESS—Apparent and genuine. In high-class restaurants, every part of the kitchen and dining room, walls, floors, shelves, and equipment are cleaned and polished daily.

FRESH AIR—Electric fans or other means of ventilation to keep the air fresh and free from odors.

EQUIPMENT AND FURNISHINGS—Arranged to give efficient and rapid service. Chairs may be filled four times an hour during the noon rush. The kitchen need not be large, but should have room for and a special place for everything needed. There should be sufficient help to keep it always in perfect order.

MANAGEMENT—Aiming to please and with constant oversight to detect leaks and improve conditions; familiarity with every smallest detail of the business; knowledge of markets and knowledge of human nature are desirable.

COURTESY—Necessary on the part of every employee toward patrons and toward one another.

GOOD FOOD—Of high quality with home-cooked flavor; carefully-tested recipes, followed accurately; dishes giving maximum food value and satisfaction for smallest expense.

RULES—For portioning all food—by weight (for meat) measure or thickness, according to the dish served.

MENUS—For plate dinners, vegetarian lunches and inexpensive meals, arranged with a knowledge of food values and dietetics and costs, so that patrons may be able to get what they should have at a reasonable price.

VEGETABLES—Properly cooked and well-seasoned; served with a poached egg they make a meal that is inexpensive and attractive to many people and oftentimes difficult to find.

READY-TO-EAT-DISHES—Essential in a lunch room that caters to business people who want to be served at about the same hour—from 12 to 2 or 5 to 7 o'clock.

  For example:
    Soups
    Stews
    Scalloped dishes
  Casserole dishes
  Vegetables
  Sandwich fillings—which can be mixed beforehand to be made up to order
  Salad materials—which can be prepared for serving and will keep without being "dressed," and so can be utilized the following day, if not sold.
  Gelatine, Cornstarch, or other Molded Deserts.
  Pies
  Ice Cream

COFFEE—This must be beyond criticism.

The manager of a chain of restaurants states that 20% of their receipts come from coffee. For each one hundred dollars taken in is served:

Coffee	$20.00
Griddle products	16.50
Hot dishes ready to serve	13.00
Desserts	12.00
Egg dishes	9.50
Special dishes	5.70
Bread, etc.	5.40
Sandwiches	4.25
Oysters	3.50
Soups	2.75
Cereals	2.65
Hot dishes to order	2.35
Vegetables	1.50
Salads, cold dishes, misc.	.90
	$100.00

Cost of Recipes and Portions

The cost of every recipe used should be accurately worked out, and the cost of individual portions of each dish that is listed on your bill of fare should be known, in order that prices may be intelligently made. If lunches at 30c, 35c, 40c, 60c, etc., are served, the per capita overhead cost and the expected profit per person should first be subtracted from the proposed special lunch price. The cost of bread and butter and coffee may be taken out; the remainder may be used for the special dishes. For regular customers the cost may vary slightly from day to day.

Recipes for serving a large number of people are written by accurately increasing the amounts of each ingredient in a family recipe, as explained on pages 50 and 51.

The checks received for food each day should be analyzed in order that the manager may know what kinds of foods are most popular, which pay the best, and which are losing money.

Dishes that must be sold at a loss should not often be put on a bill of fare. Those that are not profitable should be taken off. Low-priced nutritious attractive dishes should be featured. A daily comparison of food issued, and food sold should be made, to show you each day just where you stand—whether you are making or losing money. This can be known only by the most careful attention to details, the most accurate knowledge of costs and income.

The following menus have been used in a lunch room managed by a woman, where 1,500 people are fed daily:

APRIL

Chicken Soup, Rice........ .25
Escalloped Chicken and
  Macaroni .... .30
Creamed Cod Fish, Potato.. .30
Hot Corned Beef, Cabbage,
  Potato .... .35
Baked Sausage, Potato..... .35
Hashed Brown Potato,
  Bacon .... .30
Tomato Rarebit .... .25
Hashed Brown Potato, Tur-
  nip, Cabbage .... .25
Rice Custard Pudding..... .10
Chocolate Bread Pudding... .10
Caramel Nut Tapioca...... .10
Pineapple Whip .... .10
Charlotte Cream Pie....... .15

Russian Sandwich .... .15
Macaroni and Cheese...... .10
Buttered Cabbage .... .10
Mashed Turnip .... .10
Creamed Carrots and Peas. .10
  Bread served with vege-
  tables .05 extra.
Potato and Egg Salad...... .25
Fruit Salad .... .25
Cherry and Pineapple Short-
  cake .... .15
Grape Fruit Cocktail ...... .10
Loganberry Jelly, Custard
  Sauce .... .10
Vanilla and Strawberry Ice
  Cream 05-.10
Orange Cream Pie........ .15

OCTOBER

Oyster Stew .... .30
Baked Haddock a la Rarebit .30
Spiced Mackerel, Hashed
  Brown Potato .... .30
Chicken Stew, Dumpling... .40
Hot Roast Lamb Sandwich.. .35
Fried Liver, Bacon, Potato. .30
Baked Peas, Corn Cake.... .25
Sweet Potato (Southern),
  Bacon .... .30
Boiled Onions in Cream.... .10

Cocoanut Bread Pudding.... .10
Apple Tapioca Pudding..... .10
Chocolate Walnut Pudding. .10
Coffee Spanish Cream...... .10
Hermits or Cookies (2).... .05
Squash Pie .... .15
Macaroni and Tomato..... .10
Squash .... .10
Mashed Turnip, Potato..... .10
Cheese and Apple Jelly
  Sandwich .... .20

Stewed Corn and Lima
Beans .... .10
Bread served with vege-
tables .05 extra.
Date, Cheese and Nut Salad. .30
Vegetable Salad .... .30
Loganberry Shortcake .... .15

Lady Baltimore Cake........ .10
Bananas and Cream........ .10
Prune Sauce, Whipped
Cream .... .10
Frozen Pudding ....05 & .10
Vanilla Ice Cream.......05 & .10

PREPARATION FOR MANAGEMENT

Training in a home economics is the best fundamental preparation for cafeteria or lunch room management. This should if possible be followed by one year's experience as an employee in some well run cafeteria.

The woman without complete technical training, but with a good knowledge of food and cookery and some experience in catering to the public taste should spend at least three months as a worker in a well-run establishment and become familiar with equipment and methods of operation before opening a place of her own. To one who understands the business, the machinery of operation is simple. The cafeteria is a democratic method of public feeding. Excellent food, courteous service, absolute cleanliness of surroundings together with attractiveness are sign posts of success. Above all the home-cooked "come again" flavor of the food served must be maintained.

IN CONCLUSION

Food service outside the home is one of our country's largest and most essential industries. It is estimated that over nine million people eat daily in lunch rooms, cafeterias and restaurants. Many millions of dollars are invested in these enterprises and the business has been highly developed. Apparently the demand is well supplied, but there are hundreds and thousands of eating places where the food service is bad, very bad. There is a wide field for expert cooking and service—food with the home flavor will find demand and, with good management, the business will give handsome profits.

Beginning with the sale of home-cooked food, specialties and home-made candy, through catering in all its many branches, to guest house, tea room, cafeteria and lunch room management, there is a splendid opportunity for professional food service—*Cooking for Profit.*

It is the hope of the author that these lessons may serve as a guide, point the way, give courage and inspiration to many women to push ahead into creative work which will increase their value to the world and to themselves.

QUESTIONS ON COOKING FOR PROFIT

XII

Cafeteria and Lunch Room Management

1. What would be the cost in your locality of trays, silver and glass listed in this lesson, page 265?
2. Make out one day's menu which could be served in a cafeteria.
3. List cost of each dish per person and usual selling price of above menu.
4. Using the figures of 250 daily with an average check of 40 cents how much would you have daily for overhead expenses?
5. Figure out your profit for one year, one month, one day according to per cent given on page 270.
6. How much could your payroll be for one week, your rent for one month?
7. From suggestions given in this lesson, draw a floor plan of cafeteria and dining room as you would like to have it.

REFERENCE BOOKS

Equipment for Cafeterias, Lunch Rooms, Restaurants and Dining Rooms (illustrated). Published by Albert Pick & Co., Chicago.

The Lunch Room, by Paul Richards, $2.50

The Lunch Room as a Money Maker, by C. A. Patterson, $2.00

Institution Recipes, by Emma Smedley, $3.00

Recipes and Menus for Fifty, by Frances L. Smith, $2.00

Paul Richards' Pastry Book, $2.50

Hotel St. Francis Cook Book, by Victor Hirtzler, $5.00

Selection of Dishes and a Chef's Reminder, by Charles Fellows, $1.25

A Culinary Handbook, by Charles Fellows, $2.50

The Hotel Butcher, Garde Manger and Carver, by Frank Rivers, $2.50

Vachon's Economical Soups and Entrees, $1.25

Cafeteria Standards and Methods of Obtaining Them, by Treat and Richards, Bulletin 44, Extension Division, University of Minnesota, St. Paul

Present Day Cafeterias, by Gilbert Cowan, in Hotel Monthly, Sept., 1919

Cafeteria Records, by Elizabeth Anselm, Y. M. C. A., in Hotel Monthly, Nov., 1921

Any of the above books and all others listed in these lessons may be ordered of the Am. School of Home Economics, Chicago.

Magazines

The Journal of Home Economics, Baltimore, Md., $2.50 a year

American Cookery, Boston, Mass., $1.50 per year

Hotel Monthly, Chicago, Ill., $1.00 per year

American Restaurant, Chicago, Ill., $2.00 per year.

Plant-Restaurant Management, Chicago, Ill., $2.50 per year

The Caterer, New York City, $2.00 per year

Bulletins, Free from U. S. Department of Agriculture, Washington, D. C.

No. 142 Nutrition and Nutritive Value of Food
No. 256 Preparation of Vegetables for the Table
No. 275 Care of Food in the Home
No. 391 Economical Use of Meat in the Home
No. 535 Sugar and its Value as Food
No. 712 School Lunches
No. 771 Homemade Fireless Cookers and Their Use
No. 808 How to Select Foods: I, What the Body Needs
No. 817 How to Select Foods: II, Cereal Foods
No. 824 How to Select Foods: III, Foods Rich in Protein
No. 851 The House Fly
No. 879 Home Storage of Vegetables
No. 927 Farm Home Conveniences
No. 1099 Home Laundry
No. 1109 Preserving Eggs
No. 1136 Baking in the Home
No. 1180 House Cleaning Made Easier
No. 1228 A Week's Food for an Average Family
Bulletin No. 28, Composition of American Food Materials (sent for 10 cents (coin) from Supt. of Documents, Washington, D. C.)

INDEX

Note—Recipes and chapter headings are given in heavy faced type.

www.ingramcontent.com/pod-product-compliance
Lightning Source LLC
Chambersburg PA
CBHW011202090426
42742CB00019B/3381